# PRAISE FOR *COLLEGE, QUICKER*

"I am very impressed with the practical, applicable information in *College, Quicker*. Kate writes in a style that is easy to relate to, with anecdotal examples that should make students—and parents—see that the steps are doable. I seriously think that every student should get a copy in 8th or 9th grade. Even if students only choose a few of the options, the opportunity to save time, money, and stress during college is huge."

—*Roger Wilson, Director for Financial Aid Services, Northwest University*

"As a graduating high school senior, looking at the cost of my next four years in college can be daunting. Reading about smart and efficient ways to stay on track (and even get ahead!) with college credits has been so valuable. I highly recommend *College, Quicker* to anyone trying to sort through the challenge of paying for college!"

—*Emily Jane Hanaway, incoming freshman, Texas Christian University*

"*College, Quicker* is jam-packed with college information, including credits, finances, and even covering resources for those in the military. As the mother of four boys, with two in college and one in the military, I will use this book to help guide their next steps. This is a must-read for new and returning students of all levels, as well as parents. If you ever wanted a compact, easy-to-read resource covering the ins and outs of options in college, this is it!… Save immense time, money, and frustration with just one book!"

—*Mollie Sharp, BSN, RN, and ARNP student, military wife, and mother of four*

"My husband and I are planning to help our three teenagers pay for college within the next six years. When we added up the cost, that dream seemed daunting. I wish I had all the resources Kate Stephens compiled in *College, Quicker* when we began planning. It would have saved us so much time and second guessing… Think of this as a book of college discounts where you can save tons of money without sacrificing the quality of education. Kate's research…is extensive. Her personal experiences provide insight and entertaining information. I would highly recommend this book for parents and students with their sights set on a college education."

—*Stephanie Ivan, mother of a first-year college student,*
*a high school junior, and a high school freshman*

"Clear, concise, and conversational, while also practical, informative, and motivating! I wish a one-stop guide such as this was available when I first forayed into college classes; I earned my bachelor's degree by taking nine years of night classes while working a day job, paying along the way. Talk about the slow boat to a degree! Kate has outlined how to bypass the slow boat by taking advantage of practical and realistic ways to engage in systems already in place. This is a must-read for anyone embarking on a college education, or for anyone who has already started in college and needs some guidance on creating a realistic and attainable graduation plan."

—*Cynthia Reese, NW Marketing Manager, Environmental Science Associates*

"I never knew there were ways to get college credits quicker! Kate's book is very informative and easy-to-read. The chapter about CLEP exams is of particular interest to me since I fall into the category of a nontraditional student. Having step-by-step instructions on how to prepare for and take this test is extremely helpful! I'll be using this book in the near future."

—*Alla Karpenko, student*

"This book is a treasure map to your life's success! Not only does Kate show you how to make college quicker and less expensive, but she also gives you steps that are the cornerstones to a successful life: research, plan, execute, and follow up, then do it all again. Every student about to enter high school should have this book in their must-read and study plan. Parents should be reading this with their students to help them see the possibilities and integrate the steps into a lifetime practice."

—*John C. Erdman, President and CEO, Ideal Companies*

# COLLEGE, QUICKER

## 24 PRACTICAL WAYS TO SAVE MONEY AND GET YOUR DEGREE FASTER

# Kate Stephens

S

Published by Sourcebooks, Inc.
P.O. Box 4410, Naperville, Illinois 60567-4410
(630) 961-3900
Fax: (630) 961-2168
www.sourcebooks.com

Library of Congress Cataloging-in-Publication data is on file with the publisher.

Printed and bound in the United States of America.
VP 10 9 8 7 6 5 4 3 2 1

*There's a popular saying that "behind every great man is a great woman." In my case, the opposite is true and has one very important addition. Behind this woman is not only a great man, but an even greater God.*

*I dedicate this book to them both.*

# CONTENTS

# *INTRODUCTION*

LIFE. During childhood, I played this game incessantly. I delighted in the virtually endless combinations. I could work as a doctor, a lawyer, or an accountant; live in a mansion, log cabin, or Tudor style; and drive a purple, yellow, or green car. But while I often chose different occupations, residences, and automobiles, I almost always selected the college before career path. Even as young as five, I understood the value of a bachelor's degree. You'd have more career options and could earn more money. So without much thought, I asked the banker for $100k in loan slips to cover my education costs. Even with the interest, I would accumulate enough to settle my debt after a couple PAY DAYs.

Although this decision was easy in the game, it was much harder in the real world. As I grew older, I discovered the truth about the price of college. It didn't cost one or two PAY DAYs; it cost 10 years of barely scraping by. Not wanting this life, I decided to create my own path. I would still graduate with a college diploma but without student loans. Obviously, this was easier said than done. I didn't have an Education Savings Account, a 529 Plan, or a trust fund. Just a few hundred dollars at a local bank. Nearly broke, I would need to roll up my sleeves and bring in the money myself.

I first tried the government aid route. While I didn't live on skid row, I didn't reside on Park Avenue either. I came from a middle-class family. And due to our income bracket, I expected some state or federal grants. To attain this money, I filed the FAFSA and patiently waited for my official financial aid award letters. In the spring, they arrived from the colleges I'd been accepted to. Most of the schools awarded me a small amount of scholarship money, but Uncle Sam offered me only loans. The land of the free didn't give me a penny free. Yet even though the state and federal financial aid systems had failed me, I wasn't ready to quit. I had a couple other moneymaking options. One down, two to go.

Next, I tried the private scholarships route. Like thousands of other high school students, I searched Fastweb for scholarships offered by organizations other than colleges. Unfortunately, I wasn't eligible for many. But the few I did qualify for, I applied to over the next several weeks. I spent hours on the computer; I wrote essay after essay after essay. Yet my valiant effort was all for naught. I didn't win one. That's right, not even one. And with schoolwork continuing to mount, I decided to move on to the most reliable moneymaking venture. Two down, only one to go.

For my last attempt, I tried the job route. Although I started babysitting at age 12, I never worked more than a few hours a week. And $50 wouldn't pay for a textbook, let alone tuition. I needed steady employment. Since an espresso shop exists on literally every corner in Seattle, I applied for a barista position. Within a month, I was manning the cash register and the coffeemaker. But between serving and studying, I had little free time. And with my minimum-wage paycheck, I couldn't tuck much away. By the time I gave my two-weeks' notice, I had stashed only around $2,000 in savings. A far cry from the $120K college sticker price. Three down, none left.

At this point, I wanted to throw in the towel, wave the white flag. Maybe my goal wasn't achievable. Just when I was ready to surrender, I remembered a line from a late-night infomercial. "There's got to be a better way." Cliché as it might sound, the TV host was right. I had tried the traditional routes: government aid, private scholarships, and part-time work. And they left me tired and tapped out. I needed an alternative. I racked my brain but came up with nothing. What was this "better way?"

Unbeknownst to me, the answer sat right under my nose. During high school, I participated in a summer scholars program and a dual enrollment program. I desired college academics as well as college experiences. In addition to fulfilling both of these wants, the programs also helped me earn almost a semester of college credit. But since I was too focused on winning essay scholarships and working extra shifts my senior year, I forgot about this perk.

However, I was quickly reminded during a visit to the registrar's office at my university. After looking over my college transcripts from the high school programs, the transcript analyst made an astute observation. Because of my previously earned credit, I could possibly graduate early.

It was my "aha!" moment. I had at last discovered the "better way." And it had nothing to do with making more money. It dealt with the root of the problem: time. Instead of attending my university for four years, I would go for only two years and complete the remaining 60 credits elsewhere. That meant having to pay just two years' worth of high tuition, room, and board costs, instead of four. But once again, a question lingered in my mind. How would I obtain these credits?

Compared to the first one, this question didn't have a single answer. I could earn credits through many different kinds of courses, exams, and activities. But as there was no universal list or comprehensive resource explaining all of these opportunities, I'd have to find them myself. I sought out suggestions from counselors, teachers, peers, and online forums. And if an idea seemed plausible and affordable, I gave it a go. Fortunately, my hard work paid off. At age 20, I graduated summa cum laude with a bachelor's degree. But my 4.0 GPA wasn't even the best part. Because college ended up costing nearly half my original estimate, I had just enough funds from university scholarships and part-time work to cover it and walk away with my diploma debt-free.

Like me, you might have tried to pay for college through the traditional routes. But as you've come to realize, four or more years of college aren't often easily paid for by government aid, private scholarships, and minimum-wage paychecks. However, by following my "better way," you can achieve an affordable education through an early graduation. Yet, unlike me, you don't have to go down this road alone. Since I've already done the research, you can forgo muddling through questionable suggestions from school counselors or confusing information on online forums. This book will serve as a clear road map, showing you exactly how to graduate in less time. While there is no surefire guarantee, my tried and tested strategies should help you earn college credits quickly and fly through your degree.

But I didn't write this book merely so you can graduate early. I wrote it so you can experience the benefits of an early graduation. And whether you shave off one semester or two years from the typical four (or more common nowadays, five or six), you'll reap these rewards. First and foremost, you'll save money. By not spending as much on tuition, room, and board, you'll reduce or even eliminate the need for student loans. Second, but no less important, you'll save time. By not spending as many terms relearning material you previously acquired in high school or taking courses that don't interest you to fulfill graduation requirements, you'll have the ability to chase after your dreams sooner. Ultimately, graduating early isn't a carefree, free ride, but it can give you the freedom from paying loans and the freedom to pursue your dreams.

# How to Use This Book

*College, Quicker* isn't intended to be read cover to cover. After learning about colleges' transfer credit policies and designing your graduation plan in Section 1, you'll have free rein to delve into and work through any of the 24 fast-track opportunities (FTOs) in Sections 2 through 6. Except for the College Credit-by-Exam and Bonus FTOs, all of them have an identical format. They open with fast facts about the opportunity, including when to start, when to complete, how much you might spend, and how much college credit you might earn. Since the cost and potential credit can vary, symbols are used instead of actual numbers. The following table shows exactly what the symbols mean.

| COST | | POTENTIAL SEMESTER CREDITS | |
|---|---|---|---|
| $ | Less than $100 | + | Less than 6 credits |
| $$ | $100–$1,000 | ++ | 6–16 credits |
| $$$ | More than $1,000 | +++ | More than 16 credits |

(If you're thinking, "$1,000! I can't afford that!" flip to The Projections on page 6 of Section 1 to gain some serious perspective on just how much these costs could save you in the short and long term.)

After the fast facts comes the meat of the opportunity. The introduction contains a lighthearted story. It's a personal account from my life or someone close to me about the FTO—because sometimes it's helpful to hear an insider's perspective. The remaining five segments get down to business. The Basics provide an overview of the opportunity, The Benefits highlight some of the opportunity's top advantages, The Bottom Line offers examples of the opportunity's financial savings, The Brief Questions help you determine whether the opportunity is right for you, and The Blueprint includes step-by-step instructions for the opportunity.

---

## ‖‖‖‖‖‖‖‖‖‖‖‖ *COLLEGE, QUICKER* SIDEBARS ‖‖‖‖‖‖‖‖‖‖‖‖

Throughout this book, you'll notice sidebars with bite-sized pieces of information, each possibly relevant and helpful in your journey toward an early graduation. The sidebars all include an icon indicating their topic, so you can quickly find the type of information you're looking for:

Suggestions on how to save even more time and money, as well as other useful tidbits of knowledge.

Warnings on common mistakes and setbacks to avoid.

Tips specific to military service members and veterans (and sometimes their families).

Advice and insights based on my own personal experiences.

Potential short- and long-term financial advantages of pursuing a given fast-track opportunity.

---

Eager to explore the "better way?" You can do it. You can afford your education. You can graduate early. And you can have an unforgettable adventure along the way. Simply turn the page and start reading.

# *ORGANIZE YOUR EARLY GRADUATION PLAN*

## The Basics of Transfer Credit Policy

"If you fail to plan, you plan to fail." You've probably heard this line from your parents or teachers. And while it's obviously cheesy, it's also inevitably true. In order to succeed, you need an outline, a model, a draft, or a layout. Or in this case, an early graduation plan. From teaching you about the all-important transfer credit policy to explaining financial advantages to debunking myths and misconceptions to revealing common pitfalls, this section will help you construct this very plan. So when you do start down the early graduation path, failure won't even be a possibility.

## The Policy

Just as with students, no two schools are the same. They're often differentiated by location, environment, size, admission requirements, academics, athletics, financial aid, cost, facilities, activities, and housing. And while all of these are significant, a factor equally as important is missing from this list. But it should be on your radar since it'll make or break an early graduation—it's the transfer credit policy.

The *transfer credit policy* outlines protocols and procedures for the transfer of credit from traditional and nontraditional sources to the college or university. The policy is not limited to transfer students; it applies to first-time freshmen as well.

Unique and specific to each institution of higher education, the transfer credit policy outlines protocols and procedures for the transfer of credit from traditional sources (usually from other accredited schools) and nontraditional sources (standardized exams, noncollegiate learning, prior learning portfolios, and military training and experience) to the college or university. Confused? If your nose and forehead just scrunched up or you raised an eyebrow, you're not alone. This definition might seem complex, but the concept is actually not. Simply put, a transfer credit policy describes what types and how much transfer credit the school will accept. Still confused? Look at this example of a policy for a fictitious college, School A:

---

## |||||||||||||||||||||||||||| TRANSFER CREDIT POLICY ||||||||||||||||||||||||||||

Must earn a minimum of 50 credits at School A

### TRADITIONAL CREDITS
> Will accept up to 60 credits for work completed at other institutions
  - Must be from a regionally accredited U.S. college or university (not a foreign or unaccredited institution)
  - Must be presented on an official transcript
  - Must be college-level, postsecondary courses (no remedial classes)
  - Must be awarded a C or better
  - Must be similar in nature, level, and content to a course offered by our school

### NONTRADITIONAL CREDITS
Maximum of 45 credits from all nontraditional sources
> Will accept up to 15 credits from AP, CLEP, and DSST exams
  - Must meet the American Council on Education (ACE) recommended score
> Will accept up to 15 credits for noncollegiate learning
  - Must be identified, evaluated, and recommended for credit by the

American Council on Education (ACE) or the National College Credit Recommendation Service (NCCRS)
> Will award up to 15 credits for a prior learning portfolio
  • Must be degree-seeking and admitted to the program of study
> Will accept up to 15 credits for military training and experience
  • Must be presented on an official JST or CCAF transcript

Obviously, the example will provide you with only a basic idea. Most transfer credit policies are much more detailed, spanning over multiple pages inside a school's course catalog and on its website. They're often wordy and complicated. Even so, *don't* skip over them. You'll need to read over the information to make an important determination. Is each policy generous or not? With a generous credit policy, you can accumulate a significant amount of credit from outside sources. And compared to credit earned on the school's campus, credit earned off campus is typically less costly and less time-consuming. Therefore, more than anything else, a generous transfer credit policy is the key to a quicker degree.

But what exactly is a generous transfer credit policy? Unfortunately, there is no perfect answer. Since the term *generous* is fairly subjective, it's all relative. You've probably noticed this with money. Scenario #1: You show up to a birthday party with a $25 gift card, while everyone else comes with at least $100. Your gift is considered stingy. Scenario #2: You go to a party with the same $25, while everyone else arrives empty-handed. Your gift is viewed as generous. Ultimately, whether your gift is stingy or generous is determined almost entirely by the gifts of others.

The same principle holds true for transfer credit policies. A school with a generous policy accepts more traditional credit as well as more types of nontraditional credit than the other schools in its comparison group. So comparing three schools (Schools B, C, and D), if School B accepts 60 traditional credits and 30 nontraditional credits from standardized exams and noncollegiate learning, School C accepts 45 traditional credits and 20 nontraditional credits only from standardized exams, and School D accepts 30 traditional credits but 0 nontraditional credits, School B clearly has the most generous policy. Fairly easy, right?

A school with a *generous transfer credit policy* accepts at least one to two years of credit from traditional sources and one year of credit from two or more types of nontraditional sources.

When your comparison group is relatively small (less than 20 schools), you can look at all the policies together and spot the most generous without much trouble. However, this strategy isn't ideal for a large comparison group (20 or more schools). You'll spend hours and might make more than a few mistakes. Therefore, you should look at each school's policy individually and figure out whether or not the school accepts at least one to two years of credit (30 to 60 semester hours) from traditional sources and one year of credit (30 semester hours) from two or more types of nontraditional sources (standardized exams, noncollegiate learning, prior learning portfolios, and military training and experience). If it does, it has a generous transfer credit policy.

So how can you use this knowledge about generous transfer credit policies? It depends on your stage in the college search and selection process. If you haven't started either yet, evaluate dozens if not hundreds of colleges and select 10 to 15 with not only your must-haves but also generous transfer credit policies. Since you'll assess 20 or more schools, use the strategy for the large comparison group. That means, unless it's your dream school, eliminate any that don't accept at least one to two years of credit from traditional sources and one year of credit from two or more types of nontraditional sources. If your efforts are coming up short and you aren't looking to take classes on campus, research Excelsior College, Thomas Edison State College, and Charter Oak State College. In the test-for-credit world, these regionally accredited colleges are commonly referred to as the Big Three because they have the most liberal credit acceptance policies among postsecondary institutions. While they all offer online courses and their own credit-by-examination programs, their very low residency requirements mean you can transfer in most credit and earn little to none at their schools.

If you've already narrowed your selections to around 10 to 15 colleges, apply to the six to eight with the most generous transfer credit policies. Since you'll assess less than 20 schools in this case, employ the strategy for the small comparison group. In some circumstances, this task will be fairly quick and easy. Suppose, for example, seven of your top schools accept 45 traditional credits and 30 nontraditional credits from standardized exams and prior learning portfolios, while your remaining choices accept only 30 traditional credits and 15 nontraditional credits from standardized exams. Obviously, those in the first group have the more generous policies. In other instances, however, you'll need to put in additional effort. For example, suppose that all of your top schools accept roughly the same amount and type of credit. Instead of drawing straws or flipping a coin, take a

Commonly referred to as the Big Three, Excelsior College, Thomas Edison State College, and Charter Oak State College have the most liberal credit acceptance policies among post-secondary institutions.

closer look at each policy. Maybe one or more have tighter time restrictions on accepting transfer credit. Or higher minimum scores for exams for credit. Or pricier fees for transferring prior learning credits. Use these stipulations to make your final decision.

If you've formally accepted admission or are already enrolled in college, either embrace your school's transfer credit policy or switch schools. However, while you technically have these two options, transferring should ideally be a last resort. You should first get to know your college's policy inside and out. Read through it thoroughly in the course catalog, and discuss it at length with your academic advisor or a staff member in the registrar's office. Only after all of this research should you even consider leaving. And since you might lose a few credits during the transfer, you should only go to an institution that has a significantly better policy (i.e., it accepts 45 credits more—not 5 more) than your current school's.

Why does a generous transfer credit policy matter? You already know two reasons. Since credit acquired off campus is typically less costly and less time-consuming, you won't spend as much money or waste as much time. In addition, there is a third not as obvious but still as important advantage. By choosing a school with a generous transfer credit policy, there's a strong possibility that you'll feel valued by your educational provider. Some colleges and universities have the "my way or the highway" mentality. You can only attend their classes with their teachers in their classrooms. A school with a generous credit policy, however, often has a more student-centered focus. It doesn't only care about its balance sheet, it also cares about you. Even if it means it loses a year or two of your tuition, the school allows you to earn credit through other schools, exams, experiences, and so on. Its ultimate goal is for you to succeed, graduate, and become a proud alum.

# The Projections

Forget staring into a crystal ball or having your palm read. You're about to see into your financial future without them. Or to be more exact, two possible futures. One where you graduate in four years and another where you graduate in less time.

Four-year graduation plan: With average tuition, room, and board costing between $11,052 and $42,419 per year, your college expenses could add up to around $44,208 to $169,676 (see Table 1).[1] And since, on average, scholarships cover only 17 percent and grants 14 percent,[2] you and your parents will have to foot the remainder of the bill out of your own pockets. Like 7 out of 10 graduates from public and private nonprofit colleges, you'll probably have to take out loans—which for the graduating class of 2013 averaged $28,400 per student—and spend the following 10 or more years paying off your debt.[3]

## TABLE 1

| AVERAGE COLLEGE COSTS (2014–2015) | | | | |
|---|---|---|---|---|
| | TUITION AND FEES | ROOM AND BOARD | COST PER YEAR | COST FOR 4 YEARS |
| PUBLIC FOUR-YEAR IN-STATE | $9,139 | $9,804 | $18,943 | $75,772 |
| PUBLIC FOUR-YEAR OUT-OF-STATE | $22,958 | $9,804 | $32,762 | $131,048 |
| PRIVATE FOUR-YEAR NONPROFIT | $31,231 | $11,188 | $42,419 | $169,676 |

1. College Board, *Trends in College Pricing 2014*, accessed March 31, 2015, http://trends.collegeboard.org/sites /default/files/2014-trends-college-pricing-final-web.pdf.
2. Sallie Mae, *How America Pays for College 2014*, accessed March 31, 2015, http://news.salliemae.com/files/doc _library/file/HowAmericaPaysforCollege2014FNL.pdf.
3. The Institute for College Access & Success, *Student Debt and the Class of 2013*, accessed March 31, 2015, http:// ticas.org/sites/default/files/legacy/files/pub/classof2013.pdf.

Early graduation plan: Although most of the fast-track opportunities aren't free, the majority are fairly inexpensive. Consequently, by earning credit through them and thus graduating early, you'll reduce your overall tuition and fees as well as avoid a full four years of on-campus housing and meal costs. Depending on your total time in school, you could potentially save thousands to tens of thousands (see Table 2) and take on only a small amount of student debt, if any. After accepting your diploma, you can start full-time employment, affording you the possibility to live on your own, buy a new car, or splurge on a 60-inch LCD sooner than anticipated. You'll also have the funds to start a decent savings account or invest in retirement at an earlier age. Just by putting away $7,500 a year beginning at age 25 instead of 35, you'll have more than an additional $1,000,000 at age 65 with an 8 percent rate of return.

## TABLE 2

| POTENTIAL SAVINGS WITH EARLY GRADUATION* | | | | |
|---|---|---|---|---|
| | 1 SEMESTER EARLY | 2 SEMESTERS EARLY | 3 SEMESTERS EARLY | 4 SEMESTERS EARLY |
| PUBLIC FOUR-YEAR IN-STATE | $8,471.50 | $16,943 | $25,414.50 | $33,886 |
| PUBLIC FOUR-YEAR OUT-OF-STATE | $15,381 | $30,762 | $46,143 | $61,524 |
| PRIVATE FOUR-YEAR NONPROFIT | $20,209.50 | $40,419 | $60,628.50 | $80,838 |

*This table assumes you spend $1,000 on FTOs per semester you graduate early. The following equation is used: (cost for # of semesters not attending) minus ($1,000 times # of semesters not attending) equals (savings).

After reading both, you probably favor the early graduation plan over the four-year plan. However, fortune-telling isn't an exact science. Your actual savings will be contingent on your selected fast-track opportunities and your individual college costs. To get a more precise picture of your future, start by going to any of The Bottom Line segments. They'll show you the short- and long-term financial advantages of completing the FTO instead of taking the traditional course of action. The short-term advantages will be pretty straightforward. An Advanced Placement Exam worth three credits, for example, will cost only $91 compared to the $4,986 it would cost to get the same three credits from Rice University; a short-term savings of $4,895.

The long-term savings are where the math gets a bit more complicated, but also where the biggest payoffs come in. Taking a loan out for that $4,895 would mean going into debt and accruing interest on the loan until it's paid off. If it took you 10 years to pay off that $4,895 and the loan had a 5 percent interest rate, you'd actually end up paying $1,335 in interest on top of the initial $4,895, for a grand total of $6,230. (That number would be even greater if the loan was unsubsidized and interest accrued on it while you were in school.) But if you took the AP Exam instead and put the money you saved into a retirement account, you could actually let your money accrue compounding returns (make interest on interest). After 40 years with just 5 percent annual returns, your initial investment of $4,895 ($4,986 minus $91 for the AP Exam) would balloon to $29,566 in retirement! This is what people mean when they say, "Let your money work for you."

Sound pretty great? Well before you sign up for a dozen AP Exams, remember that your actual savings will be contingent not only on your selected FTOs but also on your individual cost of college. So while the tuition numbers in each of The Bottom Line segments are real 2013–2014 and 2014–2015 rates published by U.S. postsecondary institutions, they each only represent one college or university and don't factor in financial aid. Therefore, you will need to subtract the cost of the FTO from *your* cost of a class, semester, or year at your school (tuition minus need- or merit-based aid). (If you aren't enrolled in college yet and don't know the cost, use the Net Price Calculator on your intended college's website for a rough estimate.) Once you've found the difference, you can discover how much you'd save in interest by avoiding a student loan of that amount. Because of factors like capitalized interest, loan fees, minimum payments, and whether loans are subsidized or unsubsidized, calculating interest on student loans can be complicated. To get accurate interest amounts, I recommend that you use the FinAid Loan Calculator (www .finaid.org/calculators/loanpayments.phtml), which I used to calculate the interest figures that are included throughout this book. I also used and recommend the Dave Ramsey Investing Calculator (www.daveramsey .com/article/investing-calculator/lifeandmoney_investing) to determine how much you'd make in interest by investing the dollars you'd save by not borrowing loans.

Do these same calculations for all of the FTOs you select, and before you know it, you'll have a good idea of your financial future. Say for instance you decide to earn a total of 30 semester credits by completing FTO #6: College-Level Examination Program (CLEP) Exams, FTO #14: Distance Learning, and FTO #21: Noncollegiate Learning (Table 3) and you attend a college that costs you $35,000 per year ($45,000 in tuition and fees minus a $10,000 academic scholarship).

## TABLE 3

| ACTUAL SAVINGS WITH EARLY GRADUATION (EXAMPLE) | | |
|---|---|---|
| | COST | CREDITS EARNED |
| FTO #6 | $500 (5 three-credit CLEP exams plus administration fees) | 15 credits |
| FTO #14 | $1,118 (2 three-credit LSU online courses through the Independent and Distance Learning program) | 6 credits |
| FTO #21 | $345 (3 three-credit StraighterLine courses plus two months of membership fees) | 9 credits |
| TOTALS | $1,963 | 30 credits |

The difference between your cost of college ($35,000) and the cost of earning 30 credits through your selected FTOs ($1,963) is how much you'll save in the short term ($33,037). In the long term, one of two things could happen, depending on your financial situation. If you're like most students with little to no funds set aside for school, you'll save even more money. You could save $9,012 in interest by avoiding subsidized student loans totaling $33,037 (assuming each loan has a 5 percent interest rate and a term of 10 years). But if you're one of the lucky few who has a good chunk of dough stashed away, you'll actually make money. You could earn a whopping $199,543 in interest by investing that $33,037 in retirement accounts (assuming each investment has a 5 percent interest rate, compounded annually), and letting them grow for 40 years.

# IIIIIIIIIII SEMESTER CREDIT VS. QUARTER CREDIT IIIIIIIIIII

Most colleges and universities in the United States have either a semester system or a quarter system. Schools on semester systems divide the academic year into halves. Each half lasts about 15 weeks, with the first part (fall semester) running approximately from August to December and the second part (spring semester) from January to May. Schools on quarter systems divide the academic year into thirds. Each third lasts about 10 weeks, with the first part (fall quarter) running approximately from September to December, the second part (winter quarter) from January to March, and the third part (spring quarter) from April to June.

Whether you attend a school on a semester system or a quarter system, you'll still earn the same four-year diploma. However, the number of credits needed to earn that diploma will differ. Schools on semester systems typically require at least 120 credits for graduation while schools on quarter systems typically require at least 180 credits. Why the huge gap? One semester credit does not equal one quarter credit. The ratio is actually two semester credits for every three quarter credits. Therefore, if you transfer credits from a school on a semester system to a quarter system (or vice versa), the credits will need to be converted.

When you officially transfer credit, a staff member in the registrar's office at your school will convert them for you. But if you want to see how much credit you will receive prior to the transfer, you can convert the credits yourself. To convert from quarter credits to semester credits, multiply the number of quarter credits by .667. To convert from semester credits to quarter credits, multiply the number of semester credits by 1.5. Since schools on a semester system are considerably more common than those on a quarter system, this book mostly uses semester credits. This means that if your school is on a quarter system, you'll have to convert rather frequently.

# The (Mis)Perceptions

You've probably heard them. Those facts about college that are often nothing more than fiction. You'll gain 15 pounds during your freshman year. You'll receive a 4.0 GPA if your roommate dies. You'll be broke and starving. But the myths and misconceptions don't stop there. Early graduation has a few of its own. And just like your weight, grades, and bank account, many aren't completely accurate. Ready for a reality check? Below are some of the most popular myths debunked.

*Myth:* *Earning credit in high school will make you ineligible for freshman scholarships.*

*Truth:* At most schools, you're only considered a transfer student if you took courses at another postsecondary institution after 12th grade. Therefore, earning credit through AP, IB, pre-college summer programs, and dual enrollment will still allow you to apply as a freshman. You won't even transfer those credits until after you've formally accepted admission.

*Myth:* *You'll have to overload your schedule with an ungodly amount of credits and classes each term.*

*Truth:* While FTO #12: Maximum Credits recommends enrolling in an above average number, you don't need to take 18 credits a semester to graduate early. You can register for a normal or less than normal course load and complete one of the other 23 FTOs instead. And with some of them requiring significantly less time and energy than an actual class (College Credit-by-Exam FTOs #6– #10, FTO #21: Noncollegiate Learning, and FTO #23: Military Transcript), you could end up with a much easier schedule than many of your peers.

*Myth:* *You'll have to sacrifice your college experience.*

*Truth:* Just because you don't attend for the typical four years doesn't mean you're banned from living the college life. It's actually quite the contrary. You can participate in all of the same activities as your peers, as well as add to your list of

Even though I participated in a pre-college summer program and dual enrollment, I completed a freshman application and competed for freshman aid. I ended up receiving two scholarships from my university, both largely (if not entirely) due to my previous academic record.

I only signed up for 14 credits each semester during my first year in college. I earned many more credits through CLEP exams than through extra classes.

I lived in the dorms, road tripped during spring break, worked as the yearbook editor, watched a sports game or two on campus, studied abroad in Europe, binged at the cafeteria, attended and hosted several theme parties, got pulled over in a limo by the authorities on the way to the annual banquet, and much, much more.

My IQ is nowhere near genius level and my SAT score was nowhere near perfect. I graduated from college early because of my drive and determination, the same D&D that helped me earn a high GPA in high school and beyond.

unforgettable college adventures and earn credit by completing FTOs from Section 5 (FTO #17: Intersession Abroad, FTO #18: Alternative Breaks (AB), FTO #19: Internship, and FTO #20: Extracurricular Activities).

*Myth: You have to be the next Freud, Newton, or Einstein.*

**Truth:** Although a few of the FTOs are academically challenging (FTO #1: Advanced Placement (AP) Exams, FTO #2: International Baccalaureate (IB) Exams, FTO #4: Dual Enrollment (DE), and FTO #12: Maximum Credits), none are reserved for those with an extremely high IQ or test score. Most are actually designed for the average student. All they require is motivation, persistence, and resolution.

## The Pitfalls

You're almost ready to create your graduation plan. But before you do, there's one more thing you should know. It's the disclaimer. Yes, you read that right. The dreaded disclaimer. You've probably seen one on a label, during a television program, or in an email. However, the disclaimer isn't necessarily bad. It actually tells you what you can or can't expect. And in this case, you can't expect to automatically earn college credit for completion of a fast-track opportunity. There is no money-back guarantee. However, as more and more students have begun to utilize the FTOs covered in this book, and as many colleges' transfer credit policies are becoming more generous in response to this growing trend, there's a good chance that you'll earn credit from one or more of these opportunities. Best of all—and unlike when you're applying for government aid and competitive scholarships—you have the power to improve your chances of earning credit and saving money by avoiding these common pitfalls:

## COMPLETING THE FTOS ON YOUR OWN

Instead, work closely with an academic advisor. Assigned by your school, your advisor will not only be your guide but also your advocate throughout this entire process. If you have yet to do so, meet with your advisor. First, mention your goal to graduate early. Then, review your degree plan (a.k.a. curriculum map) together. This plan details the exact courses required for graduation from your program of study. Following this appointment, consult your advisor again before starting a new FTO. Depending on your school's transfer credit policy and your program of study, your advisor will or will not give you the green light (and possibly also signed preapproval) to go ahead with the FTO.

## JUMPING IMMEDIATELY INTO THE FIRST STEP

Instead, do some investigative work beforehand and make any necessary modifications. Although The Blueprint steps were researched for accuracy and apply to most students, they aren't written specifically for you. If you plan on completing one of the College Credit-by-Exam FTOs, check the facts first. Read through the information for test takers on the exam provider's website. The provider may have changed its exam selections, fees, dates, and more since this book's publication. If you plan on completing any of the other FTOs, chat with a staff member at your high school or college first. Find out how to take part in and possibly earn credit for the FTO at your particular institution. The school may have some different policies and procedures from those described in the steps.

## KEEPING TRACK OF DATES AND DEADLINES IN YOUR HEAD

Instead, use a daily student planner. If you don't already own one, purchase a planner from your local office supply store or a study app (such as My Study Plan, My Homework, or iStudiez Pro) from your phone or tablet marketplace. With planner in hand, spend a few hours charting all of your upcoming commitments (classes, work shifts, extracurricular activities). Then, as you work through an FTO, block off some of your free time to complete and conquer each step. Keep your planner easily accessible (if in print format), and check it often, preferably each day but at least two or three times a week.

## STAYING IN THE DARK ABOUT YOUR ACADEMIC PROGRESS

Instead, obtain a degree audit from your institution after transferring credit or before starting a new term. Often accessed through an academic advisor or online student account, a degree audit shows you what requirements you've already met, those you're currently working on, and those you have yet to meet. Depending on your degree program and the courses you've previously taken, you might still need general education requirements (mandated courses for all students), major requirements (mandated courses only for students in a selected field of study), and electives (non-mandated courses chosen by the student). While you survey your degree audit, check for inaccuracies. If a transferred course isn't listed, wait a few weeks and then perform another audit. But for all other types of errors, contact your advisor or a staff member in the registrar's office. He or she should help to resolve the issue.

## TAKING EXAMS FOR CREDIT ON A WHIM

Instead, adequately prepare weeks to months in advance of the test date. Colleges will usually only award credits for exams like AP and CLEP if you earn a certain score (typically at or above the score recommended by the American Council on Education). But, in order to meet or beat this mark, you'll need to spend time mastering the content. You should also familiarize yourself with the timing and format of the test. At the very least, find out how long the exam will last and what types of questions might show up (multiple-choice, short answer, essay, etc.). And if you're taking an Internet- or computer-based exam, download any software made available by the exam provider to review test instructions and explore test tools.

## ACCEPTING EVERY TRANSFER CREDIT DECISION

Instead, request an appeal if deemed necessary. Upon receiving your transcript from another institution or organization (or prior learning portfolio), your school will evaluate and possibly award you credit. If credit is not granted or much less than expected is granted, consult with your academic advisor or a transfer counselor. You can likely appeal within a designated time frame. You may need to fill out a form or write a detailed narrative. In either case, you'll have to explain your rationale. You'll then submit the paperwork along with supporting documentation (or a significantly altered portfolio) to the appropriate office and wait for a reply. If credit is not granted or much less than expected is granted once again, you may be able to appeal to an even higher authority, such as the vice president for academic affairs.

# The Plan

You're probably done with talk and ready for some action. Your wish has been granted. You can now design your early graduation plan. Out of the 24 fast-track opportunities, you can pick and choose which to complete. (But don't feel limited to just 24. If you discover FTOs on your own, you can do those as well.) To help you decide, read through the introduction paragraphs of the next five sections, skim through the FTO content, and consult Appendix A: Which Fast-Track Opportunities Are Right for You? and Appendix B: Sample Schedules. After you've selected at least a few FTOs, organize them in the Do-It-Yourself Schedule in Appendix B. But write only with a pencil. That way, you can add or drop some at a later date.

Once your graduation plan is laid out, it's go time! Work through each of your selected fast-track opportunities, starting with the first in your plan. Since you can complete or skip any of the 24 FTOs and can do so in any order, your first fast-track opportunity might be FTO #1, FTO #24, or another FTO somewhere in between. After you've finished with all of your selected fast-track opportunities, jump to Final Thoughts, positioned between FTO #24 and Appendix A. It'll leave you with hope and excitement for your future after graduation.

# UTILIZE COLLEGE-LEVEL COURSEWORK IN HIGH SCHOOL

According to an article by *U.S.News & World Report*, 30 percent of students drop out of college after their first year.[4] Luckily, I wasn't one of them. How did I escape this fate? While many of my high school peers enrolled in the easiest classes available, I took college-level courses. Obviously, this decision afforded me less leisure time. But the trade-off paid off. I was not only granted almost a semester of college credit, I was also ready for college curriculum. Those students who had previously skated by until now couldn't keep up in college, and watching them struggle to adjust to the demanding coursework was disheartening. I, on the other hand, could hold my own and received straight As. And by staying above 90 percent on most of my assignments and tests, I didn't end up leaving school with the 30 percent.

Whether you're in 9th, 10th, 11th, or 12th grade, you can utilize college-level coursework in high school. Depending on your preference of a high school or college setting, complete one or more of the next four FTOs. Try FTO #1: Advanced Placement (AP) Exams or FTO #2: International Baccalaureate (IB) Exams if you want to take college-level courses at a high school. Or try FTO #3: Pre-College Summer Programs if you want to take college-level courses at a college. Or try FTO #4: Dual Enrollment (DE) if you would be willing to take college-level courses at either location (where you attend will be contingent on your state and school district). But

4.   Mike Bowler, "Dropouts Loom Large for Schools," *U.S.News & World Report*, August 19, 2009, accessed August 7, 2014, http://www.usnews.com/education/articles/2009/08/19/dropouts-loom-large-for-schools.

whichever you choose, make sure you're up for the task. These FTOs require you to be a motivated and driven student, capable of thriving in an academically challenging environment.

Do you plan on earning a technical certificate or associate's degree in applied science? Explore the mini fast-track opportunity (*Bonus FTO #5*: Articulated Credit/Tech Prep) at the end of this section.

# INTRO TO COLLEGE CREDIT-BY-EXAM (FOR HIGH SCHOOL STUDENTS)

## The No. 2 Pencil Is Mightier than the Sword

Born 10 years apart, my younger brother and I don't seem related. Although we share the same father and mother, we aren't anything alike. He's tall, tan, and blonde. I'm petite, pale, and brunette. He's a class clown. I'm a brainiac. He enjoys history, hamburgers, and heavy metal. I prefer science, smoothies, and soundtracks. While most would chalk up these differences to our gender or age gap, I wasn't as quick to write them off. I wanted answers. And, after skimming through the tabloids and searching the Web, I uncovered a potential explanation: switched at birth.

Even though it seemed far-fetched, it wasn't impossible. Hospitals have made this mistake before. Maybe shortly after his arrival, my brother was given to another couple. So somewhere out there is my actual sibling. A short, scholarly, smoothie-loving sophomore. For more than a decade, I actually considered this scenario. But at the start of this school year, I began to doubt my theory when my brother enrolled in AP European History. He not only wanted to learn about the subject, but also earn college credit.

Over the past several months, he's accomplished his first goal. He's gained knowledge of Peter the Great, the Protestant Reformation, and Marxism. And in May, he'll try for his second goal. He'll sit for his first AP Exam. With serious studying and a little luck, he should achieve a high score and bank a few credits. But he doesn't intend to stop there. He plans to take several more AP Exams and accumulate up to a semester of credit before he finishes high school. In turn, he'll graduate from college early, just like me. No point testing our DNA; we're not so different after all.

# The Basics

You're used to getting A's for more than just effort. You're a smart student, and you want to take challenging classes. No show-and-tell or arts and crafts—you're looking for push-the-limits academics. Fortunately, you have not one but two options: Advanced Placement (AP) and International Baccalaureate (IB). However, these programs don't just provide intellectually stimulating high school courses in a variety of subjects. They also offer exams for college credit at the end of the school year. You can sit for one or more of these exams and, depending on your scores, receive credit from colleges and universities across the globe. Now that's an A for awesome.

Although participation in either will impress college admissions and potentially earn you college credit, AP and IB are not one and the same. These high school programs are actually quite different. Present in more than 19,000 schools and with greater than 2.3 million students in 2014,[5] AP is much more widespread and, specifically in the United States, well-known. The program offers an individualistic approach, allowing 10th, 11th, and 12th grade students to register for AP courses and exams in one or more of their choice of subjects. Students also have the choice between taking an AP course and then sitting for the AP Exam or skipping the course and simply taking the exam.

On the other hand, IB isn't nearly as prevalent or nationally recognized,[6] with the Diploma Programme (DP) in around 800 schools in the United States and the Career-related Programme (CP) in less than 100 schools worldwide. The Diploma Programme (DP) offers a holistic approach, requiring 11th and 12th grade students to register for six courses and take the IB exams in those six subject areas as well as complete the DP core. The Career-related Programme (CP) offers a similar approach to that of the DP but with a career focus, requiring 11th and 12th grade students to

5.   "About the Exams," College Board, accessed October 25, 2014, http://professionals.collegeboard.com/testing/ap/about.
6.   "IB World School Statistics," International Baccalaureate, accessed October 25, 2014, http://www.ibo.org/facts/schoolstats/progsbycountry.cfm.

register for at least two DP courses and take the IB exams in those subject areas as well as complete the CP core and an approved career-related study. While students can forgo either program and take individual IB exams, they still must take an IB course in that subject area first, as some in-class assignments count toward the final score. For a side-by-side comparison of AP and IB, check out Part 1 of Appendix C: College Credit-by-Exam (for high school students).

## ⅢⅢ ACADEMIC CREDIT VS. ADVANCED PLACEMENT ⅢⅢ

Sometimes, colleges and universities may choose not to award you college credit for your scores on AP or IB exams, but rather grant you a course exemption or advanced placement. (See where that AP name comes from?) Advanced placement means that you're exempt from having to take intro-level courses and can jump ahead to higher-level ones, and it may help you satisfy general education requirements, too.

For example, suppose you score a 4 on the AP English Language and Composition Exam. It's a good score, but as you come to think, not good enough. While your school gives college credit for a 5, you're only granted a course exemption from ENGL 101: Introduction to College Writing for a 4. But don't feel discouraged; this exemption is still an advantage. Although it won't help you graduate early, you're no longer required to complete ENGL 101 and can fulfill these credits with another more advanced and potentially even more interesting course instead. You could possibly take a class on creative writing, the world of publishing, or the craft of poetry. Or, if your school allows, take a class in an entirely different academic discipline. Either way, you'll have a bit more freedom and flexibility when selecting your course schedule.

# The Benefits

- *Remain in a high school setting.* Many parents reminisce about their "glory days." Often, these stories center on their high school years (circa 1980–1990). Whether you roll your eyes, plug your ears, or actually listen, you clearly understand the message. High school can foster some unforgettable memories: spirit week, Spanish club, and spring formal. Fortunately, you don't have to sacrifice these experiences for college credit. You can take AP or IB courses with students your own age and maybe even at your current high school. So just like your mom and dad, you'll experience a few "glory days" of your own. But since you won't be sporting parachute pants, shoulder pads, or a Flock of Seagulls hairdo, these days will be even more glorious than theirs. Or as they would have said, "more radical."

- *Earn a higher GPA.* As a high school student, your age is possibly the most important number. Since it determines what you can and cannot do, you probably wish you were older. Unfortunately, you can't change your birth date; you can only wait for another year to pass. However, you can influence an equally significant number: your GPA. Many high schools weight AP and IB higher than regular courses. Instead of a 4.0 for an A in AP Human Geography or IB Computer Science (HL), you'll receive a 5.0. This increase not only improves your class rank, but also awes those in college admissions. So while you can't blow out the candles on your cake just yet, you'll still have one wish granted.

- *Transition smoothly to college-level work.* If you coast through high school, your first day of college might cause a panic attack. Upon opening the syllabus, you'll quickly notice the coursework required. Two chapters of reading a night, three forum posts a week, four quizzes a month, five tests a semester. Because of the sheer volume of work, you might end up dropping out or failing the class. By taking AP or IB, however, this amount won't seem out of the ordinary. In these programs, the workload slowly increases each year. Consequently, during the second semester of your senior year, these high school courses will resemble college ones. Which means when you actually do read through your syllabus, you won't need a paramedic on standby.

- *Gain critical-thinking skills.* In high school, you might feel more robot than human. You hear, compute, memorize, and then spew data back out. But you're not AI; you have a frontal lobe. And in AP and IB, you can utilize this important part of your brain. Teachers actually encourage critical thinking in all discussions, assignments, and exams. So at the end of the year, you'll act less like C-3PO or R2-D2 and more like Luke or Leia. Even the force isn't powerful enough to cause such a transformation.

# The Bottom Line

You've probably heard every "No" response in the book from your parents. "It's not your birthday." "The budget's tight this month." "You don't need it." "Never in a million years." Whenever you ask for some spare change, their wallets seem closed for business. But maybe the issue isn't about the money; it's about the item. They won't buy you a new outfit, video game, or concert ticket. However, if you request the cash to cover an AP or IB exam—an investment in your education—you might actually get a "Yes," especially when they discover the relatively low cost of the exams. They could pay just $91 for one AP Exam or $270 ($160 candidate registration fee plus $110 candidate subject fee) for one IB exam that could earn you three college credits, compared to $4,986 for one three-credit course at Rice University (cost for tuition on a per-credit-hour basis). With such huge savings, they might finally be able to envision retiring in a condo in Boca instead of living out their golden years in your future basement. ***Short-term savings = $4,895 (AP) or $4,716 (IB).***

## AP
By taking an AP Exam instead of three semester credits at Rice University:
> You could avoid $4,895 in student loans. You'll save **$1,335** in interest*, assuming each loan is subsidized and has a 5% interest rate and a term of 10 years.

### OR
> You could invest $4,895 in retirement accounts. After 40 years, you'll earn **$29,566** in interest*, assuming each investment has a 5% interest rate, compounded annually.

## IB
By taking an IB exam instead of three semester credits at Rice University:
> You could avoid $4,716 in student loans. You'll save **$1,286** in interest*,

assuming each loan is subsidized and has a 5% interest rate and a term of 10 years.

OR

> You could invest $4,716 in retirement accounts. After 40 years, you'll earn **$28,485** in interest*, assuming each investment has a 5% interest rate, compounded annually.

*Numbers are rounded.

# The Brief Questions

Ask yourself all of the following before starting this opportunity:

- *Although you aren't guaranteed college credit upon completion, are you still willing to take an AP or IB course and/or exam?* To be awarded credit for AP or IB, your future college or university must accept the exam, and you'll need to obtain at least that institution's minimum required score. So while participating in these programs will still be advantageous (see The Benefits segment), it might not help you graduate early. If you want to earn actual credit now, take classes through a dual enrollment program instead (FTO #4: Dual Enrollment (DE)).

Answered "No"? DEALBREAKER

- *Do you have the time and energy for AP or IB courses?* To take part in classes offered by either program, you'll need to have not only the mental but also the physical capability to complete a large amount of homework. If you already have a limited schedule and are nearing exhaustion, first reduce or eliminate at least a few of your outside responsibilities. After your calendar has some room, test the waters by signing up for only one or two AP or IB courses. (As IB has a reputation for being even more difficult than AP, consider avoiding IB altogether.) If you're able to manage these classes, you can incrementally add another one or two to your schedule at the start of the following school year(s).

Answered "No"? RED FLAG

- *Are you willing to switch schools?* To meet the demand, more and more high schools are offering AP and IB classes. Even so, these programs aren't everywhere. IB, in particular, is especially limited. If you're homeschooled or your current school doesn't have AP or IB and you don't want to leave, take an AP class through independent study or an AP or IB course online. Or you can forgo a class and just sit for an AP Exam in the spring.

Answered "No"? **RED FLAG**

- *Do you score well on standardized exams (i.e., PSAT/NMSQT, SAT, ACT) or essay tests?* To earn credit for AP or IB, you'll need to receive a fairly decent score. Achieving a high grade in the class will look good on your college apps, but won't get you college credit. If you know the course material but typically perform poorly on standardized exams (AP) or essay tests (IB), practice, practice, and practice some more. For AP, take three to five practice exams spread out over several weeks to months. And for IB, answer questions from past exam papers and sit for the mock exams hosted by your high school.

Answered "No"? **RED FLAG**

- *Is your academic record strong?* To excel in a particular AP or IB class, you'll need to have a high GPA in at least that subject area. (For the full IB Diploma, you'll need a high GPA in multiple subject areas.) If your grades are more subpar than superior, don't complete this opportunity. As many counselors would advise, it's better to get an A or B in a regular course than a C or worse in an advanced course. But if you're earning high marks and you haven't responded with a "No" to any of the previous questions, strongly consider completing this opportunity.

Answered "No"? **DEALBREAKER**

Answered "Yes"? **CLINCHER**

||||||||||||||||||||||||||||||||||||||||||||||| **AP OR IB?** |||||||||||||||||||||||||||||||||||||||||||||||||||||||

Can't decide between AP and IB? Take this quiz to help guide your decision.

1.  My high school or a nearby high school offers (circle all that apply)
    A.   AP classes
    B.   IB classes

2.  My schedule has no room for anything but school and homework.
    A.   True
    B.   False

3.  I'm strong in
    A.   one or two subject areas
    B.   multiple subject areas

4.  I want most of my classes to have different students.
    A.   True
    B.   False

5.  My parents can't afford to spend more than $100 per exam.
    A.   True
    B.   False

6.  I perform better on exams with
    A.   a fairly even mix of multiple-choice and free-response questions
    B.   mostly just free-response questions

7.  I want to take the end-of-year exam but not take the yearlong class first.
    A.   True
    B.   False

8.  I'd prefer my final score to be based on the
    A.    end-of-year exam only
    B.    end-of-year exam and in-class assignments

9.  I plan to attend a college or university
    A.    nationally
    B.    internationally

Once you've finished, tally up your number of A's and B's.

> If you circled mostly A's, you might be better suited for Advanced Placement. Look at FTO #1: Advanced Placement (AP) Exams.

> If you circled mostly B's, you might be better suited for International Baccalaureate. Look at FTO #2: International Baccalaureate (IB) Exams.

> If you circled roughly the same number of A's and B's, you might be suited for either program. You can choose one or the other, or take classes offered by each.

*Note:* Even if you answered all A's or all B's, don't immediately jump in. Sit in on an AP or IB class or review practice AP Exams or past IB exams. Only after getting a feel for the actual experience should you consider signing up.

# FAST-TRACK OPPORTUNITY #1: ADVANCED PLACEMENT (AP) EXAMS

✓ Start planning in winter of 9th, 10th, or 11th grade
✓ Complete in 10th, 11th, or 12th grade
✓ Spend $ to $$ (per exam)
✓ Earn potentially + to ++ credits (per exam)

The College Board offers more than 30 AP courses in seven categories: AP Capstone, Arts, English, History & Social Sciences, Math & Computer Science, Sciences, and World Languages & Cultures. If you want more information about the process for all AP Exams, review the current version of the "Bulletin for AP Students and Parents." But if you only need specifics about a particular course and its respective exam (or for AP Studio Art, portfolio), read the course overview and course description.

Haven't yet learned about the basics and benefits of participating in AP? Refer back to the Intro to College Credit-by-Exam, starting on page 19.

## The Blueprint

### ATTEND CLASS

1. *Select an AP course(s).* Meet with your high school counselor and discuss AP. Find out about the school's enrollment requirements and procedures as

---

# Ⅲ DOES AP REALLY PREPARE YOU FOR COLLEGE? Ⅲ

The AP program has received various criticisms in recent years, one of the biggest being that not every high school AP program truly exposes its students to the challenging level of college work. In response, some colleges (particularly highly selective ones) have become stricter about what scores they'll accept, or have stopped accepting them altogether.

What does this mean for you? As a student, if you feel your high school's AP program isn't quite up to par, ask yourself three questions:

> Am I still going to be learning more difficult subject matter than if I took a regular class?
> Am I willing to put in extra effort on my own outside of class?
> Do the colleges that I'm interested in attending accept AP credit?

If you answered yes to all three and believe that taking AP would be worthwhile, then go for it! As with any opportunity in life, your AP experience will be what you make of it.

---

well as its AP course offerings. After the appointment, take the necessary steps to sign up for AP classes. If possible, enroll far in advance of the deadline. If you wait too long, all of the spots might be filled.

2. ***Show up to class.*** You won't receive an A just by making an appearance. In AP, you're expected to complete college-level work. To earn a high grade, you must actively listen to lectures, participate in group discussions, write papers, construct presentations, and study for quizzes and tests. With all these requirements, you might feel overwhelmed. But don't lose focus on the long term. Your effort will increase your knowledge and improve your organization, communication, and problem-solving skills. So come springtime, you'll not only be prepared for the exam, but for college and beyond.

## REGISTER FOR THE EXAM

3. ***Record dates and deadlines.*** The College Board provides an AP calendar

on its website. While this time line mostly remains the same with tests being offered in May, specific dates fluctuate year to year. Record them in your planner. Some deadlines only pertain to certain groups (students with disabilities and homeschooled students), so you won't need to include them all.

4. *Sign up for the exam(s).* If your school offers AP, contact its AP Coordinator in January. While your high school counselor helped you register for AP classes, your AP Coordinator will help you register for the AP Exams. In addition to this responsibility, the AP Coordinator will also order the necessary exam materials, collect the exam fees, handle administration incidents during the exams, return exams, and more. If you're homeschooled or your high school doesn't offer AP, you'll need to find a participating school. Request a list of local AP Coordinators from AP Services. Contact them before mid–March (the exact date varies from year to year). Once you locate a school willing to administer the exam(s) to you, that school's AP Coordinator will order the exam materials, collect the exam fees, and inform you when and where to report for your first exam.

5. *Pay for the exam(s).* Each AP Exam is $91. However, you may pay more or less than this amount. Fees for administration and late testing can increase it, while reductions and subsidies can decrease it. Students with significant financial need will qualify for a $29 College Board fee reduction per exam and, if provided by their state, federal and/or state funds as well. To find out the eligibility criteria and any required steps for receiving need-based aid, get in touch with your AP Coordinator.

6. *Request testing accommodations (if applicable).* If you have a documented disability, you may be eligible for extended time; large-type exams; large-block answer sheets; use of a Braille device, computer, or magnifier; an aide to read to you or write for you; a written copy of oral instructions; or some other accommodation. To gain approval for any of the aforementioned, submit your request with supporting documentation (if needed) to the College Board's Services for Students with Disabilities (SSD) by late February (the exact date varies from year to year). For more information, talk with your school's SSD Coordinator.

## STUDY FOR THE EXAM

7. *Acquire learning materials.* To get ready for an AP Exam, you can utilize a variety of resources. While the first three are accessible to all high school students, the last two aren't options if you're studying independently.

   a. *Textbook(s):* If you're an on-campus or online student, use your course textbook(s). But if you're an independent study student, borrow one from your public or school library or buy an older edition. Skim through the chapters, focusing your time and attention on topics forgotten or not fully understood. Cost: varies, possibly free.

   b. *Study guides:* Purchase one or more on your exam subject from a brick-and-mortar or online retailer. You can choose from a variety of options such as *Barron's AP* by Barron's Educational Series, *Cracking the AP Exam* by The Princeton Review, *Kaplan AP* by Kaplan AP Series, *Cliffs AP* by CliffsNotes, *5 Steps to a 5* by McGraw-Hill, and *MyMaxScore* by Sourcebooks. (Can't decide? Go with *Barron's AP* or *Cracking the AP Exam*. Many students recommend these guides above all of the others.) Read through the contents and take the included practice exams. Cost: varies.

   c. *The College Board website:* Visit apstudent.collegeboard.org. Check out free-response questions and scoring guidelines from previous years as well as test-taking tips and, if available for your specific exam, study skills. While all of these are free, many of the free-response questions and scoring guidelines are only accessible after you've logged in to your College Board account. Cost: free.

   d. *Schoolwork:* Gather all of your notes, handouts, assignments, quizzes, and tests. After organizing them by topic, look through each piece in the pile. Cost: free.

   e. *Study group:* Arrange a meeting with a few AP students. Keep the number to around three to five. Bring your textbook and other course papers. Discuss concepts, compare notes, and ask questions. Cost: free.

8. *Prepare for the exam(s).* Even if you're currently enrolled in an AP course, you'll still need to put in some work outside the classroom. About two or three months prior to the exam(s) (earlier if you're studying independently), take a practice test. You can find at least two in all of the study guides mentioned in the previous step. Then, set up a study schedule based on your results. The lower the score, the more time you

should spend hitting the books. A week prior to the exam(s), complete at least one more practice test and finish any last-minute cramming. But the night before the big day, put away your study materials and give your brain a rest.

9. ***Gather items for exam day.*** Refer to the list that follows for the College Board's guidelines on items to bring to the school and items not to bring into the testing room. This list is based on rules published in the "Bulletin for AP Students and Parents."

| BRING | DON'T BRING |
|---|---|
| • Sharpened No. 2 pencils (with erasers) <br> • Black or dark blue ink pens <br> • Six-digit school code (if you're homeschooled, you will receive this code at the time of your exam) <br> • Watch (without an alarm or that doesn't beep) <br> • Photo ID (if you're at a school other than your own) <br> • Ruler or straightedge (only for the AP Physics Exam) <br> • No more than two College Board-authorized calculators (only for the AP Biology, Calculus, Chemistry, Physics, and Statistics Exams) <br> • Social Security number (optional) <br> • SSD Student Accommodation Letter (only for students with approved disability accommodations) | • Electronic equipment (cell phone, smartphone, laptop, tablet, MP3 player, camera, handheld game console, etc.) <br> • Books (including dictionaries) <br> • Compasses, protractors, or other nonapproved measuring devices <br> • Mechanical pencils, colored pencils*, highlighters*, or other unapproved writing utensils <br> • Correction fluid <br> • Notes or scratch paper <br> • Computers* <br> • Reference guides or instructions for typing <br> • Clothing displaying information related to the exam subject <br> • Food or drink* |

*This item will be allowed only if it has been officially preapproved before the test date as an accommodation for your disability.

## TAKE THE EXAM

10. *Show up for the exam(s).* AP Exams occur during the month of May. All but one start at 8:00 a.m. or 12:00 p.m. on a school day. Most students take them on their campus. If you're in this group, you can leave your GPS at home. Simply go to your current school. But if you need to test elsewhere, leave the house early and follow the nav's directions. Upon arrival, present your ID to the school's AP Coordinator.

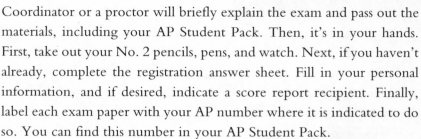

I'm no stranger to the snooze button. In high school, I would frequently wait until the last possible second to roll out of bed. To prevent a mad dash in the morning or risk showing up late, I packed the items needed for a standardized exam the night before and placed the bag right next to the front door.

11. *Settle in your seat.* You'll probably test in a classroom. The AP Coordinator or a proctor will briefly explain the exam and pass out the materials, including your AP Student Pack. Then, it's in your hands. First, take out your No. 2 pencils, pens, and watch. Next, if you haven't already, complete the registration answer sheet. Fill in your personal information, and if desired, indicate a score report recipient. Finally, label each exam paper with your AP number where it is indicated to do so. You can find this number in your AP Student Pack.

12. *Sit for the exam(s).* Most AP Exams exist in a paper-and-pencil format, last from two to three hours, and contain two different sections. In the first section, you'll find multiple-choice questions. Fill in the correct circles on your answer sheet. In the second section, you'll find free-response questions. Write your answers in your exam booklet. Between these two sections, you'll

Don't leave any multiple-choice questions blank. Unlike in previous years, wrong answers won't negatively impact your score. If you have no clue, pick C and move on to the next one.

have a scheduled break. Use this time to go to the restroom, grab a drink of water, or simply move your muscles. Just don't leave the building—it's prohibited.

## VIEW YOUR SCORE

13. *Create a College Board account.* Registered for the PSAT/NMSQT or SAT? Created a list of your favorite colleges on BigFuture? Made a CSS/PROFILE? You may have already completed this step. If not, go through the "My Account" registration portal. Fill in your personal information and pick a username and password. Shortly after, check your email for a welcome letter from the site.

14. *Withhold or cancel your score(s) (if desired).* If you performed poorly on an AP Exam, you can prevent a college or university from seeing your score. To withhold one or more scores from a particular school, fill out an "AP Score Withholding Form." The fee is $10 per score, per college. To permanently cancel one or more scores, fill out an "AP Score Cancellation Form." There is no fee for this service, but you won't receive a refund for the exam(s). Once completed, submit either document by fax to (610) 290-8979 or by mail to AP Services, P.O. Box 6671, Princeton, NJ 08541-6671. While you can withhold or cancel at any time, AP Services must receive your request by mid-June (the exact date varies from year to year), so as not to send the score(s) to the college indicated on your registration answer sheet.

15. *Receive your score(s).* Starting in July, you can access your AP score(s) online. For the exact date, check apscore.org. Log in to your College Board account and enter your AP number. Based on your performance, expect a score between 1 (lowest) and 5 (highest). The American Council on Education (ACE) and the College Board recommend that credit be awarded for scores of 3 or higher—a 3 indicates that you are "qualified" to do college-level work in the given subject area. However, colleges and universities ultimately establish their own score requirements, so even if you get a 3, it doesn't guarantee that you'll earn credit. To find out a particular school's AP credit policy, use the search tool on the AP portion of the College Board website, or go straight to the college's website and search "AP credit" or "AP Exams" to ensure that you're getting the most up-to-date information.

## OBTAIN CREDIT FOR THE EXAM

16. *Verify score report delivery (if applicable).* If you designated a college or university on your registration answer sheet, the College Board will

send your AP score(s) directly to them. While some schools will notify you after receiving your score report, others will remain silent. You'll need to make the first contact. Close to the end of August, call or email the registrar's office. Ask about your score report. The school should have at least received the document. And depending on its AP policy, granted you credit or advanced placement.

Every fall, the AP Program honors high school students with AP Scholar Awards. To earn one, you must achieve high scores on several AP Exams. While these awards don't provide money or scholarships, they do get added to your official score reports and could improve your chances of admission or of receiving an academic scholarship from the colleges you apply to.

17. ***Order a score report (if applicable).*** If you didn't designate a college or university on your registration answer sheet or you want to send your score(s) to additional schools, you can request score reports any time after your exam. The cost for each report is $15 (rush processing is $25). Make this request through your College Board account, by fax, or by mail. If you choose the fax or mail option, you'll need to create and submit a document with detailed information to AP Services (see contact information in Step #14). For the exact specifications, read about score reporting services on the AP portion of the College Board website.

---

## ⊪⊪⊪⊪⊪⊪⊪⊪⊪⊪⊪ DOUBLE-CHECK YOUR WORK ⊪⊪⊪⊪⊪⊪⊪⊪⊪⊪⊪

### ATTEND CLASS
- ❏ Select an AP course(s)
- ❏ Show up to class

### REGISTER FOR THE EXAM
- ❏ Record dates and deadlines

---

- ☐ Sign up for the exam(s)
- ☐ Pay for the exam(s)
- ☐ Request testing accommodations (if applicable)

## STUDY FOR THE EXAM

- ☐ Acquire learning materials
- ☐ Prepare for the exam(s)
- ☐ Gather items for exam day

## TAKE THE EXAM

- ☐ Show up for the exam(s)
- ☐ Settle in your seat
- ☐ Sit for the exam(s)

## VIEW YOUR SCORE

- ☐ Create a College Board account
- ☐ Withhold or cancel your score(s) (if desired)
- ☐ Receive your score(s)

## OBTAIN CREDIT FOR THE EXAM

- ☐ Verify score report delivery (if applicable)
- ☐ Order a score report (if applicable)

# FAST-TRACK OPPORTUNITY #2: INTERNATIONAL BACCALAUREATE (IB) EXAMS

✓ Start planning in fall of 7th, 8th, 9th, or 10th grade
✓ Complete in 11th and 12th grade
✓ Spend $ to $$ (per exam)
✓ Earn potentially + to ++ credits (per exam)

IB offers international curriculum for students ages three to 19. Out of the four IB programs, two are designed for high school students: the Diploma Programme (DP) and the Career-related Programme (CP). While these two high school programs are available, you probably won't have a choice between them. Since the CP is relatively new, it's currently in relatively few schools worldwide. Therefore, you might have to go with the DP. Even so, you'll still have a decision to make. You can graduate with a full IB Diploma or just take individual IB subjects and earn one or more IB Certificates.

Haven't yet learned about the basics and benefits of participating in IB? Refer back to the Intro to College Credit-by-Exam, starting on page 19.

|||||||||||||||||| **CURRICULUM REQUIREMENTS** ||||||||||||||||||
**FOR THE IB DIPLOMA AND THE IB CP**

IB Diploma Curriculum: You must take six Diploma Programme courses and sit for the IB exams in those six subject areas as well as complete the DP core. The DP core includes an extended essay (an independent and self-directed 4,000-word essay on a topic relevant to one of the six DP subjects), a theory of knowledge course (an interdisciplinary course with discussion and reflection on the topic of knowledge), and creativity, action, and service activities (a minimum 150 hours of creative activity, physical exercise, and volunteer work outside of class time).

IB CP Curriculum: You must take at least two Diploma Programme courses and sit for the IB exams in those subject areas as well as complete the CP core and an approved career-related study. The CP core includes an approaches to learning course (a course aimed at developing practical and career-related skills), community and service (a minimum 50 hours of service learning outside of class time), a reflective project (a project on an ethical dilemma displayed in one of a variety of formats), and language development (exposure to and development of a second language).

# The Blueprint

## DISCOVER IB

1. *Find an IB World School.* To locate one of these schools, go to the IB website and use the search tool. Select the appropriate IB region, country, and IB programme, and then type in your state as a keyword. You'll then be provided a list of schools that meet this criteria. Click on a school name to see its contact information and some of the IB subjects it offers. But even if there isn't an IB school nearby, you can still participate in the program online. Although you can't complete the IB Diploma on your computer, you can take several courses through Pamoja Education. For more about this option, email dp.online@ibo .org or admissions@pamojaeducation.com.

2. ***Visit an IB World School (if applicable).*** Unless you plan on only completing IB courses online, as early as 7th grade, spend a day at a nearby school that offers the Diploma Programme. (If two or more schools close by your residency offer the DP, feel free to visit each of them on separate days.) First, meet with the IB Coordinator. Discuss all the aspects of the program, including admission requirements, course curriculum, and end-of-year exams. Request a copy of any important papers or forms. Then, tour the campus. Locate the main office, gym, cafeteria, auditorium, and classrooms. Finally, sit in on at least one or two actual IB courses. After the period, talk with the students and teachers about their experiences with IB. Exchange contact information if desired.

## SUBMIT YOUR APPLICATION

3. ***Meet the school's IB eligibility requirements.*** Since IB is an academically rigorous program, many schools won't accept applications from just any student. You'll have to prove you're capable of the challenge first. Complete the prerequisite (or pre-IB) courses while maintaining a high GPA, superior standard-

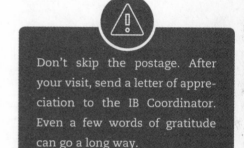

Don't skip the postage. After your visit, send a letter of appreciation to the IB Coordinator. Even a few words of gratitude can go a long way.

ized test scores, near perfect attendance, and a clean disciplinary record. Obviously, these strict standards eliminate many students. However, sometimes even the smartest and most diligent make mistakes. If you don't quite hit all of the requirements, speak with the IB Coordinator. The school might make an exception and still allow your application.

4. ***Apply to the school's IB program.*** Depending on your selected IB school, you may need to apply as early as 8th grade or as late as 10th. But in either case, start the application process several months prior to the due date. Unless you want to register only for individual IB courses, you'll probably need to write an essay, obtain recommendation letters, complete an interview, and more. After finishing each part and submitting all necessary documentation, be prepared to wait. Depending on the number of IB applicants, you might not hear word of acceptance or rejection for months.

5. ***Switch schools (if applicable).*** Because IB isn't offered at every high school, you may need to request a transfer in- or out-of-district. In-district (intradistrict) transfers are more often approved than out-of-district (interdistrict) transfers, although there are no guarantees either way. If transfer applications are reviewed and accepted in the order they are received, you can improve your chances by having your parents fill out and submit the transfer form as early as possible. Once you receive approval, visit your new school. While there, complete the registration paperwork and ask about its bus routes. Likely, you'll need to find your own transportation.

Don't wait until your junior year to switch high schools. Especially if you're switching from a private to a public school, the longer you wait, the more likely that not all of your high school credits will transfer to your new school. This loss of credit could mean a summer or two in summer school or even worse, a delay in your high school graduation.

## ATTEND CLASS

6. ***Enroll in one or more IB class(es).*** If you're seeking an IB Diploma, you must take six IB courses. You can take one course from each of the six subject groups (studies in language and literature, language acquisition, individuals and societies, sciences, mathematics, and the arts) or forgo the arts course and take an additional languages, individuals and societies, or sciences course instead. At least three but no more than four courses must be taken at the higher level (HL), while the remaining can be taken at the standard level (SL). Higher level courses are not only more in-depth and often more rigorous, they also require 240 teaching hours compared to 150 hours for the standard level. Therefore, HL courses typically last two years and SL courses typically last one year. If you're not seeking the IB Diploma, you don't have these restrictions. You can choose any IB courses at the standard or higher level.

7. ***Excel in your IB class(es).*** Whether you take AP or IB, your coursework will determine your final grade. But with IB, you have even more incentive to succeed inside the classroom. Unlike with your AP score, your IB score likely isn't based just on the end-of-year exam. Teacher

assessments such as oral work, fieldwork, investigations, lab work, and artistic performances may contribute from 20 percent to 50 percent. Therefore, you should strive for top marks throughout the year, not just at the very end.

## REGISTER FOR THE EXAM

8. *Sign up for the exam(s).* During the fall of 11th or 12th grade, your school's IB Coordinator will hand out the exam registration form. On the form, fill in your personal information and select your IB exam(s). Juniors can take up to two standard level exams, while seniors can take up to six standard or higher level exams. But in either case, you can only sit for an exam in a particular subject if you took the IB course in that same subject. Once the form is complete, give the paperwork along with payment back to your IB Coordinator. Payment covers the $160 candidate registration fee (paid once per year) and the $110 candidate subject fee (paid per subject exam). Since these fees can add up quickly, your school may offer scholarships, grants, and waivers to lower your total cost. Contact your IB Coordinator for information about any potential financial aid opportunities.

9. *Request testing accommodations (if applicable).* Since you're currently enrolled in the IB program, your school probably already knows about your disability. However, you should speak with your IB Coordinator regarding accommodations for the exam(s). Depending on the accommodation requested, your school may or may not need authorization from the International Baccalaureate Assessment Centre (IB's assessment headquarters in Cardiff, Wales). If authorization is required, your IB Coordinator or head of school must

Don't panic over an unexpected incident. If an adverse circumstance (bereavement, natural disaster, and civil unrest) or temporary medical condition (severe illness or accident) occurs during your written exam(s) and negatively impacts your performance, your IB Coordinator or head of school can submit a completed *Form D2* (and if relevant, medical documentation) to IB Cardiff within 10 days after your final exam, making you eligible for special arrangements or compensation.

submit a completed *Form D1* along with medical documentation to the coordinator help desk at IB Cardiff. The form must be sent at least 12 months prior to your written exam(s) (or as soon as possible after the start of your first year if you're an anticipated candidate).

## STUDY FOR THE EXAM

10. *Acquire learning materials.* To get ready for an IB exam, you can utilize a variety of resources. While this list isn't comprehensive, the following are common IB study aids:

   a. *Textbook(s):* Bring your course textbook(s) home from school. Skim through the chapters, focusing your time and attention on topics forgotten or not fully understood. Cost: free.

   b. *Oxford books:* Go to the Oxford University Press website (U.S. version). If available, buy a course book (print or online), study guide, skills and practice book, or all three. Read through the content (course book and study guide) and complete the activities and exercises (skills and practice book). Cost: $36 to $65 (print and online course book packs cost more).

   c. *Past exams:* Visit the IB's online store. Purchase and download exam papers and markschemes (recommended answers to exam questions and the point ranges corresponding to those recommended answers) from previous years. Review the questions and their respective correct answers. Cost: £1.99 (around $3.00) per paper or markscheme.

   d. *Schoolwork:* Gather all of your notes, handouts, assignments, quizzes, and tests. After organizing them by topic, look through each piece in the pile. When you come across information pertaining to a course objective (listed in the syllabus), write it down on a personalized study sheet. Create one for each course. Cost: free.

   e. *Study group:* Arrange a meeting with a few IB students. Keep the number to around three to five. Bring your textbook(s), past exams, and course papers. Discuss concepts, compare notes, and ask questions. Cost: free.

11. *Prepare for the exam(s).* In late winter or early spring, your school will likely offer mock IB exams. Even if they aren't required, take them. Then, set up a study schedule based on your results. The lower your score and the higher the number of problem areas, the more time you should hit the books. But the night before the big day, put away your study materials and give your brain a rest.

## TAKE THE EXAM

12. *Show up for the exam(s).* IB exams are offered during the months of May (most often for Northern Hemisphere schools) and November (most often for Southern Hemisphere schools). Some start after 7:00 a.m., while others begin after 12:00 p.m. on a school day. If you're enrolled in an on-campus or online IB course(s) through your local school, you don't need to test somewhere else. You'll take your IB exam(s) at your current school. But if you're enrolled in an online IB course(s) through an Open World School, you'll need to test on a campus other than your own. You'll take your exam(s) at an approved IB World School.

13. *Sit for the exam(s).* Every IB exam consists of one, two, or three papers, lasting from 45 minutes to three hours each. Typically, one or two papers are completed on the first day, and the remaining one or two papers are completed on the following day. But on either day, you won't encounter many multiple-choice questions. Unlike most standardized tests, IB exams mostly just contain essays, structured problems, short-response questions, data-response questions, text-response questions, and case-study questions.

## OBTAIN CREDIT FOR THE EXAM

14. *Receive your score(s).* After July 5 (for May exams) or January 5 (for November exams), you can access your score(s) through the IB website. On the candidate results portion, log in with the personal code and pin provided by your IB Coordinator. Based on your performance, expect a score between 1 (lowest) and 7 (highest). Although many schools only award credit for higher level exams, requirements can differ greatly among colleges and universities. To find a particular school's IB credit policy, read through the section about transferring credit in the school's course catalog or on its website. If IB isn't mentioned, contact the registrar's office and ask about your score(s).

15. *Procure transcripts (if applicable).* Before your IB score(s) is released, you must request transcripts through your IB Coordinator. During this time, you can send up to six free of charge. (However, only one of these can be delivered to a U.S. institution and one to a Canadian institution.) Once your IB score(s) has been released, you must request transcripts directly from IB. Submit the order form online with debit or credit card information or by mail with check. Each transcript costs $17. If you have any

questions about transcripts, contact IB by phone on its U.S. line at (301) 202-3025 or by email at ibid@ibo.org.

16. *Verify transcript deliveries (if applicable).* Schools should receive your transcripts within a few weeks after submitting the online or hard copy form (possibly longer during the months of December, January, July, August, and September). While some schools will notify you after receiving your transcripts, others will remain silent. You'll need to make the first contact. About a month after your request, call or email all of the schools. Each should have at least received your transcript. And depending on its IB policy, granted you credit or advanced placement.

---

## ⅢⅢⅢⅢⅢⅢⅢⅢⅢⅢⅢⅢ DOUBLE-CHECK YOUR WORK ⅢⅢⅢⅢⅢⅢⅢⅢⅢⅢⅢⅢ

### DISCOVER IB
❐ Find an IB World School
❐ Visit an IB World School (if applicable)

### SUBMIT YOUR APPLICATION
❐ Meet the school's IB eligibility requirements
❐ Apply to the school's IB program
❐ Switch schools (if applicable)

### ATTEND CLASS
❐ Enroll in one or more IB classes
❐ Excel in your IB class(es)

### REGISTER FOR THE EXAM
❐ Sign up for the exam(s)
❐ Request testing accommodations (if applicable)

### STUDY FOR THE EXAM
❐ Acquire learning materials
❐ Prepare for the exam(s)

## TAKE THE EXAM
- ☐  Show up for the exam(s)
- ☐  Sit for the exam(s)

## OBTAIN CREDIT FOR THE EXAM
- ☐  Receive your score(s)
- ☐  Procure transcripts (if applicable)
- ☐  Verify transcript deliveries (if applicable)

# FAST-TRACK OPPORTUNITY #3:
# PRE-COLLEGE SUMMER PROGRAMS
## The Early Student Catches the College Life

✓ Start planning in fall of 9th, 10th, 11th, or 12th grade
✓ Complete in summer after 9th, 10th, 11th, or 12th grade (typically summer after 10th or 11th grade)
✓ Spend approximately $$$
✓ Earn potentially + to ++ credits

Since my dad hailed from Missouri, I wanted to attend the High School Summer Scholars Program at Washington University in St. Louis. When I was awarded acceptance, my parents and I were elated. But on the flight to the muggy Midwest, my excitement morphed into panic. Much of what I knew about college came from the media—and it wasn't always good. Would my roommate seem like the psycho in *Single White Female*? Would my homework resemble the genius-level math problems in *Good Will Hunting*? Or would my lunch from the cafeteria appear as questionable as the servings in the *Wonder Years*?

When I arrived at the university, I felt unsettled and uneasy. And truthfully, the first week, I called my family crying. "Please, Mom, let me come home." She readily accepted the offer, but I chose to give the experience one more week. That week changed everything. I got acclimated to the campus, my classes, and my fellow peers. No longer did I want to leave; instead, I secretly wished the program wasn't just six short weeks.

No, not everything was perfect. About three weeks in, I accidentally deleted a PowerPoint presentation and had to stay up all night to redo it. I also barely passed the majority of my computer class exams. (I still have no clue how to bold text in Java.) And most importantly, I missed my family and friends back in Washington. But riding the Screamin' Eagle at Six Flags, reading endless *Cosmo* magazines with my roommate, showing up unannounced to an *American Idol* audition, and ordering pizza several nights in a row made this once overwhelming ordeal into an amazing adventure. Just like during the first week, I cried the last week of the program. But this time, I didn't cry because I wanted to go home; I cried because I wanted to stay. And those kinds of cries are the best.

## The Basics

Summer camp isn't just for kids anymore. While you probably won't be bouncing off "The Blob" or stitching lanyard key chains, you'll enjoy the same freedom and adventure in a pre-college summer program, but without all of the mosquito bites. Wave good-bye to Mom and Dad and welcome your new home: the dorms. During your stay, enjoy ice cream for breakfast and midnight study sessions. And since most programs last only a few weeks, you'll still be able to watch reruns in your pajamas for most of the summer.

Yet pre-college summer programs are more than just camps with junk food and late nights. Offered at several colleges and universities across the United States, they're designed to expose high school students to the rigors of college academics and the flexibility of college life before even graduating. Students enroll in actual college classes, share quarters with roommates, and engage in campus activities. But be aware that your opportunities to enroll in one of these programs can be limited. While many programs encourage participation from students between 9th and 12th grades, some only accept applications from students in their sophomore or junior year.

## The Benefits

- *Experience the freedom of college life.* Your parents aren't down the hall anymore; they're now several states away. No obligation to clean your room (although it's still advised), eat your vegetables (some say french fries count), or finish your homework before dinner (the predawn hours can be extremely productive). While your folks may still text unsolicited advice—"Remember to take your vitals every morning. XOXO, Mom...Oops! I meant vitals...No, I meant vitamins...Autocorrect again. XOXO, Mom."—feel free to silence your phone. You obviously love them, but absence makes the heart grow fonder, right?

- **Meet students from around the globe.** Sharing a locker with a foreign exchange student may not be your only interaction with people from other countries. In your pre-college summer classes, you might encounter students from the four corners of the world. Introduce yourself and engage in conversation with them. *Et il ne serait pas mal pour étudier certaines phrases clés en langue étrangère avant de partir.* (For those who don't speak French: "And it wouldn't hurt to study some key foreign language phrases before you go.")

- **Test out a school.** Ever purchased a seemingly perfect pair of shoes, only to be limping from pain a week later? To make matters worse, they cost an arm and a leg and aren't refundable. Think of college as a very, very expensive pair of shoes. Even if you tour the campus and sit in on a few classes, it can take a few weeks, or sometimes even longer, to really discover if it's a good fit for you. And if you hate it, you're stuck there for at least a semester, unless you're willing to lose money and forgo credits to transfer to a new school. Fortunately, just like borrowing your friend's shoes, with a pre-college summer program, you can try out a college before buying a semester or more of tuition. So once you do seal the deal, you won't feel a smidge of buyer's remorse.

- **Explore a new city.** You aren't Christopher Columbus or Marco Polo, but you can still survey lands with a pre-college summer program. Many of these programs organize off-campus events and activities and encourage students to visit local sites on their own as well. If that's an option, tie up your laces, grab a couple friends, and hit the town. While you won't claim any new worlds, you still might discover a few great places.

## The Bottom Line

Although early-bird specials are most popular among senior citizens, students can also take advantage of these discounts. But instead of saving a couple of bucks by going to dinner a few hours early, save a couple thousand by going to college a few years early. As a pre-college summer student, you'll receive the same quality education as a regular student, but at a fraction of the cost. For example, by attending the University of Miami's Summer Scholars Program as a residential student, you'll only pay $6,980 for six semester credits, textbooks, a room, a meal plan, and access to student services. Or if you're a commuter student simply desiring credit, a lunch meal plan, and access to student services, you'll pay even less: only $5,853. On the other hand, if you attend this university during a typical school year, you'll pay $10,740 for six credits alone (cost for tuition on a per-credit-hour basis). *Short-term savings = $4,887 (or $3,760 for a residential student).*

By earning six semester credits as a commuter student during the Summer Scholars Program instead of during the regular school year at University of Miami:

› You could avoid $4,887 in student loans. You'll save **$1,333** in interest*, assuming each loan is subsidized and has a 5% interest rate and a term of 10 years.

OR

› You could invest $4,887 in retirement accounts. After 40 years, you'll earn **$29,518** in interest*, assuming each investment has a 5% interest rate, compounded annually.

*Numbers are rounded.*

# The Brief Questions

Ask yourself all of the following before starting this opportunity:

- *Can you or your parents afford the costs?* To pay for a pre-college summer program, you'll probably need around $4,000 to $10,000 for the tuition, room, and board. And depending on the location, you might also need to cover travel expenses. If you or your parents don't have this much available, apply for financial aid through the school. Often based on need and sometimes on merit, you might qualify for scholarships and/or grants. In addition to trying for aid, you should also choose a program close to home if possible. You'll not only save on travel costs, but also on housing and meals as a commuter student. If, after doing both of these things, you and your parents still don't have enough funds for the program, don't complete this opportunity.

## Answered "No"? **RED FLAG** or **DEALBREAKER**

- *Do you have availability this upcoming summer?* To commit to a pre-college summer program, you'll need to be available for the entire session. Pre-college programs offer one or more sessions each summer (e.g., Session A: June 30–July 25 and Session B: July 28–August 22), which typically last between two and six weeks. If your summer is booked solid, cut out some of your previously arranged activities and events, or if you're a freshman or sophomore in high school, wait one more year before applying.

## Answered "No"? **RED FLAG**

- *Are you comfortable living away from your parents?* To attend a pre-college summer program, you might need to fly and stay thousands of miles away from home. While some students consider this exhilarating, others find it frightening. If you panic at the thought of being apart from family, enroll in a program as a commuter student. You'll go to classes on campus during the day, but reside at home in the evening. If a program isn't relatively close, select one within at least a three- to four-hour drive. That way, as long as the program allows, you can visit your parents on weekends.

## Answered "No"? **RED FLAG**

- *Do you want a taste of the college experience?* To live in the dorms, take classes like Elementary Arabic and Intro to International Politics, and wear pajamas at any time of day, you usually need to finish 12th grade first. But with a pre-college summer program, you can do all these and more while in high school. If you're itching to pack your bags, move out of your parents' place, and unload on campus, and if you haven't responded with a "No" to any of the previous questions, strongly consider completing this opportunity.

Answered "Yes"? CLINCHER

# The Blueprint

## SELECT YOUR IDEAL PROGRAMS

1. *Locate colleges with high school summer programs.* To find results quickly, search the Web. Use keywords like "pre-college summer," "high school summer college," and "summer scholars." You'll find several programs, all with different strengths. For example, you could enjoy the academics at Harvard's Secondary School Program, the culture and diversity at University of Chicago's Summer Program for High School, or the nice weather at University of Southern California's Summer Program.

2. *Select your favorite eight to 10 schools.* Then, compare your choices based on several criteria, including location, program duration, tuition and other fees, GPA and test score requirements, courses offered, and interest level on a scale of 1 (least) to 5 (most). Consider creating a spreadsheet similar to the example on the next page. Include additional categories if desired.

Not all pre-college summer programs award credit. Before applying, make sure the program's classes offer college credit. If they do, also find out the amount.

| COLLEGE | LOCATION | DURATION | TUITION & FEES | GPA & TEST SCORE REQUIREMENTS | COURSES OFFERED | INTEREST |
|---------|----------|----------|----------------|-------------------------------|-----------------|----------|
|         |          |          |                |                               |                 |          |
|         |          |          |                |                               |                 |          |
|         |          |          |                |                               |                 |          |
|         |          |          |                |                               |                 |          |
|         |          |          |                |                               |                 |          |

3. *Review your choices.* Ask yourself a few questions about each program: Will I live in the dorms or commute? Will the dates conflict with any of my summer plans (e.g., family reunion, summer job, or Mediterranean cruise)? Can I afford the tuition and fees? Am I eligible based on my grades and test scores?

4. *Reduce your list of favorite schools.* Based on your comparisons, pick around four to five schools. You should choose two "match" schools (your grades and test scores are in-line with their average student) for every one "reach" school (your grades and test scores are below its average student) and one "safety" school (your grades and test scores are above its average student).

## PREPARE YOUR APPLICATIONS

5. *Record the application deadlines.* In your planner, note the application deadlines for your favorite four to five schools. A school may have regular admission or rolling admission. With rolling admission, you can send in your application anytime within a large window. However, you should still apply early to increase your chances of acceptance. By waiting until the end of the application window, you risk all of the spots filling up and your application being denied.

6. ***Request copies of your high school transcript.*** You'll either need to make a phone call or drive to your school's administration office. The program may prefer that your high school directly mails your transcript or you include a sealed transcript with your application package. A quick word to those whose grades aren't valedictorian-worthy: it's never too late to improve them. However, if a major event (e.g., a health crisis or cross-country move) impacted your GPA for a brief period of time, explain the reason on your application.

7. ***Take one or more standardized exam(s).*** You may need to sit for the PSAT/NMSQT, SAT, ACT, and/or TOEFL. While the PSAT/NMSQT is offered in October by your high school, the SAT happens seven times a year and the ACT six times a year at a testing center. If English is not your first language, you may also need to take the TOEFL. Unlike the limited test dates of the PSAT/NMSQT, SAT, and ACT, the TOEFL is offered over 50 times a year at various testing center locations. Choose a test date several months before your applications are due. Indicate a score report recipient during the exam. If this option is unavailable, formally request your scores afterward.

8. ***Obtain recommendation letters.*** Don't seek out just any teacher; find teachers who know you well and grade your work highly. When approaching your teacher with the request, bring your high school transcript, a current résumé, and basic information about the program you're hoping to attend. Your résumé should include your most recent extracurricular activities and work history (if applicable). If your program has not set any specific guidelines for the letter, have your teacher adhere to a general paper format: introduction, body, and conclusion. In the introduction, your teacher should include your name and the context of your relationship. The body should highlight your achievements and explain why you're the right student for the program. The conclusion

By participating in the PSAT/NMSQT your junior year, you're automatically eligible for recognition and scholarships. The largest scholarship granting organization for the PSAT/NMSQT is the National Merit Scholarship Corporation (NMSC), which gives more than 10,000 scholarships to 11th grade students each year.

Don't give a teacher a one-day notice to complete your letter of recommendation. To allow for some flexibility, ask your teacher to finish at least two weeks before your first application is due.

Since I was pretty clueless at 16 about my family's finances, I didn't tackle the FAFSA on my own. My mom not only helped compile the necessary paperwork, but also helped fill out the forms. With her assistance, I scored a partial scholarship for the program from the university.

should contain your teacher's name and contact information.

9. ***Compose the essay.*** This essay will showcase your writing ability as well as display your interest in a pre-college summer program. Some schools request a general essay, but picking a topic can be tricky. If you're stumped, ask yourself the following questions and base the essay on your answer to one of them. Who is your biggest inspiration? What hardships in your life have you overcome and how? What are your top three personal goals? What is your opinion on _____? (Fill in with a political, cultural, or religious issue.) Other schools, however, require a more specific essay. You'll explain why you chose their school and summer program. After finishing your general or school-specific essay, wait at least a day and then read it over slowly. Correct mistakes and delete any extraneous parts to be within the designated word count. For more in-depth help, refer to the most current edition of *Fiske Real College Essays That Work* by Edward B. Fiske and Bruce G. Hammond.

10. ***Complete the financial aid forms (if applicable).*** Some schools may award money to pre-college summer students. To be eligible, you'll likely need to file a Free Application for Federal Student Aid (FAFSA) at fafsa .ed.gov. Obtain your parents' tax return from the previous year and fill in all of the required information. If your parents aren't together, use the financials for your custodial parent (the parent you've resided with the most over the past 12 months). After submitting and electronically signing your FAFSA, you and your selected colleges will receive a copy of your student aid report within seven to 10 days.

## APPLY FOR ADMISSION

11. *Submit your applications.* Meet the deadlines and include all of the necessary paperwork (including your transcript, test scores, recommendation letters, essay, and application fee). If you're sending your applications through the U.S. Postal Service, consider purchasing delivery confirmation. This extra service provides you with the date and time of package delivery, but doesn't require the recipient's signature.

12. *Wait for news.* You might not have to camp outside your mailbox for months—some schools offer a window of time when they'll respond with news of acceptance or rejection. But if you're left in the dark, avoid pacing or biting your nails. Continue with your normal routine instead. Once the first envelope arrives, breathe deeply and open. If it's a rejection, don't panic or lose all hope. That's the beauty of applying to multiple schools—you only need one acceptance.

13. *Accept admission into a program.* However, hold off on any decisions until you've received an acceptance or rejection letter from every school. Complete the admissions acceptance form and pay the enrollment deposit (if applicable) by the school's deadline. If you have questions, contact the school directly.

## ATTEND THE PROGRAM

14. *Pack for the program.* If you're staying in the dorms, remember to pack bedding (likely extra-long twin), clothes, toiletries, medicines, and school supplies. If you're in contact with your future roommate, try to divide the load. Maybe just one person brings a blow-dryer or a gallon of laundry detergent. Finally, consider buying a laptop, if you don't already have one. Even if you'll have full access to campus resources, having to make constant trips to the computer lab can become inconvenient and may restrict the hours during which you're able to work on assignments.

15. *Experience the program.* Although homework is important, building friendships, seeing the local sites, and experiencing dorm life will make the program unforgettable. Also, remember the following tips while away: wear flip-flops in the shower, stay by the washer and dryer on laundry day, save your work on the computer every few minutes, and walk with a buddy at night. By following this advice, you'll save yourself

I loved living in the dorms, but not so much studying with distractions. Instead of yelling "Keep it down" every 10 minutes, I found another place to work: the library basement. Because it was summer and a ghost town, I could take up an entire table, spread out all of my books and materials, and spend hours there undisturbed.

athlete's foot, missing pants, a retyped paper, and possibly a scary call to your parents from the program's director.

16. ***Finish the program and head home.*** To shorten the period of adjustment, reestablish your old routine immediately. Wake up early. Meet up with friends for coffee at your favorite café. Run the local trails. Enjoy a long bath. Indulge in Mom's homemade chili. Before long, you'll feel like you never left. And even if the pre-college summer program was incredible, deep down you'll know—there's no place like home.

## DOUBLE-CHECK YOUR WORK

### SELECT YOUR IDEAL PROGRAMS
- ❏ Locate colleges with high school summer programs
- ❏ Select your favorite eight to 10 schools
- ❏ Review your choices
- ❏ Reduce your list of favorite schools

### PREPARE YOUR APPLICATIONS
- ❏ Record the application deadlines
- ❏ Request copies of your high school transcript
- ❏ Take one or more standardized exam(s)
- ❏ Obtain recommendation letters
- ❏ Compose the essay
- ❏ Complete the financial aid forms (if applicable)

### APPLY FOR ADMISSION
- ❏ Submit your applications

❏   Wait for news
❏   Accept admission into a program

## ATTEND THE PROGRAM
❏   Pack for the program
❏   Experience the program
❏   Finish the program and head home

# FAST-TRACK OPPORTUNITY #4:
# DUAL ENROLLMENT (DE)
## Kill Two Courses in One Period

✓ Start planning in winter of 8th, 9th, 10th, or 11th grade
✓ Complete in 9th, 10th, 11th, or 12th grade (typically 11th and 12th grade)
✓ Spend approximately $ to $$$
✓ Earn potentially + to +++ credits

During my final year in high school, I contracted a bad case of senioritis. I exhibited all of the usual symptoms including boredom, frustration, and an intense itching to graduate and start college. I patiently waited for the "illness" to subside; unfortunately, it only worsened. Looking for answers, I made an appointment with a professional: an academic advisor. Within a matter of minutes, she diagnosed my disease and recommended a remedy. She suggested participation in a dual enrollment program called Running Start, allowing me to stop attending high school and begin attending college. Eager to alleviate my ailments, I promptly followed her prescription and signed up for two courses at a local community college.

Even though leaving high school eased my senioritis, I soon confronted another common woe. Since I didn't know the campus, the teachers, or the students at my new school, I developed college jitters. My anxiety and confusion caused sweaty palms, uncontrollable shaking, a queasy stomach, and a myriad of mishaps. On my first day, I ended up in the wrong class. On my second day, I received a pricey parking ticket. And on my third day, I encountered computer trouble.

Wanting a quick fix, I considered heading back to the halls of high school. But before I even had time to seek out treatment, my nerves had run their course. And with my panic diminished, I could now see several advantages of college over high school. I could attend fewer classes, complete less busywork, and endure PE only if desired. (I rejected that tempting offer.) Even better, by the end of the quarter, I'd earned not only my high school diploma, but also 10 college credits. My college experience was just what the doctor ordered.

# The Basics

As you've probably suspected, you're not a wizard. So unlike Hermione Granger, you can't reverse the clock in order to take two different classes offered at the same time. You can, however, earn high school and college credit simultaneously. By participating in dual enrollment (DE), you'll graduate 12th grade with not only a high school diploma, but a handful of college credits or an associate's degree as well. Even better, your DE courses may be entirely free. No tuition fees, no book costs. With a program this bewitchin', who even needs magic in the Muggle world?

With more than 1.2 million students participating nationwide during the 2010–2011 academic year,[7] dual enrollment (also called dual credit) is rapidly catching up with the AP program as one of the most common ways to make college degrees more affordable. The popularity of DE is largely due to its guarantee of college credit. Unlike with AP or IB, high school students in dual enrollment take actual college classes offered through two-year community colleges or traditional four-year colleges and universities. Depending on the region, the courses are taught by college-certified instructors in high school classrooms or by college professors in college classrooms. But in either case, as long as a student passes his or her classes, he or she will not only receive actual high school credit, but also actual college credit.

---

7.    U.S. Department of Education, Dual Enrollment Programs and Courses for High School Students at Postsecondary Institutions: 2010–11, February 2013, prepared by the National Center for Education Statistics in cooperation with the U.S. Department of Education, http://nces.ed.gov/pubs2013/2013002.pdf.

# The Benefits

- *Impress those in college admissions.* Forget about rapping your extensive list of extracurricular activities on YouTube. You can wow university bigwigs by taking dual enrollment classes instead. Like with Advanced Placement (AP) and International Baccalaureate (IB), participation in dual enrollment (DE) demonstrates your readiness for the rigor of college academics. So as long as you do well in your courses, you won't need to rely on gimmicks to get noticed. Even without a music video, college admissions officers will be singing your praises.

- *Select diverse classes.* A typical high school day consists of English, math, history, science, foreign language, and an elective (PE, music, drama, or art). Forget choice or originality; you're trapped in Generic Class 101 in Room 101 for the next four years. Unlike high schools, colleges offer numerous classes to interest and excite students, including anthropology, economics, and modern dance. By participating in a dual enrollment program at a college, you can take advantage of its thick course catalog and learn more than just reading, writing, and arithmetic.

- *Utilize state-of-the-art facilities.* Your high school facilities seem stuck in the Stone Age—and you're eager for an upgrade. You want mega-sized exercise and athletic gyms, cutting-edge research libraries, and high-tech computer labs. Lucky for you, many colleges have these facilities, and as a dual enrollment student, you'll probably have access to them. So you can exit Bedrock and enter into the 21st century.

- *Create a flexible schedule.* Most high school students aren't morning people. Waking up before noon makes them cringe. But with early school start times, the jolt of a "beep…beep…beep" at dawn is a daily occurrence. Wouldn't you prefer to hit the snooze button and leave hibernation on your own time? In a dual enrollment program at a college, you can take classes almost any day of the week at almost any time of the day. You're not confined to courses only between 8:00 a.m. and 3:00 p.m.; you can also choose evening, weekend, and even online classes. So you can rise long after the sunrise.

# The Bottom Line

BOGO. Although not as well-known as BRB or BTW, this acronym is understood by most savvy shoppers and crazy couponers. It stands for "buy one, get one." Instead of paying $10.99 for one T-shirt, you hand over the same amount for two. Dual enrollment is another example of BOGO, yet with much larger savings. You shell out money for only one class, but receive high school *and* college credit. At Green River Community College in Washington, dual enrollment students spend absolutely nothing for tuition for up to two years, compared to regular student costs of $1,333.35 per quarter. *Short-term savings = $8,000.10 for six quarters (or, 90 quarter credits).*

By enrolling in 90 quarter credits as a dual enrollment student instead of as a typical, in-state student at Green River Community College:

> You could avoid $8,000.10 in student loans. You'll save **$2,182** in interest*, assuming each loan is subsidized and has a 5% interest rate and a term of 10 years.

### OR

> You could invest $8,000.10 in retirement accounts. After 40 years, you'll earn **$48,321** in interest*, assuming each investment has a 5% interest rate, compounded annually.

*Numbers are rounded.*

# The Brief Questions

Ask yourself all of the following before starting this opportunity:

- *Can you or your parents afford the costs?* To pay for a dual enrollment program, you might need up to several thousand for tuition, books, and fees. While your postsecondary institution, school district, or state organization may help with some or all of the expenses, don't expect the federal government to cover any of the amount. As per the Higher Education Act of 1965, students enrolled in a secondary school (i.e., high school) are not eligible for federal student aid. If the program you're interested in doesn't take care of the costs, and the tuition and fees are beyond your family's budget, don't complete this opportunity.

## Answered "No"? **DEALBREAKER**

- *Are you willing to leave high school?* To participate in a dual enrollment program, you might need to sign up for classes at a community or state college. While you can probably still attend your high school's prom and graduation, you'll miss out on the day-to-day school activities. If you're already counting the hours until senior sneak or some other much-anticipated high school event, register for dual enrollment and high school classes, take dual enrollment classes on a high school campus, or complete FTO #1: Advanced Placement (AP) Exams or FTO #2: International Baccalaureate (IB) Exams instead.

## Answered "No"? **RED FLAG** or **DEALBREAKER**

- *Do you meet the eligibility criteria?* To even apply for a dual enrollment program, you'll likely need to fulfill several requirements, such as a minimum GPA or standardized test score, completion of certain high school courses, and permission from a teacher or principal. If you don't satisfy them all, talk with the counselor at your high school or the college that offers the program and explain your situation. He or she might still grant you entrance into the program. But if you're discouraged from proceeding further, wait another year or don't complete this opportunity.

## Answered "No"? **RED FLAG** or **DEALBREAKER**

- *Do you have a working vehicle?* To get to your dual enrollment classes on a college campus, you can't simply catch the school bus. You'll need your own form of transportation. If you're not within walking or biking distance and don't own a car, purchase a bus pass. Many schools have a bus stop nearby. But if you don't have access to any reliable mode of transportation, take your classes via an online format. While you should still complete the steps in The Blueprint that follows, you should also refer to FTO #14: Distance Learning.

## Answered "No"? **RED FLAG**

- *Are you bored with high school academics?* To provide a more intellectually challenging alternative to regular or honors classes, dual enrollment programs offer college courses to high school students. If your current classes feel too easy and you haven't responded with a "No" to any of the previous questions, strongly consider completing this opportunity.

## Answered "Yes"? **CLINCHER**

# The Blueprint

## SECURE A SPOT IN THE PROGRAM

1. *Meet with your high school counselor.* Discuss the possibility of dual enrollment. Choose an appointment time that works with your parents' schedules. While in the meeting, ask some or all of the questions below.
   - What classes are offered through dual enrollment?
   - Who teaches these classes?
   - Where are the classes located?
   - Are there any restrictions on the number of credits I can earn? If yes, what is the limit?
   - Is it possible to earn an associate's degree through the program?
   - How much are the tuition and fees? Are any of the costs covered?
   - What are the deadlines to enroll?

2. *Schedule a doctor's appointment (if applicable).* It's always wise to go for an annual checkup, but if you're switching schools to take dual enrollment courses, your new school might also require an updated list of your vaccines. During the visit, your doctor or other health-care provider might simply fill out an immunization form, or they might ask you to roll up your sleeve. If you haven't gotten them already, you might

Don't wait too long after a tuberculosis skin test. You must return to the doctor within 48 to 72 hours post injection. If you forget, you'll have to retake the test.

need one or more vaccinations (such as Tdap, meningitis, hepatitis B, varicella, or MMR), and if you're enrolling in any health-care classes, a test for tuberculosis.

3. ***Sign up for the program.*** Start by applying to the college offering dual enrollment. In addition to completing the application form, you might also need to request your high school transcript and provide the immunization form. After submitting all of the necessary paperwork and paying the application fee, wait for a letter of acceptance and then fill out the dual enrollment form. It will require signatures from your high school principal and counselor along with a John Hancock from one or both of your parents. Hand in this form, but don't expect to never see another one. You may need to turn in a new dual enrollment form every term or year.

If you've previously taken the SAT or ACT, see whether or not you can opt out of the placement test. As long as you reach their SAT and ACT minimum scores, many colleges won't need you to complete another standardized exam.

## REGISTER FOR THE PROGRAM

4. ***Take a placement test (if applicable).*** A placement test examines your skill level on particular subjects. By obtaining this information, the school can place you in the most appropriate courses. To sit for this test, go to your college's testing center. They may require an appointment or allow walk-ins. After signing in and paying the fee (often free), start the test. It will likely include writing, reading, and math sections.

5. ***Experience orientation (if applicable).*** Your college might mandate an on-campus or online orientation. With either format, you'll attend an information session. You'll learn about the college's policies and procedures such as registration, transcripts, and accommodations for students with disabilities. With an on-campus orientation, you'll also go on a campus tour. You'll see the grounds, classrooms, and facilities.

6. ***Enroll in classes.*** Since you're earning both high school and college credit simultaneously, work closely with your high school counselor and maybe also a college academic advisor. If available, choose classes that aren't offered at your high school. Satisfy a science lab requirement with geology. Or a foreign language requirement with Italian. Or a PE requirement with white-water canoeing. The possibilities are virtually endless.

I wish that I had purchased study materials and spent at least several days preparing for the COMPASS placement test required by my dual enrollment program. While it wasn't an extremely difficult test, I couldn't remember several concepts and consequently guessed on a handful of questions.

## ACQUIRE NECESSARY ITEMS

7. ***Get a student ID card (if applicable).*** You'll have access to the library, computer labs, testing center, and shuttle services, as well as discounts to local restaurants, theaters, and attractions. Grab your government-issued ID and student schedule, but feel free to leave your cash at home. Most schools only charge a fee for a replacement ID. Then, head to the campus card office or student services center. A staff member will snap your photo and hand you a student ID card within minutes. Keep it in your wallet for convenience and safety.

Don't schedule all of your classes in one day. Instead, spread out your classes over at least two or three days (T/Th or M/W/F), if feasible, to minimize your risk of mental fatigue.

8. ***Obtain a parking or bus pass (if applicable).*** Don't be saddled with a parking ticket or kicked off the bus on your first day of classes. Purchase a parking permit or a subsidized bus pass through the college early. If your school doesn't offer subsidized bus passes, plan out your route and buy enough tickets to cover multiple trips. Keep track of your ticket count throughout the year (in the event you need to reorder).

## PARTICIPATE IN THE PROGRAM

9.  ***Review all of your syllabi.*** A college syllabus provides an overview of a course, detailing the goals and objectives, prerequisites, required texts and materials, instruction topics, schedule, and policies. During the first week of classes, carefully read through each syllabus. Then, take out your student planner and record every single assignment, quiz, and exam. Unlike with high school teachers, college professors won't remind you about an upcoming paper or test. They'll expect you to already know that information.

10. ***Show up to every class.*** Although college professors rarely do roll call or check in-class assignments, attendance and participation are vital to your grade. And since your grades will appear on your college academic record, other undergraduate and graduate schools might one day see them. Therefore, skipping class shouldn't even be an option. However, if you can't attend due to an illness or emergency, first email your teacher (profs usually list their email address on the syllabus) and let him or her know of your absence. Then, contact another student to get a copy of the notes and an extra set of handouts.

11. ***Enroll in classes for the next term (if applicable).*** If you are in the second semester of your senior year, you can skip this step. All other students will need to sign up for classes for the following term. To help you select courses that will satisfy high school requirements, you may want or even need to schedule a meeting with your high school counselor or college academic advisor before registration. Continue this step for every term that you're in the program.

Don't expect a curved grading system. If your exam is too difficult and all or most of the students score poorly, your teacher might grade on a curve and raise everyone's scores. But since you won't know whether this will or will not take place until after the exam, continue to study and learn the information without any expectation of an adjustment later on.

12.  ***Take your final exam(s) (if applicable).*** In college, final exams are fairly common. Start by finding out if any of your classes require a final (look in the syllabus or ask the teacher). Then, determine whether each final will be comprehensive. A comprehensive final will cover all of the material from the first day of

class while a final that is not comprehensive will only cover new material since the last exam. Although you'll likely spend more time preparing for a comprehensive exam, you should begin studying for your final at least a few weeks in advance regardless of the type. As the final often accounts for a large portion of your total grade, you might need to achieve a good final exam grade in order to pass the class.

13. *Graduate.* Don your Sunday best, complete with cap and gown. Regardless of whether you'll only be gracing the auditorium stage once to accept your high school diploma or twice for your associate's degree as well, be proud of your accomplishments. By participating in a dual enrollment program, you possess more of the tools to college success than many of your fellow classmates. So grab your family and friends and throw a moderately priced graduation party. (Just because you saved on tuition doesn't make you Beyoncé rich.)

---

## ⫞⫞⫞⫞⫞⫞⫞⫞⫞⫞⫞⫞⫞⫞⫞⫞⫞⫞ DOUBLE-CHECK YOUR WORK ⫞⫞⫞⫞⫞⫞⫞⫞⫞⫞⫞⫞⫞⫞⫞⫞⫞⫞

### SECURE A SPOT IN THE PROGRAM
- ❏ Meet with your high school counselor
- ❏ Schedule a doctor's appointment (if applicable)
- ❏ Sign up for the program

### REGISTER FOR THE PROGRAM
- ❏ Take a placement test (if applicable)
- ❏ Experience orientation (if applicable)
- ❏ Enroll in classes

### ACQUIRE NECESSARY ITEMS
- ❏ Get a student ID card (if applicable)
- ❏ Obtain a parking or bus pass (if applicable)

### PARTICIPATE IN THE PROGRAM
- ❏ Review all of your syllabi

- ☐ Show up to every class
- ☐ Enroll in classes for the next term (if applicable)
- ☐ Take your final exam(s) (if applicable)
- ☐ Graduate

# BONUS FTO #5:
## Articulated Credit/Tech Prep

If your end goal isn't a four-year diploma in the arts or sciences, you don't have to feel left out—you can still reduce your overall time in college. Similar to a dual enrollment program but designed for students interested in a vocational or technical discipline, an Articulated Credit or a Tech Prep program will help you receive credit for high school courses comparable to college ones. Meet with your counselor to ask for a list of articulated courses offered by your high school. You'll typically take these classes during your junior or senior year. When selecting a college or technical institute, be sure to choose one that has an articulation agreement with your high school. As long as you meet the criteria upon graduating (e.g., earning good grades in your articulated courses, enrolling in the school within the designated time frame, and pursuing a technical certificate or applied science degree), you can petition for and get college credit.

# STANDARDIZE YOUR TESTING

During her reign on network television, Oprah aired an annual special called "Oprah's Favorite Things." The items differed each year from pajamas to CDs to perfume to cookware. If I had the same segment, I'd include some popular favorites like Netflix streaming movies, Pizza Hut pizzas, *US Weekly* magazines, and Ray-Ban Wayfarer sunglasses. But I'd also mention a not as predictable and familiar one. It'd be—drum roll, please—college credit-by-exams. I know, I know, weird answer. However, they're that good. While I initially resisted sitting for more standardized tests, these cost only a few dollars and took only a few hours, but awarded at least a few credits each. Had she taken them too, even Ms. Winfrey would have made these a part of her favorite things.

Even if exams for credit will never make your top 10, you can still standardize your testing. Start by looking at your degree plan and finding at least one class needed to graduate. Choose a general education course, a major course (primarily in business or nursing), or an elective. Then, fulfill this requirement by completing any of the five FTOs in this section. Try FTO #6, #7, #8, or #9 if you need an exam in English composition, humanities, social sciences, history, sciences, mathematics, or business. Or try FTO #7, #8, or #9 if you need an exam in technology. Or try FTO #6 or #10 if you need an exam in a foreign language. Or try FTO #8 if you need an exam in nursing. But whichever you choose, make sure your school will award you credit for the exam. CLEP and DSST exams (FTOs #6 and #7) are more widely accepted by colleges and universities, while UExcel, ECE, TECEP, and NYU School of Professional Studies Foreign Language Proficiency exams (FTOs #8, #9, and #10) are not as well recognized.

# INTRO TO COLLEGE CREDIT-BY-EXAM

## The No. 2 Pencil Is Mightier than the Sword

What would you do for $50,000? For several years, the television show *Fear Factor* answered that question. Through a series of stunts, contestants faced their worst phobias, from acrophobia to trypanophobia to entomophobia. Even with the lure of thousands of dollars, I never applied. However, at least on a few specific days each school year, I would have preferred a spot on the show to a seat in a school. Because while I could brave heights, needles, and creepy crawlers, I panicked from even the mention of a standardized exam. I had a severe case of testophobia.

I first noticed my standardized test anxiety in elementary school. However, since my scores didn't much matter, my nerves felt manageable. But during the SAT, I lost control and froze. I read and reread the questions, but with little to no comprehension. Pressured by the time limit, I guessed or left many of them blank. By some miracle, I didn't completely bomb the exam. But I didn't receive a number anywhere close to 1600 either. In an attempt to raise my score, I tried again. After weeks of studying vocab words and math equations, I sat for the SAT a second time. Although my testophobia still negatively impacted my performance, my hard work paid off. I bid farewell to my heart palpitations and irregular breathing and welcomed in a more Zenlike period—one free from standardized exams.

However, this phase didn't last long. In my quest to graduate early, an enrollment counselor at my college recommended CLEP. Through this program, I could earn up to 30 college credits. Although initially intrigued,

I suspected a "catch." My gut was right. CLEP stood for College-Level Examination Program. Another dreaded standardized test. But unwilling to sacrifice credits, I decided to sign up. Luckily, CLEP was unlike my SAT experience. It didn't involve scads of students, packs of pencils, or weeks of waiting. I sat solo with only a keyboard and mouse. And within minutes of finishing, I received my score. I had passed! In only six short months, I banked the full 30 credits. And while I didn't win $50k, I saved a year of tuition by facing my fear. Joe Rogan would be proud.

# The Basics

Good-bye to a semester of gen-ed requirements. Farewell to coma-inducing early morning classes. So long to homework, in-class assignments, and textbook reading. Instead, say hello to acronyms. Use the information you learned in school, at work, on the news, or via the Web to complete a CLEP, ECE, TECEP, or other college credit-by-exam opportunity and earn multiple college credits.

Exams for credit aren't just reserved for adult learners—students from high school to retirement can register and sit for them (you must be in college to take a TECEP exam). You don't even need previous coursework in your exam subject. Simply schedule a date and time, study independently (see the list of learning materials in Appendix D), take the test under the supervision of a proctor, and earn several college credits. But if you can't find a specific subject out of the hundreds offered, check with your school to see if it offers any departmental or challenge exams. Unlike national standardized tests, these exams are created and graded by your school.

While the college credit-by-exam options in this part of the book basically work the same way, each has its own particular details and requirements to be aware of, which are explained in the FTOs that follow this overview. For a side-by-side comparison of all of the exams in this section, check out Part 2 of Appendix C: College Credit-by-Exam.

---

######### UPPER-LEVEL VS. LOWER-LEVEL CREDIT #########

Three credits earned on a CLEP exam aren't necessarily equivalent to three credits earned on a DSST exam, nor are three credits earned on one DSST exam necessarily equivalent to three credits earned on another DSST exam. Even though the number of credits and possibly even the college credit-by-exam program are identical, the type of credit might be different. Some exams are at the lower level while others are at the upper level. Although your school can set its own policies, typically lower-level exams award credit at the 100 or 200 level (usually satisfying general education courses) and upper-level exams award credit at the 300 or 400 level (usually satisfying major courses).

Not sure whether the exam you're considering is an upper- or lower-level exam? If you're taking CLEP, you don't need to do any research. All CLEP exams are at the lower level. But if you're taking a DSST, UExcel, ECE, or TECEP exam (NYU School of Professional Studies Foreign Language Proficiency Exams aren't classified as upper or lower level), you'll need to do a little investigation. Lower-level exams are labeled as lower-level baccalaureate or lower-level or have an exam number starting with a 1 or 2. Upper-level exams are labeled as upper-level baccalaureate or upper-level or have an exam number starting with a 3 or 4.

# The Benefits

- *Satisfy multiple course requirements.* Unlike typical college classes, exams for credit require only one assignment. Visit a local testing center, spend a few hours on an exam, and voilà—you're three to 16 college credits richer. After only a handful of exams, you may be finished with a whole year or more of school.
- *Utilize past learning.* Your dad dragged you to a reenactment of the Battle of Gettysburg. You've watched the movie *Glory* four times. You starred as Robert E. Lee in an elementary school production. Learning happens everywhere, not only in a classroom. Just because you haven't completed Civil War 101 doesn't mean you don't know

the subject. By taking a college credit-by-exam, you can translate all those family vacations, movie marathons, and tireless rehearsals into college credit.

- *Complete the exams on your schedule.* You can take an exam for credit almost any weekday of the year. Monday at 3:30 p.m. or Tuesday at 10:00 a.m. or even Friday at 11:30 a.m. Several testing centers even offer Saturday appointments (Sunday appointments are rare). So stop grumbling because your midterm falls on the day after the biggest party on your floor, the season premiere of your favorite show, or the 24-hour flu. And start scheduling exams at your optimal convenience.

- *Understand the material, not the class or the teacher.* Odd exam questions written by college profs aren't uncommon. What country was mentioned during the discussion last Friday? What was the color of the man's shirt in my PowerPoint presentation? Am I a Democrat, a Republican, or an Independent, and why? These examples might be a bit exaggerated, but in order to reinforce class attendance and participation, professors do make a point of testing information that only gets covered in class. Unlike tests written by individual teachers, however, college credit-by-exam questions are uniform and virtually unbiased. Since they only test your knowledge of the subject matter, you can toss your index cards with the names of Professor Smith's 12 pets in the trash (unless you foresee an animal adoption in your future).

# The Bottom Line

DIRECTIONS: Read the question carefully and circle the best possible answer. Use a No. 2 pencil only. Calculators and scratch paper are allowed, but not required.

1. You need a semester of general education credits. You can spend $15,047, $11,101.50, $4,446.50, or $400. Which would you prefer?

    a.  $15,047 (average cost for one semester at a private, nonprofit institution)

    b.  $11,101.50 (average cost for one semester at an out-of-state public institution)

    c.  $4,446.50 (average cost for one semester at an in-state public institution)

    d.  $400

Obviously, this question isn't on any standardized test. However, it isn't hypothetical either. By taking an exam for college credit, you can earn credit for hundreds instead of thousands of dollars. And the more exams you take, the more you'll save. For 15 credits, you'll spend at most $400 through CLEP, compared to $13,178 as an out-of-state student at Texas A&M University. *Short-term savings = $12,778.*

By earning 15 semester credits through CLEP exams instead of through classes at Texas A&M:

› You could avoid $12,778 in student loans. You'll save **$3,486** in interest*, assuming each loan is subsidized and has a 5% interest rate and a term of 10 years.

OR

› You could invest $12,778 in retirement accounts. After 40 years, you'll earn **$77,179** in interest*, assuming each investment has a 5% interest rate, compounded annually.

*Numbers are rounded.*

# The Brief Questions

Ask yourself all of the following before starting this opportunity:

- *Are you capable of learning without an instructor?* To prepare for an exam for credit, you'll need to study independently, utilizing resources like textbooks, OpenCourseWare (OCW) courses, and study guides. If you need guidance, study with a family member, friend, or tutor knowledgeable about your subject.

## Answered "No"? **RED FLAG**

- *Can you commute to a testing center?* To sit for an exam for credit, you may need to drive far. If the nearest facility isn't within reach, select a proctor and test in a more ideal location (only available for TECEP and NYU School of Professional Studies Foreign Language Proficiency Exams). Or if you own a computer and webcam, take a TECEP exam in your home or dorm through ProctorU.

## Answered "No"? **RED FLAG**

- *Do you score well on standardized tests?* To earn credit, you'll need to achieve a minimum score or grade set by the American Council on Education (ACE) or your school. If you have a history of well-below average scores on standardized tests, spend a significant amount of time studying and take several practice exams before sitting for the actual exam. But if you typically get above-average results and haven't responded with a "No" to any of the previous questions, strongly consider completing this opportunity.

## Answered "No"? **RED FLAG**

## Answered "Yes"? **CLINCHER**

- *Do you possess significant knowledge on a college subject?* To receive a passing score or grade, you'll need to demonstrate understanding of the exam subject. If you've formally learned about a particular college-level topic and you haven't responded with a "No" to any of the previous RED FLAG questions, strongly consider completing this opportunity.

## Answered "Yes"? **CLINCHER**

# FAST-TRACK OPPORTUNITY #6: COLLEGE-LEVEL EXAMINATION PROGRAM (CLEP) EXAMS

✓ Start planning a few months prior to testing
✓ Complete any year in high school or college (typically freshman or sophomore year of college)
✓ Spend $ to $$ (per exam)
✓ Earn potentially + to ++ credits (per exam)

The College Board offers more than 30 Internet-based CLEP exams in five categories: History & Social Sciences, Composition & Literature, Science & Mathematics, Business, and World Languages. If you want more information about the process for all CLEP exams, review the current version of the "Information for Test-Takers Bulletin." But if you only need specifics about one exam, head to the "CLEP Exams" page on the CLEP portion of the College Board website. There you will find a content outline, sample questions, and recommended resources for each CLEP exam.

## The Blueprint

### SELECT A TEST CENTER

1. **Create a College Board account.** Registered for the PSAT/NMSQT

Haven't yet learned about the basics and benefits of taking a CLEP exam? Refer back to the Intro to College Credit-by-Exam, starting on page 73.

or SAT? Viewed an AP Exam score? Made a CSS/PROFILE? You may have already completed this step. If not, go through the "My Account" registration portal. Fill in your personal information and pick a username and password. Shortly after, check your email for a welcome letter from the site.

2. *Search for a testing center.* Over 1,800 institutions across the United States and overseas administer CLEP exams. To find a center nearby, search in your College Board account. Some centers are available only to admitted or enrolled students (limited), while others are accessible to all (open).

If you're on active duty in the military or you're a spouse or civilian employee of the Air Force Reserve, Army National Guard, Army Reserve, or Coast Guard, select an on-base or base-sponsored test center. At these locations, you won't pay an exam or administration fee. If you're a veteran, you may also be eligible for reimbursement from the Veterans Administration (VA).

3. *Request testing accommodations (if applicable).* If you have a documented disability, you may be eligible for ZoomText (screen magnification), modifiable screen colors, an aide to read to you or write for you, a sign language interpreter, extended time, or untimed rest breaks during your CLEP exam. To gain approval for any of the aforementioned, contact your selected test center and ask for instructions on requesting and receiving an accommodation. You might need to show official documentation of your condition and prognosis. However, if one of the previously listed accommodations doesn't meet your needs, don't register online. Contact CLEP Services at (800) 257-9558 or clep@info.collegeboard .org instead.

## SCHEDULE THE EXAM

4. *Sign up for the exam.* Log in to your College Board account to order your CLEP exam. During this process, ensure your contact information is current, choose your preferred test center (optional), take a general survey, indicate which school should receive your score (optional), review your selections, and pay the $80 fee. Once your order is complete,

you'll receive immediate confirmation with a PDF of your registration ticket. Print out the ticket and bring it with you to the testing center. It is valid for six months. If you want to see a step-by-step of registration, watch the "CLEP Exam Registration Tutorial" on the CLEP portion of the College Board website.

5. ***Book the exam appointment.*** Contact the test center directly to set up an exam date and time. Some facilities only operate Monday through Friday during normal business hours, while others stay open on evenings and Saturdays as well. During the call, ask about a proctor fee (charge for administering the exam). Obtain details on the amount and acceptable payment methods.

Don't pick just any date for your CLEP exam. Choose one that allows for adequate study time. If you don't meet your school's minimum qualifying score, you cannot repeat the exam for 180 days. And if you're in the military, the retest won't be free.

## PREPARE FOR THE EXAM

6. ***Watch the CLEP tutorial.*** No need to wait until test day. Download and watch the "CLEP Tutorial-Testing Platform" on the CLEP portion of the College Board website. In this instructional video, you'll familiarize yourself with the CLEP testing platform by learning about the testing tools, types of exam questions, and types of calculators. While this tutorial won't ease all of your anxiety, it will at least eliminate some uncertainty and decrease the likelihood of unexpected surprises.

A few nights prior to an exam, I would take a practice test. If I didn't receive a passing score, I would try to push back the test for another week or two.

## TAKE THE EXAM

7. ***Show up for the exam.*** Arrive at the testing center 30 minutes early. Eat a light snack and use the restroom. Once you feel ready, check in for your CLEP test. Present your registration ticket, any registration

If you're a military service member, bring your Uniformed Services Geneva Conventions Common Access Card (CAC). If you're a spouse or civilian employee, bring your Uniformed Services Identification and Privilege Card (DD Form 1173) or DoD Guard and Reserve Family Member Identification and Privilege Card (DD Form 1173-1).

Since a wrong answer won't hurt your score, don't leave any multiple-choice questions blank. If you have no clue, pick C and move on to the next one.

paperwork required by the testing center, a government-issued ID (or a completed "CLEP Student ID Form" provided on the CLEP website), and the administration fee payment. Students taking the optional essay for College Composition Modular, American Literature, Analyzing and Interpreting Literature, or English Literature will also need to pay an additional fee of $10. If you have any questions, ask the exam proctor.

8. **Sit for the exam.** Depending on the exam subject, the exam will last for 1.5 or 2 hours (the optional essays for the composition and literature exams will increase exam length) and will contain just a multiple-choice portion or multiple-choice and essay portions. For the multiple-choice portion, eliminate any obviously wrong answers and then make an educated guess. If needed, skip a question and return to it at a later point. For the essay portion, construct an outline and then piece together a few paragraphs. Read over your writing and correct any spelling or grammatical errors.

## OBTAIN CREDIT FOR THE EXAM

9. **Receive your score.** Except for College Composition and the essay portions for College Composition Modular, American Literature, Analyzing and Interpreting Literature, and English Literature, you'll know your results immediately. Based on your performance, expect a scaled score between 20 and 80. If your school awards credit based on ACE recommendations, you'll need at least a 50 (higher for some foreign language exams) to earn three, four, six, or 12 college credits.

10. **Procure additional transcripts (if applicable).** If you selected a score

report recipient during registration, your $80 exam fee covered your first transcript. However, if you did not select a score report recipient at that time or you want to send your score to additional schools, you can request a transcript by fax or by mail. On the College Board website, find and fill out the "College-Level Examination Program Transcript Request Form." Indicate whether to send one, some, or all of your CLEP scores. Either fax this document with credit or debit card information to (610) 628-3726 or mail with check or money order to CLEP-Transcript Services, P.O. Box 6600, Princeton, NJ 08541-6600. Each transcript costs $20.

Members of the military should submit a "Military Transcript Order Form." To send your current institution scores from any or all of your CLEP and DSST (see FTO #7) exams taken while in the military, fax this document with a credit card number and expiration to (651) 603-3008 or mail with a certified check or money order to Prometric, ATTN: DSST/CLEP Transcripts, 7941 Corporate Drive, Nottingham, MD 21236. Each transcript costs $30.

---

## ⸿⸿⸿⸿⸿⸿ DOUBLE-CHECK YOUR WORK ⸿⸿⸿⸿⸿⸿

### SELECT A TEST CENTER
- ☐ Create a College Board account
- ☐ Search for a testing center
- ☐ Request testing accommodations (if applicable)

### SCHEDULE THE EXAM
- ☐ Sign up for the exam
- ☐ Book the exam appointment

### PREPARE FOR THE EXAM
- ☐ Watch the CLEP tutorial

## TAKE THE EXAM
- ❐ Show up for the exam
- ❐ Sit for the exam

## OBTAIN CREDIT FOR THE EXAM
- ❐ Receive your score
- ❐ Procure additional transcripts (if applicable)

# FAST-TRACK OPPORTUNITY #7:
## DSST EXAMS

✓ Start planning a few months prior to testing
✓ Complete any year in high school or college (typically freshman or sophomore year of college)
✓ Spend $ to $$ (per exam)
✓ Earn potentially + to ++ credits (per exam)

Prometric offers more than 30 Internet- and paper-based DSST exams in six categories: Business, Humanities, Math, Physical Science, Social Sciences, and Technology. If you want more information about the process for all DSST exams, review the current version of the "Test Taker Information Bulletin." But if you only need specifics about one exam, read through its content fact sheet. Each sheet includes exam information, a content outline, references, sample questions, and credit recommendations.

## The Blueprint

### SELECT A TEST CENTER

1. **Search for a testing center.** Over 1,200 institutions and 500 military installations administer DSST exams. To

Haven't yet learned about the basics and benefits of taking a DSST exam? Refer back to the Intro to College Credit-by-Exam, starting on page 73.

If you're on active duty in the military or you're a spouse or civilian employee of the Air Force Reserve, Army National Guard, Army Reserve, or Coast Guard, select a DANTES-funded military test center. At these locations, you won't pay an exam or administration fee. If you're a veteran, you may also be eligible for reimbursement from the Veterans Administration (VA).

I shopped around for testing centers. I ended up finding a center charging a mere $10 administration fee. It was not only $15 cheaper than another center a few miles away, but also had Saturday time slots.

find a center nearby, use the institution database on the DSST website. You can search by name, city, state, or site code.

2.     *Pick a test format (if applicable).* Computer and keyboard or paper and pencil? As previously mentioned, DSST has Internet- and paper-based testing (iBT and PBT). However, testing centers don't offer both types; they administer one or the other. If you live near two or more testing centers, you might have the choice between iBT and PBT. While many students prefer iBT, those with limited exposure to technology should strongly consider PBT instead.

## SCHEDULE THE EXAM

3.     *Book the exam appointment.* Contact the test center directly to set up an exam date and time. Some facilities only operate Monday through Friday during normal business hours, while others stay open on evenings and Saturdays as well. During the call, ask about a proctor fee (charge for administering the exam). Obtain details on the amount and acceptable payment methods.

4.     *Request testing accommodations (if applicable).* If you have a documented disability, you may be eligible for a special accommodation or arrangement during your DSST exam. Contact your selected test center and ask for instructions on requesting and receiving an accommodation. You'll need to submit professional documentation of your disability to the center, and then it will forward the documentation to Prometric for approval. Start this process well ahead of your exam date as Prometric requires 30 days' advanced notice.

# PREPARE FOR THE EXAM

5. *Try out the DSST software (if applicable).* If one is available in your exam subject area, take a practice test through Prometric. Unlike other companies' tests, Prometric's practice tests offer the same look and feel of an actual DSST exam. That means, instead of waiting until exam day, you can familiarize yourself with the testing tools ahead of time. While this test won't ease all of your anxiety, it'll at least eliminate some uncertainty and decrease the likelihood of unexpected surprises.

Don't pick just any date for your DSST exam. Choose one that allows for adequate study time. If you don't meet your school's minimum qualifying score, you cannot repeat the exam for 90 days. And if you're in the military, the retest won't be free.

6. *Gather items for exam day.* Avoid the mad rush by packing the night before. Refer to the list that follows for Prometric's guidelines on items to bring to the test center and items not to bring into the testing room. This list is based on rules published in the "Test Taker Information Bulletin."

| BRING | DON'T BRING |
|---|---|
| • Government-issued ID with current photo and signature<br>• Military ID (if you are military and want DANTES to fund the exam)<br>• Light snack<br>• Sharpened No. 2 pencils with erasers (only for paper-based exams)<br>• Black ballpoint pens (only for paper-based exams)<br>• Nonprogrammable calculator (only for the Business Mathematics, Fundamentals of College Algebra, Introduction to Computing, Personal Finance, Principles of Finance, Principles of Financial | • Electronic equipment (cell phone, smartphone, laptop, tablet, MP3 player, camera, handheld game console, etc.)<br>• Papers or study materials<br>• Personal items (digital watch, coat, purse, backpack, scarf, etc.) |

| BRING | DON'T BRING |
|---|---|
| Accounting, and Principles of Statistics exams) <br> • $80 exam fee (only credit cards are accepted for Internet-based exams, but certified checks and money orders are also accepted for paper-based exams) <br> • Administration fee <br> • School's four-digit DSST code, located in the institution database (if you want to indicate a score report recipient during the exam) | |

## TAKE THE EXAM

7. ***Show up for the exam.*** Arrive at the testing center 30 minutes early. Eat a light snack and use the restroom. Once you feel ready, check in for your DSST test. Present your ID and pay the exam fee plus administration fee. If you have any questions, ask the exam proctor.

8. ***Sit for the exam.*** Depending on the subject, the exam will last for two hours and contain just a multiple-choice portion, a multiple-choice and an optional essay portion, or a multiple-choice and speech portion. For the multiple-choice portion, eliminate any obviously wrong answers and then make an educated guess. If needed, skip a question and return to it at a later point. For the essay portion, construct an outline and then piece together a few paragraphs. Read over your writing and correct any spelling or grammatical errors. For the speech portion, find out about your topic and audience and then deliver a persuasive oral presentation. Speak slowly and clearly and be mindful of the three- to five-minute requirement.

Since a wrong answer won't hurt your score, don't leave any multiple-choice questions blank. If you have no clue, pick C and move on to the next one.

9. ***Indicate a score report recipient (if applicable).*** During the exam, enter

your institution's four-digit DSST code. On an Internet-based exam, enter the code into the field for "Institutional Score Report Recipient." On a paper-based exam, write the code in the space for "Score Report Recipient Institution Code." With this information filled in, Prometric will send your DSST exam score directly to your school.

## OBTAIN CREDIT FOR THE EXAM

10. *Receive your score.* Internet-based test takers will receive their results immediately, with the exception of those completing the Principles of Public Speaking exam and the optional essay portions for the Ethics in America and Technical Writing exams. Paper-based test takers, on the other hand, will receive their scores by mail after approximately four weeks. Based on your performance, expect a score between 200 and 500. If your school awards credit based on ACE recommendations, you'll need at least a 400 to earn three college credits (or in the case of the Criminal Justice exam, six college credits).

11. *Procure additional transcripts (if applicable).* If you selected a score report recipient during the exam, your $80 exam fee covered your first transcript.

However, if you did not select a score report recipient at that time or you want to send your score to additional schools, you can request a transcript by fax or by mail. On the DSST website, find and fill out the "DSST Transcript Order Form." Indicate whether to send one, some, or all of your DSST scores. Either fax this document with credit card information to (651) 603-3008 or mail with a certified check or money order to Prometric, ATTN: DSST Transcript Request, 7941 Corporate Drive, Nottingham, MD 21236. Each transcript costs $30.

Members of the military should submit a "Military Transcript Order Form." To send your current institution scores from any or all of your DSST and CLEP (see FTO #6) exams taken while in the military, fax this document with a credit card number and expiration to (651) 603-3008 or mail with a certified check or money order to Prometric, ATTN: DSST/CLEP Transcripts, 7941 Corporate Drive, Nottingham, MD 21236. Each transcript costs $30.

||||||||||||||||||||||||| **DOUBLE-CHECK YOUR WORK** |||||||||||||||||||||||||

## SELECT A TEST CENTER
- ❏ Search for a testing center
- ❏ Pick a test format (if applicable)

## SCHEDULE THE EXAM
- ❏ Book the exam appointment
- ❏ Request testing accommodations (if applicable)

## PREPARE FOR THE EXAM
- ❏ Try out the DSST software (if applicable)
- ❏ Gather items for exam day

## TAKE THE EXAM
- ❏ Show up for the exam
- ❏ Sit for the exam
- ❏ Indicate a score report recipient (if applicable)

## OBTAIN CREDIT FOR THE EXAM
- ❏ Receive your score
- ❏ Procure additional transcripts (if applicable)

# FAST-TRACK OPPORTUNITY #8:
# UEXCEL EXAMS AND EXCELSIOR COLLEGE EXAMINATIONS (ECES)

✓ Start planning a few months prior to testing
✓ Complete any year in high school or college (typically freshman or sophomore year of college)
✓ Spend $ to $$ (per exam)
✓ Earn potentially + to ++ credits (per exam)

Excelsior College offers more than 70 computer-delivered exams in seven categories: Business, Education, Humanities, Natural Sciences & Mathematics, Nursing, Social Sciences/History, and Technology. While the majority are UExcel exams, a handful are Excelsior College Examinations (ECEs). If you're not an Excelsior College student, these ten ECEs (all nursing theory exams) require authorization from your school to request materials or register. If you want more information about the process for all UExcel exams and ECEs, review the current version of "Exam Registration and Information: A User's Guide." But if you only need specifics about one exam, read through its content guide. Each guide includes recommended resources, a content outline, sample questions, and rationales for sample questions.

Haven't yet learned about the basics and benefits of taking a UExcel exam or an ECE? Refer back to the Intro to College Credit-by-Exam, starting on page 73.

# The Blueprint

## REGISTER FOR THE EXAM

1. *Create a MyExcelsior account.* Fill in your personal information and pick a username and password. Shortly after, check your inbox. You should have received an email with your newly assigned student ID. Since you'll need this number to schedule an exam online through Pearson VUE (the company that administers UExcel exams and ECEs), don't delete the email.

2. *Sign up for the exam online or by phone.* With online registration, you can order a UExcel exam or an ECE 24/7 through your MyExcelsior account. With phone registration, however, you're limited to typical business hours. You must call Excelsior College at (888) 723-9267 or (518) 464-8500 between 8:30 a.m. and 5:00 p.m. ET, Monday through Friday. Either way, you'll need to pay for the exam to complete the registration process. While the majority of the exams are $95, some cost as much as $325 to $440 (mostly nursing exams). After finishing your registration, you'll receive an Authorization to Test (ATT) letter within 24 to 48 hours. This letter will contain instructions on scheduling and taking your UExcel exam or ECE.

If you're in the military, ask your local education office if Tuition Assistance (TA) or other military education benefits can be used to pay for your exam.

## SCHEDULE THE EXAM

3. *Look for a nearby testing center.* Head to the UExcel and ECE portion of the Pearson VUE website. Click on the "Find a test center" tab. In the search box, enter your current full address or just your city and state or zip code. You'll receive a list of centers, arranged by distance. Scan your options and choose one.

4. *Request testing accommodations (if applicable).* If you have a documented disability, you may be eligible for additional time, a reader, a recorder of answers/amanuensis, scheduled breaks, a separate room, special mechanical devices, or some other accommodation during your UExcel exam or ECE. To gain approval for any of the aforementioned, complete the

"Online Disability Registration and Request for Accommodation Form," accessible through the Disability Services portion of the Excelsior College website. Once you've electronically sent this form, you'll take part in a telephone interview with the disability services coordinator and must submit documentation of your condition and prognosis from a qualified professional on official letterhead. Your documentation will then be reviewed and processed, and you'll receive an updated Authorization to Test (ATT) letter. With letter in hand, call Pearson VUE at (800) 466-0450 and speak with the accommodations coordinator. This call will be free of charge.

5. *Book the exam appointment.* Set up an exam date and time through Pearson VUE within an approximate six-month window for an administration fee of $50 (for two-hour exams) or $60 (for three-hour exams). You can book via phone, but select the online option instead. While you'll have to create a Pearson VUE account first, by using the Internet Scheduling System (www.pearsonvue.com/uexcel), you can schedule, reschedule, confirm, or cancel your testing appointment around the clock. However, by using the phone, you can only call (888) 926-9488 between

Members of the military can also pick a Pearson VUE Authorized Test Center on U.S. military installations. On the test center search page, click the link for U.S. service members looking for on-base test centers.

I usually scheduled my exams immediately after lunch. Since most students were in classes at that time, the center was generally slower and the check-in process went fairly quickly.

Don't pick just any date for your UExcel exam or ECE. Choose one that allows for adequate study time. If you don't meet your school's minimum qualifying grade, you cannot repeat the exam for 60 days after your first attempt and 120 after your second and subsequent attempts. Even worse, you can only take the same test up to three times in a given year and four times total.

7:00 a.m. and 7:00 p.m. CT, Monday through Friday. You'll also have to pay an additional $15 transaction charge ($20 if you're rescheduling or canceling an appointment within seven calendar days of your original test date).

## PREPARE FOR THE EXAM

6. *Purchase practice tests.* For most UExcel exams and ECEs, you can register for their respective practice tests directly through your MyExcelsior account. Each test contains two forms and costs $25 (for two-hour exams) or $75 (for three-hour exams); the one exception is Research in Nursing, which costs $35. For the Calculus, Introduction to Psychology, Introduction to Sociology, Physics, Political Science, Spanish Language, and Statistics exams, go to www.starttest.com instead. Although these practice tests only include one form for $18, you can buy one more for the same price.

7. *Try out the Pearson VUE software.* Download and install the Pearson VUE "Tutorial and Practice Exam" on the UExcel and ECE portions of the Pearson VUE website. In the first part of the tutorial, you'll learn all of the possible computer-based test functions. Topics include getting started, answering items, item reviewing, and finishing the exam. In the second part of the tutorial, you'll use each function during a practice exam. While these questions won't relate to your exam subject, answering them will still help you feel more prepared for test day.

## TAKE THE EXAM

8. *Show up for the exam.* Arrive at the testing center 30 minutes early. Eat a light snack and use the restroom. Once you feel ready, check in by presenting at least one but possibly two valid forms of ID. A test center staff member will then take your photo, signature, palm vein scan, and fingerprints; ask you to put away all of your personal belongings; and give you a Candidate Rules Agreement to read and complete. If you have any questions, ask the Test Administrator.

9. *Sit for the exam.* Depending on the subject, the exam will last for two or three hours and contain multiple-choice questions (objective), essay questions (extended response), or multiple-choice and free-response

questions (mixed-format). For multiple-choice questions, eliminate any obviously wrong answers and then make an educated guess. If needed, skip a question and return to it at a later point. For essay questions, construct an outline and then piece together a few paragraphs. Read over your writing and correct any spelling or grammatical errors.

Since a wrong answer won't hurt your score, don't leave any multiple-choice questions blank. If you have no clue, pick C and move on to the next one.

## OBTAIN CREDIT FOR THE EXAM

10. ***Receive your grade.*** With an objective exam, you'll know your results immediately. But with an extended response or mixed-format exam, you'll have to wait for a mailed report. Either way, expect a letter grade of A, B, C, D, or F. If your school awards credit based on ACE recommendations, you'll need at least a C to earn one, three, four, six, or eight college credits.

11. ***Procure a transcript report.*** Unlike CLEP and DSST, UExcel exams and ECEs are transcribed on an official college transcript. To send this form to your current institution, make a transcript request through your MyExcelsior account, by fax with credit card information to the attention of the Bursar's Office at (518) 464-8700, or by mail with personal check or money order to Bursar's Office, Excelsior College, 7 Columbia Circle, Albany, NY 12203-5159. Each transcript costs $12, but can be rushed for a $30 fee and overnighted for another $30.

---

|||||||||||||||||||||||||||||| **DOUBLE-CHECK YOUR WORK** ||||||||||||||||||||||||||||||

### REGISTER FOR THE EXAM
- ❐ Create a MyExcelsior account
- ❐ Sign up for the exam online or by phone

## SCHEDULE THE EXAM
- ❏ Look for a nearby testing center
- ❏ Request testing accommodations (if applicable)
- ❏ Book the exam appointment

## PREPARE FOR THE EXAM
- ❏ Purchase practice tests
- ❏ Try out the Pearson VUE software

## TAKE THE EXAM
- ❏ Show up for the exam
- ❏ Sit for the exam

## OBTAIN CREDIT FOR THE EXAM
- ❏ Receive your grade
- ❏ Procure a transcript report

# FAST-TRACK OPPORTUNITY #9:
## THOMAS EDISON STATE COLLEGE EXAMINATION PROGRAM (TECEP) EXAMS

✓ Start planning a few months prior to testing
✓ Complete any year in college (typically freshman or sophomore year)
✓ Spend $ to $$ (per exam)
✓ Earn potentially + credits (per exam)

Thomas Edison State College (TESC) offers more than 30 online and paper-based TECEP exams in seven categories: English Composition, Humanities, Social Sciences, Natural Sciences/Mathematics, Business and Management, Computer Science Technology, and Applied Science and Technology. For more information about a specific exam, read through its test description. Each description includes a brief synopsis, covered topics, recommended resources, and sample questions.

## The Blueprint

### REGISTER FOR THE EXAM

1. *Apply for admission*. To have access to Online Student Services, you must formally apply to Thomas Edison

Haven't yet learned about the basics and benefits of taking a TECEP exam? Refer back to the Intro to College Credit-by-Exam, starting on page 73.

State College. On the school's website, click on the "Apply Now" button on the top of the homepage, and then click "Apply Now" on the right-hand side of the next page. Create an account and then log in. At the bottom, you can start your application. To avoid paying a fee, make sure to select the application for nonmatriculated students (a.k.a. nondegree-seeking students). Fill in the required information, and then certify and submit. After your application is processed, you'll receive an email with additional details.

2. *Sign up for the exam.* You can register for a TECEP exam through Online Student Services; by phone at (609) 633-9242 between 11:00 a.m. and 3:00 p.m. ET, Monday through Friday; by fax at (609) 292-1657; or by mail at Office of the Registrar, ATTN: Course Registration/TECEP Registration, Thomas Edison State College, 101 W. State St., Trenton, NJ 08608-1176. If you choose to fax or mail your request, download, complete, and send the "Undergraduate Course Registration Form" located on the "Student Forms" page on the TESC website. But before you can finalize your registration, you'll need to pay for the exam. All except for one cost $105 for New Jersey residents and $111 for out-of-state residents. (Medical Terminology (APS-100) costs $35 for New Jersey residents and $37 for out-of-state residents.)

3. *Pick your testing arrangements.* Computer and keyboard or paper and pencil? You can select from online or paper-based testing, with the exception of Music History II (MUS-221), which is only offered online. With online testing, you don't even need to leave your home. You'll take the exam in front of your monitor, using an Online Proctoring Service (OPS). While this option is undeniably convenient, if you don't have a computer with a microphone and speakers, a webcam, and high-speed Internet and you aren't able to get all three before the exam, go with paper-based testing instead. With paper-based testing, your exam is administered by your own selected proctor or by a staff member in the testing facility at Thomas Edison State College. This means that you'll unfortunately have to venture outside, but at least you won't have to fuss with any technical equipment.

## SCHEDULE THE EXAM

4. *Locate an exam proctor (if applicable).* If you're taking an online

TECEP exam or a paper-based TECEP exam at Thomas Edison State College, you can skip this step. All other students must find an acceptable proctor. You can't choose your neighbor, mom, best friend, or piano teacher; you can only ask a full-time member of a testing office, a full-time professor or professional staff member, or a full-time librarian. If he or she accepts the responsibility, check your email for a "Proctor Request Form" from TESC. Fill out and send this document back to the college. Wait for a response concerning proctor approval.

If you're in the military, you can select a commissioned officer of your unit but not in your direct chain of command, NCPACE representative, Test Control Officer (TCO), Education Services Officer (ESO), career counselor, base librarian, or chaplain as your TECEP exam proctor. However, if you're unable to find a proctor outside of your direct reporting chain, contact the Office of Test Administration at testing@tesc.edu.

5. ***Book the exam appointment.*** This process is contingent on your testing arrangement. For online testing, you must schedule with ProctorU. Create an online account, test your technical equipment, and then pick a date and time. For paper-based testing with an approved proctor, schedule directly with the individual. Select a date and time as well as a meeting place (an accredited college or university or a public library). Finally, for paper-based testing at Thomas Edison State College, schedule through their web-based test scheduling service or by calling the Office of Test Administration at (609) 984-1181, ext. 2265. You can choose from either an 8:30 a.m. or 10:30 a.m. time. Regardless of your scheduling method, you'll likely pay a small administration fee.

6. ***Request testing accommodations (if applicable).*** If you have a documented disability, you may be eligible for a special accommodation or arrangement during your TECEP exam. Go to the "Students with Disabilities" page on the Thomas Edison State College website and download the "Student Guide to Accessing Disability Support Services." Print out everything in the appendices, and then complete and send the "Disclosure of Disability" form (Appendix II), a "Verification of

Don't wait to schedule your TECEP exam. At Thomas Edison State College, each term lasts 12 weeks. Whether you sign up at the beginning or at the end of the term, you must test within those 12 weeks. Otherwise, you'll need to register and pay the exam fee again. For term dates, visit the TESC website.

Don't pick just any date for your TECEP exam. Choose one that allows for adequate study time. If you don't pass, you cannot repeat the exam for three months. Even worse, you can only take the same test two times total.

Disability" letter from a professional or agency (Appendix III), and, if desired, the "Permission to Release Student Information to Another Source" form (Appendix V). Once the first two are on file and you've received your mentor's name and email address, complete and send the "Term Accommodation Request" form (Appendix IV) at least three weeks prior to your TECEP exam. You can submit these documents by fax to (609) 943-5232, by mail to Thomas Edison State College, Office of Student Special Services, 101 W. State St., Trenton, NJ 08608-1176, or by email to ada@tesc.edu. If any questions or concerns arise during this process, contact the ADA Coordinator in the Office for Disability Support Services at (609) 984-1141, ext. 3415 or at ada@tesc.edu.

## TAKE THE EXAM

7. *Show up for the exam.* This step will depend on your selected proctor. If you chose ProctorU, begin your preparation at least a half hour before. Grab your photo ID and a reflective surface (CD, DVD, or mirror); close out all of the programs, applications, and websites on your desktop computer or laptop; and turn on the lights and reduce as much noise as possible in the room that you'll test in. At your scheduled exam time, head to the ProctorU website, log in to your account, and click on the "Go" button. You'll then connect to a live proctor, connect your screen to the proctor, show your ID, and answer some authentication questions. After you've finished with these parts, your proctor will officially start your online TECEP exam. If you chose your own proctor or a

proctor at Thomas Edison State College's testing facility, begin your preparation at least a few hours before. You may need to gather some sharpened No. 2 pencils, pack a snack, and study directions to the designated meeting spot or testing center. (The TESC testing facility is located at 101 W. State St., Trenton, NJ.) Arrive at the exam site 30 minutes early. Eat a light snack and use the restroom. Once you feel ready, check in. You may need to present your ID, complete paperwork, and pay an administration fee. After you've finished with these parts, your proctor will officially start your paper-based TECEP exam.

8. **Sit for the exam.** Depending on the subject, the exam will last for two or three hours. While most of the tests contain multiple-choice questions, a few test your knowledge through other methods. You might have to write a research paper, define a term, construct a persuasive business letter, solve a computational problem, or something else entirely. For multiple-choice questions, immediately eliminate any obviously wrong answers and then make an educated guess. But for any other type, take your time and make sure you completely understand the request before crafting a response.

Since a wrong answer won't hurt your score, don't leave any multiple-choice questions blank. If you have no clue, pick C and move on to the next one.

## OBTAIN CREDIT FOR THE EXAM

9. **Receive your grade.** No matter your testing arrangements, you won't find out your results instantaneously. However, although your wait time is unknown, exams with only multiple-choice questions are typically scored faster than those with short answer or essay questions. Once your grade is available, Thomas Edison State College will post it in your Online Student Services account and send you a hard copy report. Based on your performance, expect either a CR (Credit) or NC (No Credit). To be awarded a CR and earn three college credits (or in the case of the Medical Terminology exam, one college credit), you'll need at least a score equivalent to a letter grade of C.

10. **Procure a transcript report.** While your file will show your grades for

all attempted TECEP exams, an official Thomas Edison State College transcript will only display the titles you successfully passed and the number of credits earned. To send this document to your current institution, you'll need to go to the National Student Clearinghouse website. (TESC has authorized this company to provide online transcript ordering.) Enter in your information and the recipient's information, and then complete the order by paying the transcript and processing fees with a credit card and signing your consent. Your request will be processed within five business days.

---

## DOUBLE-CHECK YOUR WORK

### REGISTER FOR THE EXAM
- ❏ Apply for admission
- ❏ Sign up for the exam
- ❏ Pick your testing arrangements

### SCHEDULE THE EXAM
- ❏ Locate an exam proctor (if applicable)
- ❏ Book the exam appointment
- ❏ Request testing accommodations (if applicable)

### TAKE THE EXAM
- ❏ Show up for the exam
- ❏ Sit for the exam

### OBTAIN CREDIT FOR THE EXAM
- ❏ Receive your grade
- ❏ Procure a transcript report

---

# FAST-TRACK OPPORTUNITY #10:
# NYU SCHOOL OF PROFESSIONAL STUDIES FOREIGN LANGUAGE PROFICIENCY EXAMS

- ✓ Start planning a few months prior to testing
- ✓ Complete any year in high school or college (typically freshman or sophomore year of college; 9th, 10th, and 11th grade high school students must obtain permission from NYU School of Professional Studies to test)
- ✓ Spend $$ (per exam)
- ✓ Earn potentially + to ++ credits (per exam)

Were you raised by Vietnamese-speaking parents? Have you traveled to Norway for an extended period? Shared a dorm with a student from Russia? Studied Arabic on your own? You can acquire a second language through a variety of ways. And through the NYU School of Professional Studies, you can earn college credit for this knowledge. This school offers 12-, 16-, and 4-point exams in more than 50 foreign languages.

The 12-point NYU School of Professional Studies Foreign Language Proficiency Exam tests your listening, reading, and writing skills through the following four components: (1) Listen to a passage and then answer questions based

Haven't yet learned about the basics and benefits of taking an NYU School of Professional Studies Foreign Language Proficiency Exam? Refer back to the Intro to College Credit-by-Exam, starting on page 73.

on the passage; (2) Translate a passage from the test language into English; (3) Translate a passage from English into the test language; and (4) Write a 150-word essay in the test language. The 16-point exam contains the same four components plus a 350-word essay. But you don't have to take the harder exam initially. If you opt for the 12-point exam and earn a perfect score, you can try for the extra points (4-point exam) at a later date. You'll just write the 350-word essay.

# The Blueprint

## REGISTER FOR THE EXAM

1. *Locate an exam proctor (if applicable).* If you reside in New York City, you can skip this step. All other students must find an acceptable proctor. But you can't choose just anyone; you can ask only a college faculty member, administrator, or a government or company official. Once someone agrees to administer your exam, he or she must formally commit in writing and on official letterhead. Retrieve this document and keep it accessible for registration.

2. *Complete the exam registration form.* Visit the Foreign Languages, Translation, and Interpreting department's portion on the NYU School of Professional Studies website. Find, download, and print out the "Registration Form" for the NYU School of Professional Studies Foreign Language Proficiency Exams. Fill in all of the required information, including your college's complete address, so that the NYU School of Professional Studies can send your exam results there (high school students can leave this section blank). If you want more than one school to receive your score, use a separate form and pay an additional $15 fee per school.

## SCHEDULE THE EXAM

3. *Book the exam appointment.* If you don't reside in NYC, you'll need to register before you can schedule your exam. Send in your proctor's letter, completed registration form, credit card information or money order for the exam and registration fees (4-point exam: $120, 12-point exam: $300; 16-point exam: $400; registration fee: $20), and money

order or certified check for the shipping and handling fee ($20) to the NYU School of Professional Studies. You can then arrange a date, time, and meeting place with your chosen proctor. If you do reside in NYC, you won't need to mail in any registration paperwork. Since you must test at the NYU Midtown Center, scheduling will be easy. Simply call (212) 998-7030 and provide your name, NYU Student ID number or passport number, daytime telephone number, and specifics about the exam (language and point number). You can then pick either a Tuesday or Saturday appointment.

4.  ***Request testing accommodations (if applicable).*** If you have a documented disability, you may be eligible for a special accommodation or arrangement during your NYU School of Professional Studies Foreign Language Proficiency Exam. If you're taking the exam at a school other than NYU, contact the institution's disability office directly. But if you're taking the exam at NYU, contact the Moses Center for Students with Disabilities (CSD) by phone at (212) 998-4980 or by email at mosescsd@nyu.edu. In either case, you'll be provided instructions on requesting and receiving an accommodation at its specific facility.

## TAKE THE EXAM

5.  ***Show up for the exam.*** If you're taking the exam off campus, go to your agreed upon meeting place. While you may need to provide your ID and pay an administration fee, you won't have to supply the exam. NYU School of Professional Studies sends the test directly to your proctor. If you're taking the exam on campus, head to the NYU Midtown Center, 11 West 42nd Street, Room 1039, New York, NY 10036. Present your ID, completed registration form, and a credit card or money order for the exam and registration fees. (You won't have to pay a shipping and handling fee.) But regardless of whether you test on or off campus, arrive at the exam site 30 minutes early. This way, you'll have time to eat a light snack and use the restroom beforehand.

6.  ***Sit for the exam.*** The exam will last one hour (for a 4-point exam), two hours (for a 12-point exam), or three hours (for a 16-point exam). While the types of questions (multiple-choice, short answer, etc.) may vary depending on the test language and/or point value, every exam includes at least one essay. The 12- and 16-point exams require a short 150-word

essay on an easy topic relating to everyday activities and subjects. The 16- and 4-point exams require an extended 350-word essay on a more complex topic relating to abstract ideas.

## OBTAIN CREDIT FOR THE EXAM

7. *Receive your score.* Up to eight weeks after your exam, an official letter with your exam results will be mailed to the institution you indicated on your registration form (or mailed directly to you if you didn't indicate a score report recipient). Based on your performance, expect a score between 0 and 4 (for a 4-point exam), 0 and 12 (for a 12-point exam), or 0 and 16 (for a 16-point exam). Since the ACE doesn't provide credit recommendations for NYU School of Professional Studies Foreign Language Proficiency Exams, you'll need at least the minimum score set by your school to earn up to 16 college credits.

8. *Procure an official transcript (if applicable).* While most schools accept the official letter with your NYU School of Professional Studies Foreign Language Proficiency Exam score, some require an actual transcript. You can order a paper transcript free of charge through the registrar's office at NYU. Complete the "Official Transcript Request Form" online or write a request letter by hand. Send either document by fax to (212) 995-4154, by mail to the Office of the Registrar, Academic Records, P.O. Box 910, New York, NY 10276-0910, or by email to academic .records@nyu.edu. If you have any questions, call (212) 998-4280.

---

## |||||||||||||||||||||||| DOUBLE-CHECK YOUR WORK ||||||||||||||||||||||||

### REGISTER FOR THE EXAM

- ❏ Locate an exam proctor (if applicable)
- ❏ Complete the exam registration form

### SCHEDULE THE EXAM

- ❏ Book the exam appointment
- ❏ Request testing accommodations (if applicable)

## TAKE THE EXAM

❒   Show up for the exam

❒   Sit for the exam

## OBTAIN CREDIT FOR THE EXAM

❒   Receive your score

❒   Procure an official transcript (if applicable)

# OPTIMIZE YOUR TIME

Two years. While the idea of earning a degree in this short span initially felt overwhelming, this goal wasn't as petrifying upon further review. When converted into much smaller units, two years became 63,072,000 seconds. And by declaring just one academic major, class sessions and homework only took up around one-third of that time. I still had a good two-thirds remaining. Winter break, spring break, and summer break. Before school, after school, and weekends. Filling in some of these gaps with more credits and more courses meant less college and less cost. And achieving my goal of graduating in two years—all by making every second count.

Whether you attend for just one year or stay for almost four, you can better optimize your time in college. Start by working through FTO #11: One Major, No Minor. Then, complete one or more of the next three FTOs. Try FTO #12: Maximum Credits if you have availability during the school year. Or try FTO #13: Summer Classes if you have availability during the summer. Or try FTO #14: Distance Learning if you need flexibility regardless of the season. But whichever you choose, make sure you have room in your calendar. Adding even one more credit to an already jam-packed schedule could produce high cortisol levels and low course grades. Even an early graduation isn't worth that.

Do you want to study a subject mostly on your own? Explore the mini fast-track opportunity (*Bonus FTO #15:* Independent Study) at the end of this section.

# FAST-TRACK OPPORTUNITY #11:
# ONE MAJOR, NO MINOR
## Less Is More Manageable

✓ Start planning as early as 11th or 12th grade in high school
✓ Complete before junior year in college
✓ Spend $0
✓ Earn 0 credits

When I grow up, I want to be… Throughout childhood, my response rarely remained the same. I wavered between teaching ABCs and 123s, nabbing murderers and thugs, or treating colds and flus. Right before college, I switched my career path one final time—or so I assumed. My new dream involved a corner office and a steep climb up the corporate ladder. To pursue these aspirations, I selected business administration as my major and enrolled in a host of management classes.

Unsurprisingly, after my first year in college, my executive ambitions faded. Like the many times before, it didn't take long for me to change my mind. Instead of supervising staff, training teams, and balancing budgets, I decided that I desired a profession without a profits-only mindset. My younger brother has high-functioning autism, and I felt drawn to helping children with special needs. I considered special education and speech-language pathology, but settled on occupational therapy (OT). However, I wasn't exactly in the right field of study for this line of work. As OT requires a master's or doctorate degree, many hopeful therapists earn a bachelor's in a science or social science. A far cry from my soon-to-be business degree.

I debated switching my major, but knowing that my new career goal would require additional graduate-level coursework (and thus, more money), I stayed in the business program and achieved my original goal of graduating early. Although my enthusiasm for finance and marketing had diminished, I maintained my high grades throughout my second year. After graduation and a brief venture into the business world, I applied to an OT program. Although confident in my GPA and volunteer experiences, I feared that my lack of an exercise physiology or psychology degree would hinder my chances of acceptance. Instead, it had the opposite effect. During an admissions interview, the chair of the department praised my focus on management, acknowledging the importance of having a business mentality in health care. Since that meeting, I've never again questioned my major, and thankfully, it hasn't much mattered. In many career tracks, employers will require a bachelor's degree, but not a specific type. My major, it turned out, wasn't actually that major.

# The Basics

Should I study animal sciences? Ask again later. What about hospitality management? My sources say no. Maybe creative writing? Without a doubt. Don't leave your future to a Magic 8 Ball. By completing this fast-track opportunity, you can find the major that's right for you and avoid the added stress of a minor or double major. You'll just have to ask yourself one final question: "Should I make this important decision on my own, instead of relying on fate?" Even the Magic 8 Ball would give a resounding "Yes."

While you can wait until your freshman or sophomore year in college to declare a major, you should start to explore your career options in high school and, if possible, settle on a major in your junior or senior year. By beginning this process early, you can select a college offering your intended field of study, which would be especially beneficial if you're interested in an uncommon major like aerospace engineering or one that can best be studied in specific locations, such as marine biology. Another advantage is that you can start planning which general education, elective, or major requirements you can knock out before you even enroll, by way of FTOs like AP, dual enrollment, CLEP, and others. However, if you're already in college and unsure what to major in, don't panic. Although limited by your school's offerings, you'll likely still encounter a long list of majors. And with careful planning, you can still map out a path to an early graduation.

# The Benefits

- *Specialize in your field of study.* Employers often aren't looking for a Jack-of-all-trades. They'd typically much rather hire a candidate with deep knowledge of one subject than a candidate with broad or surface-level knowledge of multiple subjects. What does that mean for you? You can forget about taking on a minor or additional major to impress potential employers. It might even cause more harm than good if you end up learning only a little because you're trying to learn a lot. Instead, choose a single major and devote all of your time and energy to becoming an expert in that field of study through relevant classes, clubs, internships, and volunteer experiences. While you won't become a Jack-(or Jill)-of-all-trades, you will become a master of one.

- *Demonstrate commitment to a program.* Automatically admitted into your selected major? Think again. Many departments require an application for entrance. While this process may exist merely as a formality, competitive programs typically accept or reject students based on their applications. The unlucky few without an offer of acceptance may have to wait up to a year before reapplying. You can potentially avoid this delay by picking only one major and building up your experiences in that area of study. Your loyalty and dedication to the program might earn you a few brownie points and make those reviewing your application think again before tossing it into the reject pile.

- *Exhibit decisive behavior.* Dinner out with a wishy-washy friend can leave you hungry. "I want Thai...no Mexican...wait, maybe Italian." By the time a particular cuisine has been chosen, you're already munching on last week's leftovers and questioning whether you'll invite your friend to grab a meal ever again. Constantly changing your mind about dinner, just like constantly switching majors, portrays you as *fickle* and *capricious* (bonus! SAT words). While you may be one of those "I don't care what others think of me" people, the world won't stop judging you. Drifting from finance to biology to architecture might prevent you from being hired, especially if the potential boss knows you personally. On the other hand, by sticking with your original major, you'll be viewed not only as *steadfast* but also as *employable*.

- **Avoid mental overload.** If you've ever taken midterms or finals, you're probably no stranger to brain strain. It occurs after you've used your noggin nearly nonstop for days, leaving you completely exhausted and unable to think clearly. Luckily, you'll likely only experience this feeling about two weeks each semester. However, with a minor or additional major, it could happen a lot more frequently. To prevent this unnecessary mental fatigue, go with only one major and no minor. It's just a no-brainer.

# The Bottom Line

Maybe you "don't know much about history," but you'll know about biology. Depending on how many course requirements overlap, selecting only one major instead of a major and minor or double major could save you one to two years of tuition. At University of Montana, a history major requires 40 credits of history, a number almost equal to three semesters of school. With tuition and fees for in-state students costing $3,091 per semester, just by opting for biology instead of biology and history, you'll keep thousands more in your pocket. *Short-term savings = $9,273 (three semesters of tuition).*

By choosing a single major in biology instead of a double major in history and biology at University of Montana:

> You could avoid $9,273 in student loans. You'll save **$2,530** in interest*, assuming each loan is subsidized and has a 5% interest rate and a term of 10 years.

### OR

> You could invest $9,273 in retirement accounts. After 40 years, you'll earn **$56,009** in interest*, assuming each investment has a 5% interest rate, compounded annually.

*Numbers are rounded.

# The Brief Questions

Ask yourself all of the following before starting this opportunity:

- *Can you graduate without a minor?* To obtain a bachelor's degree, you will most often need just a major. If your school requires a minor as well, you can work through each of the steps in The Blueprint that follows, but disregard the advice in Step #10 to forgo a minor.

## Answered "No"? **RED FLAG**

- *Do you stick with your decisions?* To save on tuition by opting for only one major, you can't switch to another academic discipline later on. If you frequently change your mind, don't rush into a major. Take the time to find the one that's right for you. And after making your decision, write down a list of reasons for your intended major and glance at it periodically as a reminder.

## Answered "No"? **RED FLAG**

- *Is your major still undecided?* To enter your junior year, you'll need to have chosen a major. But often, you can elect one much earlier in your college career. If you've already officially declared a major that you feel confident about, keep your original pick for the remainder of your time in school, but don't spend time on the steps that follow. If you have yet to select a major, however, and you haven't responded with a "No" to any of the previous questions, strongly consider completing this opportunity.

## Answered "No"? **DEALBREAKER**

## Answered "Yes"? **CLINCHER**

# The Blueprint

## DISCOVER SUITABLE CAREER OPTIONS

1. *Reflect on your passions and abilities.* Answer the questions that follow with or without help from family and friends. Write down your responses for later reference.
   - What subjects, causes, and political issues captivate my interest?
   - What talents, skills, and innate capabilities do I possess?
   - Which of my previous school, extracurricular, and work-related activities have challenged me while still remaining enjoyable?

2. *Meet with your school's counselor.* If you're in high school, schedule an appointment with your high school counselor. But if you're in college, schedule an appointment with a career counselor in your school's career services office. During the first half of the meeting, discuss your answers to the questions in the previous step. Your counselor might also ask you additional questions and give you one or more career assessments. During the second half of the meeting, listen to your counselor's career suggestions as well as information on said careers.

---

### NAVIANCE

Naviance is a college and career readiness software provider. Thousands of schools worldwide partner with Naviance to provide their students with college and career tools and assessments. To see if your school is a partner, ask your high school counselor. If your school is, you can log in and use the Naviance student and family portal (Family Connection) to search colleges, explore careers, and take personality assessments, among other things. You can also download the Naviance Student mobile app on your iPhone or iPod Touch for access on the go.

3. ***Take a career assessment test.*** Career tests recommend specific professions based on an individual's aptitude (natural competency) and expertise. If your high school or college career counselor didn't give you at least one, complete this type of test now. You can find several online. Some good and decently priced career tests are offered by Career Maze,

When I started college, I didn't immediately enter the business program. But from day one, I chose classes based on the degree plan for this major.

www.CareerPlanner.com, and Career Key. But don't plan your future around the results. Instead, use the findings only as another tool for self-discovery.

4. ***Go online.*** Head to bigfuture.collegeboard.org/explore-careers. On this site, you can find majors and careers based on your interests as well as look through dozens of major and career profiles in several categories (Business, Health and Medicine, Public and Social Services, Trades and Personal Services, and so on). While you use these tools, write down any careers that you would like to explore further and maybe actually pursue.

5. ***Narrow down your choices.*** Pick three or four careers and, if you haven't already, determine the type of degree and major needed for each profession. For example, to work as a news anchor, you should get a bachelor of arts in broadcasting or journalism. Or to work as a crime lab analyst, you should get a bachelor of science in chemistry, biology, or forensic science. If you are already in college, guarantee your school offers the degree program required for each of your selections.

As most colleges do not offer pre-med and pre-law majors, don't pick either as potential major choices. Instead, pick a science or social science major whose requirements fulfill the prerequisites for your advanced degree.

## EVALUATE YOUR CAREER CHOICES

6. ***Enroll in classes.*** As a freshman, sign up for three or four courses related to your selected careers to

Don't haphazardly select a major that is only applicable to very specific professions. Unless you're 100 percent sure you want to work in a hospital or classroom, shy away from majors like nursing and education.

Before my informational interview with a high-level manager, I devised a list of potential questions to ask him. That way, I wasn't left coming up with something brilliant on the spot.

start testing the waters. Make sure the classes will fulfill graduation requirements. Take sociology, politics, and chemistry if you're torn between helping people in need, fighting for justice, or formulating cutting-edge pharmaceuticals. At the end of the term, weigh the pros and cons and name a favorite.

7.     *Job shadow at one or more companies or organizations.* During a job shadow, you'll watch a seasoned professional work. Considering a job in sales? Tag along with a rep during a few sales pitches. Contemplating a job in health care? Follow a doctor or nurse during rounds. Keep in mind that no matter who or where you shadow, the experience will be short. It'll probably only last between a couple hours and a couple days. If you want to try out a job for longer and possibly even earn college credit, consider an internship instead (FTO #19: Internship).

8.     *Schedule one or more informational interviews.* Unlike a normal interview, an informational interview puts you in the driver's seat. You ask the questions and a working employee answers them. Since you aren't looking to land a specific position, you'll seek out more general information about the company and the industry, including but not limited to job growth, average salary, working conditions, and job satisfaction.

9.  *Research the job market.* Don't choose a career based on salary and bonus alone. But don't ignore the numbers, either; the fact is that some degrees pay more than others, and not taking that into consideration could leave you broke. Instead of these two extremes, investigate employment figures and factor them into your career decision. Search for this information in the "Occupational Outlook Handbook" on the U.S. Bureau of Labor Statistics website. This handbook not only

contains actual figures (median pay and number of jobs), but also projections on the change in employment over a 10-year span (job outlook and employment change) for a myriad of professions. For wages in a specific geographical area, check out salary .com as well. While you might notice that salaries in some areas are higher, keep in mind that the cost of living in those areas is probably much higher, too.

## DETERMINE YOUR MAJOR

10. *Pick only one major and no minor.* Meet with your advisor for instructions on how and when to officially declare a major. If you choose a competitive program (often computer science, economics, engineering, and nursing), you may need to declare pre-major status. During this phase, you'll complete prerequisites. But be careful not to let your grades slip; pre-major status doesn't guarantee you a spot in the program.

11. *Declare your major.* Depending on the competitiveness of the major, this process might involve a simple form or a lengthy application. Selective departments might even request recommendation letters, a personal statement, an interview, and for an arts program, an audition or a portfolio. Whatever the program requirements, apply early if possible. By declaring a major as a freshman or sophomore, you'll be paired with a departmental advisor and provided with a more concrete degree plan sooner.

Choose a major with a small number of required classes and a large number of general electives. Whereas major requirements typically must be filled by actual college courses, elective requirements more often can be filled by nontraditional credits (standardized exams, noncollegiate learning, prior learning portfolios, and military training and experience), which can be earned much faster and at a much lower cost.

Don't pick a general studies or interdisciplinary major. These types of majors might allow you to take an interesting variety of classes, but to future employers, they may also say that you have no idea what you want.

After you declare a major, search for more financial aid. Some scholarships are reserved only for students in a specific major. Ask the chair of your department about alumni donations, and contact professional organizations associated with your major about private scholarships. Your chances will be higher if you're part of an underrepresented group in your field of study (e.g., women in engineering).

If your major requires a capstone course, don't throw away assignments from your major courses. In a capstone course, completed during your final semester in school, you'll demonstrate and utilize the knowledge and skills gained in your major curriculum, likely through a project or paper. Therefore, you might need to refer to your old assignments to refresh your memory.

12. *Satisfy the major requirements.* Every major has a set of requirements, as outlined in the degree plan. Most, if not all, are course requirements. You must take certain classes in your field of study and achieve a satisfactory grade in them (typically at least a C). Some, however, are other types of requirements. You may have to do an internship, sit for a comprehensive exam, or go on an international trip. Whatever the requirements are for your specific major, complete all of them in order to graduate.

# ⸗⸗⸗⸗⸗⸗⸗⸗⸗⸗ DOUBLE-CHECK YOUR WORK ⸗⸗⸗⸗⸗⸗⸗⸗⸗⸗

## DISCOVER SUITABLE CAREER OPTIONS

- ☐ Reflect on your passions and abilities
- ☐ Meet with your school's counselor
- ☐ Take a career assessment test
- ☐ Go online
- ☐ Narrow down your choices

## EVALUATE YOUR CAREER CHOICES

- ☐ Enroll in classes
- ☐ Job shadow at one or more companies or organizations
- ☐ Schedule one or more informational interviews
- ☐ Research the job market

## DETERMINE YOUR MAJOR

- ☐ Pick only one major and no minor
- ☐ Declare your major
- ☐ Satisfy the major requirements

# FAST-TRACK OPPORTUNITY #12: MAXIMUM CREDITS
## The More Lectures the Merrier

✓ Start planning a few months prior to registration
✓ Complete any year in college
✓ Spend approximately $$$
✓ Earn potentially +++ credits

"You'll sleep when you're dead." Often sarcastically muttered by undergrads, this morbid saying attempts to console overwhelmed and overworked college students, usually during the exhaustion of finals. For me, this expression neither comforts nor soothes; instead, it invokes nightmares of restless, zombie-like behavior. Some individuals can't survive without daily food and water; I can't function without sleep. On less than four hours, I transform from Dr. Jekyll to Ms. Hyde—no potion needed.

To limit a string of sleepless, study-filled nights, I opted for a light credit load my first year at Northwest University. Although allowed up to 17 credits without a tuition increase, I only signed up for 14. With this schedule, I practically guaranteed myself a full eight hours of slumber. While my classmates counted atoms for chem, I would count sheep in REM. But after just a month, I started clocking in less than seven. Glued to the television, I was wasting all of my free time. And by not registering for the maximum number of credits, I was also forfeiting thousands of dollars.

While I couldn't recoup my funds, I could prevent further loss. Before my second and final year at Northwest, I decided to switch up my routine. Instead of taking a below average number of credits again, I pushed my limits. I enrolled in the maximum: a full 17. Compared to my previous semesters, my schedule held one additional course equal to three additional credits. Anticipating a tough 16 weeks (15 weeks of classes plus one week of finals), I put my TV watching days to rest. So even with the extra schoolwork, my straight-A streak continued and I experienced no shortage of zzz's. I didn't need to wait until the grave to R.I.P. after all.

## The Basics

What is the *minimum* number of pages to earn a satisfactory grade on this paper? What is the *minimum* amount of exercise to avoid the freshman 15? What is the *minimum* number of work hours to cover my rent and other bills? For many students, the word *maximum* is their Kryptonite. They frequently avoid working at this level, choosing the minimum route instead. But since you're not Superman, doing the maximum won't kill you. It'll actually help you accumulate more credits each term than your peers. And while you won't save the world from total destruction, you'll at least rescue your finances from that fate.

Unlike many of the other fast-track opportunities, no matter your class standing, you can likely sign up for a full course load. (Some schools restrict freshmen from signing up for the maximum number of credits.) However, not every college allows students to register for a range of credits (for example, between 12 and 18) without a change in tuition. Some charge incrementally less per credit hour as the number of credits increase, while others assess a flat fee per credit hour regardless of the number. For students in the latter scenario, this opportunity will facilitate a hastier graduation but not a smaller tuition bill.

## The Benefits

- *Increase your productivity.* Day 1: You only need to clean your room and finish your math homework, but you end up posting selfies on Instagram, watching cat videos on YouTube, and answering BuzzFeed quiz questions instead. Day 2: You need to clean your room, finish your math homework, study for your chem test, and write a haiku poem, and you somehow end up completing all these tasks plus running two loads of laundry. While it may seem counterintuitive, you often accomplish more with more responsibility. Still, there is a threshold for what is reasonable and what is not, so don't go crazy and enroll in 25 credits a semester. Take the maximum allowed without a tuition increase and you'll keep working at your optimal efficiency. So at the end of the term, you'll have spent only a little amount of Facebook credit, but earned a large number of college credits.

- *Prepare for graduate school.* Maybe college isn't the end of your educational journey. Immediately following graduation or a few years after, you plan on pursuing a master's or doctorate degree. In the program, you'll have to write essays and take exams, as well as possibly perform hours of research, construct and defend a lengthy thesis, and work on campus as a teaching assistant. If you're like many students, you won't be ready for this level of intensity. By successfully managing a full course load in college, however, you'll be better equipped for the heavy workload. So not only will you be able to keep up, but also earn high marks. What a great way to begin the last leg of your pilgrimage.

- *Gain desirable job skills.* You want employers to want you. But how do you become a sought-after candidate? By being able to organize and prioritize work—all while remaining steady under pressure. Unfortunately, you probably won't acquire these qualities by scooping ice cream or scanning price tags at a minimum-wage job. With a full school schedule, however, you will. So whenever you do start applying for full-time positions, likely at least one employer will put you on his or her top 10 most-wanted list.

- *Eliminate the monotony.* As a young child, your days are unpredictable, consisting mostly of imagination, exploration, and adventure. However, upon entering grade school, your life becomes more uniform and less spontaneous. Wake up at 7:30 a.m., hop on the bus at 8:05 a.m., start school at 8:30 a.m., and so on. You even maintain the same friends, hobbies, and style. Then, a new chapter of your life begins: college. With a full course load, you'll need greater flexibility while scheduling classes. Even if you prefer mornings, you might have to enroll in a cinematography class at 5:30 p.m. to reach 18 credits. While initially daunting, a packed calendar may help you meet new friends, discover a hidden passion, spice up your otherwise bland agenda—or at the very least, make you feel like a kid again.

# The Bottom Line

Would you pay $8.99 for a buffet with an unlimited selection of food? If you want an appetizer, an entrée, and a dessert, the answer might be an easy "Yes." But if you're only craving a small salad or a piece of cherry pie, you might respond differently. To receive your money's worth, you'd have to eat a large amount of food. Now imagine college as a buffet. At Coastal Carolina University, you can gobble up as little as 12 or as many as 18 credits a semester. Either way, you'll spend $11,740 in out-of-state tuition. So if you only register for the minimum number of credits for two semesters (24 total), you'll miss out on an additional 12 "free" credits. That adds up to paying for a whole semester in which you earned 0 credits. So grab a spoon and pile a few extra credits onto your plate. ***Short-term savings = $11,740.***

By signing up for 18 instead of 12 semester credits at Coastal Carolina University:

> You could avoid $11,740 in student loans. You'll save **$3,203** in interest*, assuming each loan is subsidized and has a 5% interest rate and a term of 10 years.

### OR

> You could invest $11,740 in retirement accounts. After 40 years, you'll earn **$70,910** in interest*, assuming each investment has a 5% interest rate, compounded annually.

*Numbers are rounded.*

# The Brief Questions

Ask yourself all of the following before starting this opportunity:

- ***Can you manage a large amount of schoolwork?*** To successfully handle a full course load, you'll need to have good study and time-management skills. If you lack these qualities, use an assignment planner, practice thorough note-taking, and learn test strategies.

Answered "No"? RED FLAG

- *Do you have a fairly open schedule?* To enroll in a full course load, you'll need to have significant availability for class sessions and homework. If your time is limited by a job, sport, extracurricular activity, or other commitment, reduce your hours or seriously consider quitting entirely before signing up for classes.

Answered "No"? RED FLAG

- *Does your school allow enrollment in a range of credits (e.g., 12 to 18) without a monetary increase?* To find out your school's tuition rates, look on its website or ask a staff member in the financial aid office. If your school charges a flat fee for a varying amount of credit and you haven't responded with a "No" to any of the previous questions, strongly consider completing this opportunity.

Answered "Yes"? CLINCHER

# The Blueprint

## OBTAIN A TRANSCRIPT ASSESSMENT

1. *Gather your transcripts (if applicable).* If you previously earned college credit, contact each organization or institution for a copy of your official transcript. You'll likely fill out a simple form and pay a processing fee. Send these transcripts directly to your current school. Wait a few weeks and then confirm delivery.
2. *Request a transcript review (if applicable).* During this process, the registrar's office will evaluate your previous transcripts and award college credit. Since schools can have strict transfer credit policies, some of your credit might not transfer. If this situation occurs, appeal your case.

It might involve additional work, but it'll be easier than retaking an entire class.

## CREATE A TENTATIVE SCHEDULE

3. ***Determine the course requirements (still) needed for graduation.*** If you're a new student and have not previously earned any college credit, find the course requirements for your intended degree in the school's current course catalog (for a copy, check your school's website or the registrar's office). If you're a new student and recently transferred in college credit or are a continuing student, log in to your online student account and perform a degree audit. A degree audit shows you what requirements you've already met, those you're currently working on, and those you have yet to meet. If your school doesn't allow you to perform your own audit, contact your academic advisor or a staff member in the registrar's office and ask for further instructions. You may need to fill out and submit an official request form. Your advisor or a staff member will then perform one for you and send you the results. As schools can get backlogged with paperwork, expect to wait several weeks for them.

4. ***Select courses for the upcoming term.*** On your school's website, search for a schedule of classes for the upcoming term. Many schools provide this schedule in a PDF document, with a long list of all the courses grouped together by department. The departments are organized in alphabetical order, so business and chemistry courses are before music and sociology courses. Look through this schedule to find courses that not only satisfy graduation requirements, but also spark your interest. Make sure to pick enough classes to reach the maximum number of credits allowed without incurring a fee or needing approval, and a few backups in case some of your choices end up overlapping times or being full. As you go over your options, feel free to read the description in the current course catalog for more information about a specific class (if you don't already have a copy, check your school's website or the registrar's office).

5. ***Structure your course schedule.*** Browse the Web for a class scheduling worksheet. This type of worksheet looks like an hourly planner, but it is designed to help students organize their courses. After you find one, download and print it out. Then, scan the list of scheduled classes once

Confused about the course types? General education courses are mandated by the college for all admitted students. Major courses are mandated by the college for students only in a particular field of study. Electives are non-mandated courses selected by the student, not by the college. Confused by the course numbers? 100- and 200-level classes are designed for freshmen and sophomores. The 300- and 400-level courses are recommended for upperclassmen.

again to discover the days and times of your selected courses. Write down each course in its appropriate day and time slot. If a class has more than one section (e.g., Section 1 of PSYCH 101 is offered MWF from 8:00–9:00 a.m. and Section 2 of PSYCH 101 is offered TTH from 9:00–10:45 a.m.), pick whichever section is more convenient for you. If two of your classes overlap, drop one of the classes from your schedule and add one of your backups as a replacement.

## SCRUTINIZE YOUR SELECTIONS

6. *Meet with your advisor.* Most schools require advising appointments for new students, but make them optional for continuing students. However, even if an appointment isn't mandatory for you, still get together with your academic advisor. During the meeting, show your advisor your tentative course schedule and ask for feedback. He or she will then look over your degree plan and see what requirements you have left to complete. Your advisor might recommend changes, such as swapping out one class for another. Unless your advisor encourages you to take less than the maximum number of credits, heed his or her suggestions.

7. *Uncover each teacher's strengths and weaknesses.* Head to www.ratemyprofessors.com to read reviews of professors by your fellow classmates. If a teacher isn't listed or has limited information, ask students at your university about him or her. Bearing in mind that student reviews aren't always the most objective, use your findings to help you determine whether to still register for all of the courses in your tentative schedule or enroll in some different ones.

8. *Locate your classes.* Write down the classroom numbers for each course you intend to register for. Using a map of the campus, pinpoint each stop in your daily routine (including dorm, dining hall, gym). Then, toss

on your tennies and complete a dry run. Record the time you leave and arrive at each place. If, for example, you only have a 10-minute break between two classes but they're a 30-minute walk apart, rearrange your schedule.

For every one hard class, I tried to balance it with two easy ones. For example, because I registered for Introduction to Statistics (hard), I signed up for Fitness and Wellness (easy) and Speaking in Groups (easy) in the same semester.

## FINALIZE YOUR SCHEDULE

9.  *Clear a registration hold (if applicable).* A registration hold will prevent you from registering as well as making changes to your registration (adding, dropping, and withdrawing from classes). It can occur because of a variety of reasons, including but not limited to an academic, admissions, financial, or disciplinary concern. While your school will likely send you a written or email notification about a registration hold, you can also probably access this information through your online student account (for exact instructions, ask a staff member in the registrar's or student accounts office). If your account has a registration hold, contact the department that placed the hold and resolve the issue. The solution may be as simple as paying an overdue library book fine or turning in an immunization form.

10. *Register for a full course load.* Look for a list of course registration dates on your school's website or in the registrar's office. On the earliest possible day, sign up for classes. While you may be able to register in person or over the phone, the easiest way is usually online. Log in to your student account with your username and selected password. Add classes to your schedule until you have signed up for the maximum number of credits allowed without a tuition increase or administrator

Don't expect a quick online registration. Since many students will be registering at the same time as you, your school's website will likely be exceptionally slow. Therefore, make sure that you can spend at least an hour or two on registration.

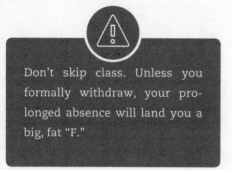

Don't skip class. Unless you formally withdraw, your prolonged absence will land you a big, fat "F."

approval. Once completed, review your selections and electronically send them to the registrar's office.

11. ***Secure a spot in a full class (if applicable).*** If a class is full, place your name on a waiting list. During the first week, attend every session and actively participate. Watch for students to drop out or not show up. If the course remains packed, ask the instructor for permission to join. If your prof agrees, head online or visit the registrar's office to enroll.

12. ***Adjust your schedule (if desired).*** If you absolutely detest a class, you can escape—but only for a small window of time. Before classes begin and often during the first week, you can add or drop courses without an extra fee. After the registration deadline, you can still withdraw from a class until close to the end of the term. However, you'll forfeit partial or full tuition and receive a "W" on your transcript.

# ⅢⅢⅢⅢⅢⅢⅢⅢⅢⅢ DOUBLE-CHECK YOUR WORK ⅢⅢⅢⅢⅢⅢⅢⅢⅢⅢⅢ

## OBTAIN A TRANSCRIPT ASSESSMENT
- ❐ Gather your transcripts (if applicable)
- ❐ Request a transcript review (if applicable)

## CREATE A TENTATIVE SCHEDULE
- ❐ Determine the course requirements (still) needed for graduation
- ❐ Select courses for the upcoming term
- ❐ Structure your course schedule

## SCRUTINIZE YOUR SELECTIONS
- ❐ Meet with your advisor
- ❐ Uncover each teacher's strengths and weaknesses
- ❐ Locate your classes

## FINALIZE YOUR SCHEDULE
- ❐ Clear a registration hold (if applicable)
- ❐ Register for a full course load
- ❐ Secure a spot in a full class (if applicable)
- ❐ Adjust your schedule (if desired)

# FAST-TRACK OPPORTUNITY #13:
## SUMMER CLASSES
### To Every Class There Is a Season

✓ Start planning in early winter of freshman, sophomore, or junior year in college
✓ Complete in summer after freshman, sophomore, or junior year in college
✓ Spend approximately $$ to $$$ (per class)
✓ Earn potentially + to ++ credits (per class)

I live near Seattle, a city famous for the Space Needle, Starbucks, and soggy weather. It's only sunny for around 70 days each year, usually during the summer season. With such a limited time frame, staying indoors between July and September is practically taboo. After months in hibernation, swarms of pasty Northwesterners desert their dens to soak up the sun. They bike, hike, swim, canoe, sail, or simply bask in the rays. And I, like most other Washingtonians, take advantage of any and every opportunity to enjoy the blue skies. Which means come October, I'm sporting a nice, healthy glow.

Between my first and second year in college, however, I sacrificed daylight for fluorescent bulbs. I needed to take a science course but couldn't fit the lab hours into my fall or spring schedule. I had two choices: push back my graduation date or enroll in summer school. Following some internal debate, I elected the lesser of two evils. And since I preferred telescopes over microscopes but my university didn't offer astronomy, I enrolled for the term at a nearby community college.

During the first class session, I questioned my decision. As I listened to the lecture, my focus shifted from my teacher to the world outside. Through the large windows, I could see the makings of a perfect day. Not a cloud above. Was the credit worth the cost? I considered quitting, but I didn't. And I'm glad I didn't. While I learned virtually the same material taught during a regular semester of astronomy, I went to class for eight weeks instead of the typical 15. The only downfall? My skin remained ghostly white. Even so, the college credits were definitely worth the cost of a spray tan.

## The Basics

Who doesn't love to brag about their summer break? I camped at the bottom of the Grand Canyon. I watched the Fourth of July fireworks in D.C. I swam with the sea turtles off the coast of Maui. But who loves to boast about their downtime? I surfed the Web. I lay by the pool. I counted tiles on my ceiling. By enrolling in summer classes, you'll eliminate some of the summer doldrums, but still have the time to indulge in a memorable vacation. Now that's a break worth tooting your horn about.

Summer term is just like any other, with three general exceptions. First, classes are shorter in length. Summer courses can range from one week to a few months, but rarely last as long as a fall or spring semester. Second, the credit load is less. Most students only register for between one and three classes, usually to fulfill a general education requirement. And third, tuition is often cheaper. To fill seats during their "off-season," some schools provide steep discounts. Financial aid is usually a possibility for summer classes, too, making them all the more affordable.

## The Benefits

- **Register for an otherwise full course.** Odds of getting a royal flush in poker? 649,739 to 1. Odds of scoring a spot in a coveted class? Seems even worse. Many students need a particular class to graduate but face the dreaded waiting list each term. Instead of letting fate decide, control your own destiny and sign up in the summer. During this time of year, enrollment generally declines and classes aren't as crowded. Go ahead, up the ante. The odds are finally in your favor.

- *Tackle a tough subject.* For many students, there's that one particular class they dread. They continually avoid the inevitable, hoping for a way out. Although not a shortcut, a less treacherous path does exist. Instead of adding a difficult course to an already packed fall or spring term, enroll in summer school. Since you won't be bogged down with a full course load, you can devote most if not all of your mental energy just on that one class. Sometimes the best course of action is the road less traveled.

- *Maintain mental acuity.* After months on the couch, you lace up your sneakers and hit the pavement. But within 10 minutes, you're gasping for breath and clutching your chest. Just like with your other organs, your brain won't function as well without consistent exercise. During school breaks, many students choose watching TV over mental training. While it may seem less stressful, students slowly lose concentration and memory, which can make the start of a new school year rough. By attending summer classes, you can help prevent this depletion, so once the fall term arrives, you can skip the warm-up and jump right into your schoolwork.

- *Attend smaller classes.* Throughout the school year, general education classes often overflow with several hundred students. But during the summer, these same courses sometimes dwindle to only a few dozen learners. By enrolling in the "off-season," you'll receive more teacher attention and interaction. Instead of, "What's your name again?" you'll hear, "Yes, Mr./Ms. [your last name here], I would love your insight on this topic."

# The Bottom Line

For the best deal, experts recommend purchasing a TV between January and February, appliances between September and October, and a car between November and December. Even tuition has a few cheap months. Due to a decrease in enrollment, many colleges and universities reduce tuition during May, June, July, and August. Some examples include Neumann University in Pennsylvania, Indiana University, and Tiffin University in Ohio, with discounts of 20, 25, and 38 percent respectively. Looking for even steeper savings? Trine University in Indiana marks off more than 100 on-campus and online summer courses by around 60 percent. Throughout the school year, tuition costs $890 or $990 (online) per credit hour. However, during the summer, the price drops down to $360 or $460 (online). For a three-credit on-campus summer course, a student would only pay $1,080 compared to the typical $2,670. ***Short-term savings = $1,590.***

By attending a three-credit course during the summer instead of during the school year at Trine University:

> You could avoid $1,590 in student loans. You'll save **$434** in interest*, assuming each loan is subsidized and has a 5% interest rate and a term of 10 years.

OR

> You could invest $1,590 in retirement accounts. After 40 years, you'll earn **$9,604** in interest*, assuming each investment has a 5% interest rate, compounded annually.

*Numbers are rounded.

# The Brief Questions

Ask yourself all of the following before starting this opportunity:

- ***Can you keep up with a fast-paced class?*** To follow along in a summer course, you'll need to be able to grasp concepts and complete assignments relatively quickly. Since summer classes are condensed, around 15 weeks of material is covered in a much shorter time frame. Teachers tend to fly through their lessons and give out homework and exams frequently. If you comprehend new ideas rather slowly and need extra time for assignments, don't complete this opportunity.

Answered "No"? **DEALBREAKER**

- *Do you still need general education classes or electives?* To find major courses (mostly upper level) offered during summer term, you may have to search far and wide. Most schools only provide general education and elective courses (mostly lower-level) during this time. If you only have major requirements left and can't locate at least one summer class needed for graduation, don't complete this opportunity.

Answered "No"? **DEALBREAKER**

- *Is your place of summer residency close to a college or university?* To attend an on-campus summer class, you'll need to be within reasonable driving distance of higher education. If the nearest school is more than an hour away, move closer or enroll in an online summer course. While you should still complete the steps in The Blueprint that follows, you should also refer to FTO #14: Distance Learning.

Answered "No"? **RED FLAG**

- *Do your summers tend to drag on and on?* To prevent boredom, staying busy is crucial. For some students, this isn't always easy between June and August. If your summer months are wide open but you want something to sink your teeth into, and you haven't responded with a "No" to any of the previous questions, strongly consider completing this opportunity.

Answered "Yes"? **CLINCHER**

# The Blueprint

## SELECT YOUR CLASSES

1. *Create a list of potential summer classes.* Request an appointment with your academic advisor to speak about attending summer school. During the meeting, determine what classes you still need to graduate. With your advisor's guidance, pick three to five suitable courses for the summer

term. While you'll probably only enroll in a couple, you'll have backup options in case your first or second choice is full by the time you register.

2. ***Choose an affordable school (if applicable).*** Unless you're staying at the same institution you're enrolled in during the regular academic year, you'll need to find another regionally accredited school for the summer (a host institution). Look for schools that not only offer courses you want to take over the summer, but also have fairly inexpensive tuition for this specific time of year. Community colleges are one of the most popular options for summer. They have a widespread presence across the country and, compared to four-year institutions, typically lower tuition. To search for a community college (or if you'd prefer, a traditional college or university) in a specific region, go to www.petersons.com /college-search.aspx or bigfuture.collegeboard.org/college-search. Once you settle on a school, verify with your advisor that the credits earned at this host institution will indeed transfer to your current institution.

## APPLY FOR ADMISSION AND FINANCIAL AID

3. ***Submit an application for admission (if applicable).*** If you plan to take summer courses at a host institution, you'll need to apply as a transient student (a.k.a. "guest student") instead of as a degree-seeking student. In addition to filling out the application forms, you might also have to obtain from your college an official transcript and a statement granting you permission to enroll somewhere else for a term. Send in all of these materials well in advance of the deadline. There might only be a limited number of spots available for transient students.

4. ***Receive grants, loans, and/or work study (if applicable).*** As long as you maintained Satisfactory Academic Progress (SAP) during the previous term and will enroll at least half-time for the summer session, you might be eligible for financial aid. If you plan to take courses at your current institution, complete the FAFSA at fafsa.ed.gov (you may need to submit the prior year's or upcoming year's forms) and any supplemental paperwork that may be required. But if you plan to take courses at a host institution, getting financial aid won't be as simple. Your current school will need to enter into a consortium agreement with your host school. For this agreement to occur, you'll need to obtain and fill out the necessary forms. Since each school has its own policies and procedures

concerning consortium agreements, speak with your academic advisor or the financial aid office at your current institution.

## ENROLL IN CLASSES

5. ***Request approval for prerequisite coursework (if applicable).*** Many courses require a prerequisite. You must complete the prerequisite before you can register for a more advanced class. For example, a common prerequisite for Anatomy and Physiology is Biology 101. At a host institution, you won't be able to automatically enroll in a class that has a prerequisite. You'll need authorization first. To get permission, send a transcript or standardized test score, as needed, to the appropriate department as proof that you've already completed the prerequisite. Due to the varying wait times for approval, submit this documentation a few weeks before the start of summer registration.

6. ***Register for summer classes.*** Registration usually opens a few months before the given term. For summer, you can enroll as early as late winter. (The precise date is specific to the school.) On the first possible day, sign up for classes. You'll probably need to go online. Type in your username and selected password to access your student account. Once you're logged in, search for courses to add to your schedule. Carefully review your selections and electronically send them to the registrar's office. If you're blocked from registering, your account might have a hold due to an academic, admissions, financial, or disciplinary reason. Fix the issue promptly.

To increase summer enrollment, some schools discount room and board as well as tuition. If you've decided to live on campus, ask the school about any housing or meal plan specials.

## GET READY FOR CLASSES

7. ***Move out and settle in (if applicable).*** Unless you've just signed a yearlong lease, you'll likely need to change housing over the summer. Schools generally don't keep all their dorms open during summer, so even if you're staying on campus, the school might require you to switch dorms. During the move, practice proper lifting techniques: keep a wide base of support and let your legs and not your back do the

heavy work. Before you leave, check and repair any damage to your room to avoid losing your deposit. Once you put down roots in your new place, set up a homework area. If you're limited on square footage, consider hitting the books outside. Simply slather on sunblock, slip on sunglasses, and study in a sling back.

8. ***Pay your tuition.*** Review your most current statement and check for errors. After addressing any concerns, take care of your debts. Expecting financial aid? Check the summer financial aid disbursement date and the tuition deadline. If the tuition deadline is prior to disbursement, apply for a fee deferment (this might be automatic) or pay out-of-pocket. Not expecting financial aid or not enough to cover the remaining balance? Depending on the available options, make a payment online, by mail, or in person. If you can't come up with the entire amount, you can also opt for a payment plan. Instead of a lump sum, you'll bear the expense over several months. But there's a negative—you'll incur a fee for this service.

9. ***Acquire your books and materials.*** Look for a list of required textbooks in each course syllabus or ask an employee in the campus bookstore (note that hours may be limited over the summer). Mention the name of the course, course code, and instructor. Then, buy the books at the campus bookstore or from another brick-and-mortar or online retailer. After this purchase, visit a local supermarket or office supply store. If you don't already own them, get a binder, planner, several spiral notebooks, college-ruled paper, pens, pencils, and a scientific or graphing calculator (for math students only). You may also want highlighters, permanent markers, and sticky notes.

Rent your textbooks for greater savings. Go to chegg.com, bookrenter.com, or campusbookrentals.com. Some universities even offer rentals in their bookstore.

I never skipped a class. Since my summer course was only eight weeks, one class session was like two classes during a regular semester.

## FINALIZE YOUR SCHEDULE

10. ***Make course changes (if applicable).*** Due to a condensed summer

schedule, the add/drop period is usually shorter than during the school year. Instead of the typical week, you may only have a few days. Therefore, immediately read through all of your syllabi after the first day. If any course seems too difficult, switch to an easier option right away. By not waiting, you'll potentially save thousands in forfeited tuition and a "W" (academic withdrawal) on your transcript.

11. *Request a transcript (if applicable).* If you were a transient student for the summer, your regular institution will need a record of your courses. To procure an official transcript, contact the registrar's office at your host school for instructions. You may need to submit your request and pay the small fee online, by mail, by fax, in person, or through a third-party provider (such as National Student Clearinghouse or Credentials Solutions). Have the transcript either sent to your school or sent to you in a sealed envelope. Due to varying processing times (typically longer at the start and end of each term), expect transcript delivery to take between a few days to a few weeks.

---

## |||||||||||||||||||||||||| DOUBLE-CHECK YOUR WORK ||||||||||||||||||||||||||

### SELECT YOUR CLASSES

- ❏ Create a list of potential summer classes
- ❏ Choose an affordable school (if applicable)

### APPLY FOR ADMISSION AND FINANCIAL AID

- ❏ Submit an application for admission (if applicable)
- ❏ Receive grants, loans, and/or work study (if applicable)

### ENROLL IN CLASSES

- ❏ Request approval for prerequisite coursework (if applicable)
- ❏ Register for summer classes

### GET READY FOR CLASSES

- ❏ Move out and settle in (if applicable)

- ☐  Pay your tuition
- ☐  Acquire your books and materials

## FINALIZE YOUR SCHEDULE
- ☐  Make course changes (if applicable)
- ☐  Request a transcript (if applicable)

# FAST-TRACK OPPORTUNITY #14:
## DISTANCE LEARNING
### Distance Makes the Learning More Accessible

- ✓ Start planning a few months prior to registration
- ✓ Complete any year in college
- ✓ Spend approximately $$ to $$$ (per class)
- ✓ Earn potentially + to ++ credits (per class)

Handball [hand-bawl]: *n*. 1. A sport involving two teams of seven players passing a ball across a court into a goal. 2. A form of cruel and unusual punishment. On one fateful afternoon, my PE teacher selected me as keeper in handball. In an attempt to block shots to my head and heart, I left my extremities unprotected. Mere minutes into the game, a ball careened through my dominant hand, causing searing pain down my thumb. I had torn a ligament.

Although a cast covered my entire forearm, schoolwork didn't stop. My teachers still required completion of all in-class assignments, homework, and tests. Unable to write clearly or keyboard quickly, I spent several frustrating evenings scribbling words with my left hand or typing with a single finger. Concerned for my well-being, my mom suggested an alternative to my misery: homeschool. While I had never been homeschooled, I had heard the "horror" stories. Studying in a tiny room for eight hours with only your computer, books, and assignments as company. For a self-proclaimed extrovert, social isolation could cause insanity. To prevent a trip to the psych ward, I opted to stay at my current school and fight through the pain and inconvenience until my hand healed.

But in less than a year, I faced a more grown-up type of homeschool opportunity: distance learning. While in dual enrollment, I had to register for an online course due to a scheduling conflict. Immediately after signing up, I imagined an entire quarter of seclusion. It turned out my fears were unjustified. I communicated often with the other students via email, discussion boards, and chat rooms. And the ability to attend class in sweats but without makeup was worth a couple pangs of loneliness. After that positive experience, I took a few more distance learning classes throughout college. While I still prefer a traditional school environment, I'd pick the solo sport of homeschool over a team tournament of handball any day.

## The Basics

You can shop, play, socialize, and work from almost anywhere. Why not add learning to the list? Through distance learning, you gain credit without stepping foot on campus. Instead of showing up to college and sitting in a traditional classroom, you receive your education in a much more convenient and comfortable spot. So toss out your backpack, save your gas, and find a relaxing place to study. School's in session.

With distance learning, you have the choice of synchronous or asynchronous learning. Synchronous learning occurs when you attend class at the same time as the teacher, as in audio or video conference courses. Asynchronous learning is the exact opposite. It includes online and correspondence courses. In online (or elearning) classes, you have frequent deadlines and communicate with your teachers and peers via discussion boards and chat rooms. On the other hand, correspondence (or independent study) classes are entirely self-paced with few deadlines or social interaction. The combination of these two types of learning (synchronous and asynchronous) is hybrid or blended courses. While you meet on campus for instruction, you complete classwork online.

## The Benefits

- *Maintain your current schedule.* No need to switch to the night shift; college doesn't have to dictate your calendar. With distance learning, you can attend class wherever and whenever. At the DOL during the early morning rush. Or in the doctor's office before an evening appointment. Or at the airport on a layover right after lunchtime. You'll no longer be scheduling your life around school, which means you can preserve your already established routine. So sign up for distance learning courses and keep your day job—or at the very least, your precious freedom.

- **Learn at your own pace.** Your teacher flies through the first concept. Too fast. Then, your teacher lingers on the second one. Too slow. While listening to a classroom lecture, it's easy to feel like Goldilocks from "The Story of the Three Bears." The pacing never seems to be perfect. But unlike classroom learning, distance learning allows you to spend more time on material you don't understand and less on material you do. Which means before long, you'll be uttering those two famous words, "Just right."

- **Choose from a wider selection of classes.** You aren't limited to the courses in your school's course catalog. Even if your college doesn't offer art history and you can't find a professor who will teach the material through independent study, you can still enroll in and complete the class. How is that possible? By taking the course outside of the classroom through another school. Many institutions offer nonmatriculated students (a.k.a. nondegree-seeking students) access to their vast array of distance learning courses, some of which may not be provided by your college. Art history, anatomy, accounting—the sky's the limit!

- **Reduce your carbon footprint.** In recent years, words like *eco-friendly* and *green* have become commonplace. But who has the time to separate garbage into recyclable, compostable, or trash; the money to buy hemp clothing; or the energy to plant a tree for each piece of paper used? Instead, fight global warming by signing up for distance learning courses. Since your home is also your classroom, you can keep the car in the driveway and decrease your auto emissions. So the next time you forget to turn off the lights, don't feel guilty. You're saving the planet in another way.

# The Bottom Line

Cyber Monday only happens once a year, but you can save online the other 364 days through distance learning. While not every college discounts online classes, Louisiana State University does through its Independent and Distance Learning program. As an out-of-state student, you'll only pay $559 in tuition and fees for a three-credit online class, compared to $1,809 for a three-credit on-campus course (cost for tuition on a per-credit-hour basis). But if you're commuting, the savings don't stop there. Not needing to drive to and from school, you'll greatly reduce your auto expenses. With the average small sedan costing around $0.60 per mile to operate,[8] you could keep an additional $1,152 in your wallet compared to a student commuting 20 miles each way, three times a week for a typical 16-week LSU semester. *Short-term savings = $2,402 ($1,250 tuition savings plus $1,152 gas savings).*

By participating in a three-credit semester course online instead of on campus through Louisiana State University:

> You could avoid $2,402 in student loans. You'll save **$655** in interest*, assuming each loan is subsidized and has a 5% interest rate and a term of 10 years.

OR

> You could invest $2,402 in retirement accounts. After 40 years, you'll earn **$16,910** in interest*, assuming each investment has a 5% interest rate, compounded annually.

*Numbers are rounded.*

# The Brief Questions

Ask yourself all of the following before starting this opportunity:

- *Can you handle a class with a larger than normal homework load?* To

8.   AAA, *Your Driving Costs*, accessed October 6, 2014, http://publicaffairsresources.aaa.biz/wp-content/uploads/2014/05/Your-Driving-Costs-2014.pdf.

compensate for the lack of in-class sessions, distance learning courses often require more work than their on-campus counterparts. Before you register for a distance learning course, ask the instructor for a copy of the syllabus. While you should eventually read through the entire document, just look over the section with the list of assignments and exams for now. If the amount seems unmanageable and might negatively impact your grade, change to a different distance learning course or the same one in an on-campus format.

## Answered "No"? **RED FLAG** or **DEALBREAKER**

- *Are you self-disciplined?* To avoid falling behind on readings and assignments, you'll need to stay motivated throughout the entire distance learning class. If you regularly procrastinate without an instructor's prompting, find a family member; friend, or another student in the course to keep you accountable and on track.

## Answered "No"? **RED FLAG**

- *Can you filter out constant distractions?* To thrive while learning from home, you'll need to be able to ignore disruptions. If you easily lose focus, turn off all your electronics and study in a quiet, secluded area.

## Answered "No"? **RED FLAG**

- *Are you comfortable on a computer?* To participate in an online distance learning class, you'll need to have the ability to formulate emails, create documents, and browse the Web. If you lack significant exposure to technology, take a few computer classes for free at your public library or enroll in a different type of distance learning (e.g., a correspondence course).

## Answered "No"? **RED FLAG**

- *Are you unable to attend on-campus classes?* To listen to lectures, understand the material, and sit for quizzes and exams in a traditional course, you'll need to show up to the majority of class sessions. If you live too far from a school, have an extremely busy schedule, or can't leave the house for at least a few hours at a time, and if you haven't responded with a "No" to any of the previous questions, strongly consider completing this opportunity.

Answered "Yes"? CLINCHER

# The Blueprint

## REGISTER FOR CLASS

1. *Select a distance learning class(es).* First, figure out what courses you still need to graduate. Out of these, choose at least one that you want to take via distance learning. If needed, ask your academic advisor for help. Next, pick the type of distance learning best suited to your personality and learning style. If you're introverted, correspondence courses might be a good fit. But if you're a social butterfly, hybrid or video conference classes might be better. Keep in mind your schedule as well. If you're fine waiting, online classes often have concrete start dates, similar to those of on-campus classes. But if you're eager to begin now, correspondence courses typically have flexible start dates, allowing enrollment at any time.

2. *Ensure accreditation (if applicable).* If you're already enrolled in a traditional college or university, your school might offer distance learning courses, but those courses might not help cut your tuition costs or expedite your graduation. To achieve these objectives, consider taking distance courses at a host institution. But before you do, make sure the school is regionally accredited. Accreditation means a college or university meets a minimum standard of quality in education. Credit from unaccredited institutions will likely not be transferable.

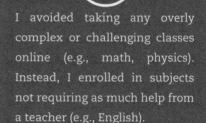

I avoided taking any overly complex or challenging classes online (e.g., math, physics). Instead, I enrolled in subjects not requiring as much help from a teacher (e.g., English).

Don't trust the school's word. Since phony credentials do exist, beware of scams. Do the legwork up front and save potentially wasted credits and tuition in the long run.

Additionally, credit from institutions with national accreditation might not transfer as easily as credit from those with regional accreditation. Therefore, visit ope.ed.gov/accreditation and search for the school in the Database of Accredited Postsecondary Institutions and Programs. You can view not only the institution's accrediting organization, but any specialized accreditations as well.

3.      *Enroll in class(es).* If you plan to take a distance learning course at a host institution, you'll need to apply for admission. Submit the application for a transient student (a.k.a. "guest student") instead of for a degree-seeking student. After you've been formally accepted to the college or, if you're taking the course through your regular institution, register for the course. Log in to your student account with your username and selected password. Add classes to your schedule. Once completed, double-check your choices and electronically send them to the registrar's office.

4.    *Attend the distance learning orientation (if applicable).* Whether or not it's required, complete the orientation offered by the school. It'll likely take place online with a self-paced format. In the first part, you might assess your distance learning readiness through a questionnaire. Many schools use SmarterMeasure to show students' strengths and weaknesses in an online environment. In the second part, you might read through sections (such as "Using Course Technology," "Keys to Success," "Navigating through an Online Course," and "Student Resources") and answer questions on the material. Once you're done with the orientation, you may have the option to send your score report or a certificate of completion to your professor.

## OBTAIN THE NECESSARY EQUIPMENT

5.    *Meet the technical requirements (if applicable).* On your school's website, find a list of the technical requirements for distance learning. In addition to a broadband Internet connection (DSL, cable, satellite), you'll need specific hardware and software. In terms of hardware, you'll probably

need a computer (PC or Mac), monitor, printer, headset with microphone, and, especially for video conference courses, a webcam. In terms of software, you'll probably need a compatible browser (Internet Explorer, Mozilla Firefox, Google Chrome) with the correct configured settings, office suite (word processing, spreadsheet, and presentation program), plug-ins (Adobe Reader, Java Runtime Environment, QuickTime Player), and antivirus software. If you don't already own these items and can't afford them, use the equipment at your public library or your school's computer lab.

6. ***Create a homework space.*** Even if you live in a dorm or cramped apartment, you'll just need a spot to fit a desk, an adjustable chair, and a lamp. To promote a healthy posture and avoid injury, adjust and arrange the items on and around your desk until your feet are flat on the floor, wrists are in a neutral position, monitor is

If your school doesn't require Microsoft Office, look into Libre Office (www.libreoffice.org). It's free, open-source software.

at eye level, and mouse is near the keyboard. After your workstation is ergonomically correct, dress up the area with pictures and a few knick-knacks. Make it an inviting place to study.

## FINANCE YOUR CLASS AND MATERIALS

7. ***Pay your tuition.*** Before the due date, access your bill electronically. Review the most current statement and check for errors. You may incur a technology or distance learning charge on top of the course tuition. After addressing any concerns, take care of your debts. Since you might not be near the campus, you can probably pay your bill one of two ways, by mail or online. If you elect to pay by mail, send a personal check or money order to the student accounts or bursar's office. If you elect to pay online, log in to your account and then enter your bank account information and routing number (no transaction cost) or credit card number (potential transaction cost) into the secure online bill pay form. If you can't come up with the entire amount, you can also opt for a payment plan. For a fee, you'll bear the expense over several months instead of in one lump sum.

8. ***Obtain your textbooks.*** Your course tuition may or may not include the cost of materials. If you need to buy your books separately, start by determining which are required. You can find a list in the course syllabus or call and ask an employee in the campus bookstore. Make sure to mention that you're taking a distance learning class, as the books might vary from the ones used in the equivalent on-campus course. Once you've discovered exactly what you need, order the items through the online campus bookstore or another online retailer. You can purchase physical textbooks or, since you'll already be on your computer frequently for class, go with ebooks.

## ATTEND CLASS

9. ***Explore the online portion of your class(es) (if applicable).*** After logging in, read any messages or announcements on the homepage. Then, browse through the remaining pages by clicking all tabs and hyperlinks. If you experience problems, try some basic troubleshooting before calling in the big guns. Can't access the Internet? Unplug your router and plug it back in. Can't log in? Verify your credentials and ensure Caps Lock is off. Can't view the web page? Double-check the address and, if it's correct, try back in a few hours. Your school's server might be temporarily down. Can't use specific functions on the website? Open the page on a different computer or in a different browser. You might also need to install a plug-in. As a last resort, perform a full reboot. If these simple suggestions don't fix the problem, contact your school's IT department for further assistance.

10. ***Pass your distance learning class(es).*** To achieve this goal, first create a study plan. Take out your planner and block out several hours each week for readings, assignments, and tests. Although you don't have to work at your desk or computer during these times, treat them like actual class sessions and show up ready to learn. Second, stay in contact with your instructor, and if applicable, your classmates. Ask your teacher for help by email or phone. Use the discussion board or chat room to communicate with the other students. Third, take advantage of the distance learning resources. You might be able to use an online library, tutoring center, and writing lab—all free of charge.

11. ***Locate an exam proctor (if applicable).*** Many distance learning courses,

especially correspondence courses, require proctored exams. A proctor provides the directions as well as supervises the exam. If you live close to the college offering the distance learning course, an administrator in the school's testing office will probably proctor your exam. You simply make an appointment, show up on test day, and pay the administration fee. If you live far from the college,

If you're in the military, check with your Education Center, Navy College Office, or installation's testing center, library, or learning center for an acceptable proctor.

you'll need to find your own proctor. Your choices might be limited to a full-time faculty member, administrator, or librarian. Once one of these individuals agrees to the job, send the proctor form to the college well in advance of the deadline. After he or she is approved, arrange a test day and time along with a meeting spot.

12. *Request a transcript (if applicable).* Transient students will need to send a record of their distance learning course to their regular institution. To procure an official transcript, contact the registrar's office at your host school for instructions. Unless you're close to the campus and can visit the office in person, you'll need to submit your request and pay the small fee online, by mail, by fax, or through a third-party provider (such as National Student Clearinghouse or Credentials Solutions). Have the transcript either sent to your school or sent to you in a sealed envelope. Due to varying processing times (typically longer at the start and end of each term), expect transcript delivery to take between a few days to a few weeks.

---

||||||||||||||||||||||||| **DOUBLE-CHECK YOUR WORK** |||||||||||||||||||||||||

## REGISTER FOR CLASS
- ☐ Select a distance learning class(es)
- ☐ Ensure accreditation (if applicable)

❏ Enroll in class(es)

❏ Attend the distance learning orientation (if applicable)

## OBTAIN THE NECESSARY EQUIPMENT

❏ Meet the technical requirements (if applicable)

❏ Create a homework space

## FINANCE YOUR CLASS AND MATERIALS

❏ Pay your tuition

❏ Obtain your textbooks

## ATTEND CLASS

❏ Explore the online portion of your class(es) (if applicable)

❏ Pass your distance learning class(es)

❏ Locate an exam proctor (if applicable)

❏ Request a transcript (if applicable)

# BONUS FTO #15:
## Independent Study

Contrary to its name, independent study is not reserved for loners and recluses. Independent study courses are an option for any self-motivated college student. And while they're sometimes provided through distance learning, they traditionally take place on campus. Maybe a class you want or need is full, doesn't fit into your schedule, or isn't even available at your college. Instead of waiting until another term, attending a different school, or learning about the topic purely for pleasure, earn credit by signing up for an independent study course at your school. First, find a faculty member competent in the subject area to act as your instructor. Next, work with him or her to alter an existing syllabus or create a brand-new one for the course. Give this syllabus as well as the independent study course form (with your instructor's signature) to the registrar's office. Once you're officially enrolled, get to work. Meet with your instructor on your mutually agreed upon times and days, and turn in all of your assignments by their deadlines.

# MAXIMIZE YOUR COLLEGE EXPERIENCE

I learned an important lesson from *The Shining*. All work and no play doesn't just make Jack a dull boy, but also a murderous maniac. Since I've never looked good in an orange jumpsuit, I couldn't skimp on play. But with my plan to graduate from college early, work could easily consume all of my time. To avoid years in jail or years in debt, I had to accomplish both activities simultaneously. With some effort, I discovered some seriously amazing ways to earn credit. In the end, Stephen King's novel remained exactly as it should: a work of fiction.

Even if you currently have a healthy work-life balance, you can still maximize your college experience. Based on your budget, complete one or more of the next four FTOs (since the numbers below don't factor in financial aid, your actual costs could be less than those stated). Try FTO #16: Gap Year Programs if you can afford to spend around $10,000 to $20,000 on approximately one to two semesters of credit. Or try FTO #17: Intersession Abroad if you can afford to spend around $3,000 to $6,000 on approximately one to six credits. Or try FTO #18: Alternative Breaks (AB) if you can afford to spend around $200 to $2,000 on approximately one to three credits. Or try FTO #19: Internship if you can't afford to spend anything and might even need to make money. But whichever you choose, make sure you can learn outside of a traditional classroom. With all four of these FTOs, your schooling will come more from exploration and experience than from textbooks and teachers.

Do you currently participate in an extracurricular, or would you like to at some point? Explore the mini fast-track opportunity (*Bonus FTO #20:* Extracurricular Activities) at the end of this section.

# FAST-TRACK OPPORTUNITY #16: GAP YEAR PROGRAMS

## Bridge the Gap Year

✓ Start planning as early as spring of 11th grade in high school
✓ Complete between high school graduation and the first day of college
✓ Spend approximately $$$
✓ Earn potentially ++ to +++ credits

Hindsight is 20/20. As a kid, I didn't quite understand this expression. I didn't make many decisions, and those I did make, I didn't care to change. As an adult, however, this statement made perfect sense. After settling on a choice, I'd see the better course of action later on. Sometimes, I'd even dream of a time machine like the one described in the science fiction novel by H. G. Wells. I could hop in, go back, and fix my mistake. Like wearing a sweater vest in my seventh grade yearbook photo. Or attempting to wax my legs on my own. Or possibly even starting college immediately after high school.

But if I could travel back only once, I obviously wouldn't waste it on those first two. However, I might use it on the third. Instead of enrolling in college at 18, I'd take time off. Back in high school, I considered a gap year. Albeit briefly, this option definitely crossed my mind. But I was persuaded against it—by teachers, counselors, and most importantly, my dad. He brought up this topic during the big talk. No, not that talk. The talk about my plans after graduation. With the best intentions at heart, he warned me about a break from school. Leaving for any length meant never coming back.

Since an undergraduate degree was my top priority, I followed everyone's advice. Unfortunately, they gave me misinformation. I wish I had known then what I know now. If I'd taken a gap year, I wouldn't have lounged around for 12 months, addicted to television and Twinkies. I might have traveled, interned, volunteered, and studied—all while earning college credit. And once my time was up, I would have returned to school like the other 90 percent of gappers.[9] Although I can't reverse the clock, I can encourage current high schoolers to look into this post-graduation possibility. Who said foresight can't also be perfect vision?

# The Basics

"Fall into the gap." An iconic tagline from a popular denim company or good advice for a soon-to-be high school grad? It's not one or the other; it's actually both. Many students go straight from high school to college, but deferring an offer of admission from a college or university (known as deferred enrollment) and taking a gap year might be a better idea. In fact, gap years are fairly common throughout the world, and in some parts, they're practically a rite of passage. Although historically not as well adopted in the United States, they have gained more credibility and popularity in recent years. And for good reason—gap years provide students with a much-needed semester to yearlong break from their formal education, while also encouraging experiential learning, personal growth, and broadened perspective.

But even though this time can be extremely advantageous, it can also be problematic for students to enter college behind their classmates, in terms of academic standing. Fortunately, more and more gap year programs today offer college credit, so you can avoid putting yourself in that position. One other caveat is that gap year programs can be quite expensive, some costing about the same as or more than a year of private college tuition. But there's good news here, too. Since you'll be earning college credit during your gap year, you can likely submit a FAFSA and potentially receive federal financial aid.

9.   Sue Shellenbarger, "Delaying College to Fill in the Gaps," *The Wall Street Journal*, December 29, 2010, accessed September 12, 2014, http://on.wsj.com/1zFBN2f.

So while you'll want to be mindful of credits and cost, there's most likely a gap program out there that will allow you to stay on budget and on track to graduate early, while at the same time getting you far ahead of your peers in life experience. Depending on the program you choose, in addition to learning and studying, you could engage in any of the following activities with others or on your own: language and cultural immersion, volunteerism and community service, paid and unpaid internships, outdoor and wilderness expeditions, domestic and international travel, fine arts and media, and conservation and sustainability. So are you ready to "fall into the gap"? No, not into a Gap store to try on a perfectly snug, practically tailored just for you pair of jeans. Into a gap program and an exciting semester or year ahead—completely free of a one-size-fits-all education.

# The Benefits

- **Recharge with a break from school.** At least two-thirds of your life has been spent in school. Years reciting the Pledge of Allegiance, listening to intercom announcements, reading textbook scripts, and sitting for multiple-choice exams. Which means after high school, you're totally, completely, 100 percent burned out. You're looking for some R&R. And although a year at the spa would more than do the trick, you don't really need 365 days of facials, massages, and body wraps. You just want to get away from the hustle and bustle of the typical classroom. With a gap program, you can accomplish this goal while rediscovering a motivation and passion for your education. In such a small fraction of time, you'll feel whole again. And that's math every student likes.

- **Stand out from the other applicants.** You might be a typical student—typical grades, typical test scores, and typical extracurriculars. And although you fit in, landing smack dab in the middle of the bell curve has its downsides. You might even have already experienced one of them. Since your college apps lacked a wow factor, you received more than one rejection letter. But you don't have to feel discouraged. You can reapply next year and complete a gap program in the meantime. And with this valuable experience under your belt, your apps will definitely stand out from the crowd and catch the eye of admissions officers, resulting in more than one acceptance. So while you won't still be like everyone else, normal is so overrated anyway.

- **Take advantage of your current freedom and flexibility.** While adulthood represents possibilities, it also represents responsibilities. College and career, spouse and house, bills and babies. And the pressure starts only a summer after high school graduation. However, it doesn't have to begin quite so soon. By pushing back your undergrad and completing a gap program, you can travel the world for up to a year. Once you're in the throes of adulthood, you'll barely have a few days free, let alone an entire 12 months. Why not go on the adventure of a lifetime now? You're only young once.

- **Acquire crucial life skills.** You've been attached to your parental units for 18 years—give or take a few. You're eager to cut the cord, but you aren't prepared to go out on your own. You don't know how to properly thaw a frozen chicken or correctly iron a dress shirt. But even more than your lack of cooking and cleaning skills is your lack of intangible skills like problem-solving, adaptability, leadership, and time management. Unfortunately, college might not address these deficiencies. A college's focus is on teaching book smarts, not street smarts. Curriculum-based gap year programs, however, do both. They'll prepare you to live independently and responsibly, apart from Mom and Dad. So go ahead, grab a pair of scissors and sever the connection. You won't need it anymore.

# The Bottom Line

The word *gap* is synonymous with the word *hole*. And as many students and parents assume, gap programs are also synonymous with large holes in their wallets. Yet while these types of programs aren't cheap, their relative costs might surprise you. A year in a gap program can be less than a year at a moderately priced institution. One such program is the Latitudes Year through Carpe Diem Education. For $18,900, you'll receive up to 36 quarter credits from Portland State University (through Carpe Diem's partnership with PSU), all food, accommodations, scheduled activities, and international health insurance. Just tuition and fees for 36 credits at PSU would set you back $18,486 as an out-of-state student. Add in $11,349 for room and board, and you'd pay a total of $29,835. *Short-term savings = $10,935.*

By spending a school year in the Carpe Diem Education program instead of at Portland State University:

❭ You could avoid $10,935 in student loans. You'll save **$2,983** in interest*, assuming each loan is subsidized and has a 5% interest rate and a term of 10 years.

**OR**

❭ You could invest $10,935 in retirement accounts. After 40 years, you'll earn **$76,982** in interest*, assuming each investment has a 5% interest rate, compounded annually.

*Numbers are rounded.*

# The Brief Questions

Ask yourself all of the following before starting this opportunity:

- *Is enjoying your time more important to you than graduating from college early?* To help students not fall too far behind, many gap programs partner with accredited schools to grant college credit. However, a year in a gap program will probably earn you less credit than a year enrolled full-time at a college. If racking up credits ASAP is your top priority, don't complete this opportunity, but consider working through one or more of the College Credit-by-Exam FTOs in Section 3 (FTOs #6–#10) instead.

## Answered "No"? **DEALBREAKER**

- *Can you live far away from home for a school year?* To participate in a gap year program, you'll need to commit for the entire length. You'll receive a long break around Christmas, and possibly another couple of breaks surrounding other major holidays. If you have a family obligation during the school year (e.g., sister's wedding in March) or are uncomfortable leaving home for that long, sign up for a gap semester. While not guaranteed, many schools allow students on deferred enrollment to return for the spring term of their freshman year instead of waiting until the following fall.

## Answered "No"? **RED FLAG**

- ***Do you crave time away from a formal school environment?*** To foster learning and growth, gap year programs offer more outside activities (such as internships, community service, and travel) than inside instruction. If you aren't quite ready for college and haven't responded with a "No" to any of the previous questions, strongly consider completing this opportunity.

## Answered "Yes"? **CLINCHER**

- ***Are you struggling to choose a college major and career path?*** To avoid wasting time and money on school, you'll need a clear direction for your future not long after starting your postsecondary education. According to an independent study by Haigler and Nelson, authors of *The Gap Year Advantage,* gap years helped 60 percent of students find or affirm their academic major or career.[10] If you have no clue what to do with your life, want between several months to a year to figure it out, and haven't responded with a "No" to the previous DEALBREAKER or RED FLAG questions, strongly consider completing this opportunity.

## Answered "Yes"? **CLINCHER**

10.   "Data & Gap Year Benefits," American Gap Association, accessed April 16, 2015, http://americangap.org/data -benefits.php.

# The Blueprint

## DISCOVER POSSIBLE PROGRAMS

1. *Determine your must-haves.* Don't visit with your high school counselor or search the Internet quite yet. You might end up wasting valuable hours. Instead, spend that time figuring out what you want and need from a gap year program. Obviously, the program must provide college credit. But you should also consider factors like length, activities, location, cost, financial aid, accommodations, food, and safety. For example, maybe you want a yearlong program offering community service projects in South America. Or you need a fall semester program costing less than $10,000 with a vegetarian meal plan. Whatever your wants and needs, write them down. While you look for and research different programs, use this list to more quickly and easily evaluate them and weed some out.

2. *Meet with your counselor.* You've likely sat in your counselor's office before. You spoke about high school. High school courses, high school activities, even high school drama. But now that you're an upperclassman, you should discuss your future. Discuss your decision to take a gap year. Request recommendations for gap year programs with your must-haves, as well as institutions with favorable policies and views on gap years. Your counselor might simply provide you with some names and websites or hand you a stack of brochures. Spend a few minutes learning about each program or institution, and then store any brochures in your backpack for easy accessibility later.

3. *Locate programs.* You can discover gap year programs through multiple avenues, but the following are the most common ways to find them: (1) Go online. Search using the keywords "gap year" and "college credit." Or directly visit the sites for LeapNow, Pacific Discovery, Carpe Diem Education, InnerPathWorks, IPSL, and ISA Gap. These third-party providers partner with a local or foreign institution to give college credit. (2) Contact schools. Check with some of your top schools to see if they offer their own gap year program (such as Elon University and St. Norbert College). These programs are organized and hosted by the schools and are typically reserved for matriculated

students (a.k.a. degree-seeking students). Therefore, unless you plan on applying to and attending the school after the program, don't even consider it. (3) Attend a gap year fair. Head to one of more than 30 fairs across the country. They take place in late winter and last a few hours. For more information and for a schedule of upcoming fairs, visit www .usagapyearfairs.org/programs.

## DEFER ADMISSION

4. *Investigate your top schools' deferment policies.* Deferred admission allows an accepted student to delay enrollment for a period of time (usually a year, but occasionally, more or less). While many schools permit and sometimes even encourage deferment, each has its own set of guidelines. Find this information on the school's website or via a staff member in the admissions office. Make sure to obtain answers to at least the following questions:

   - Does the school allow deferred admission? If yes, what are the required steps and deadlines?
   - Can I enroll in another institution during the deferral period? If yes, how many college credits can I earn?

5. *Apply to some or all of your top schools (if applicable).* During your senior year in high school, submit applications to any of your top six to eight schools that not only allow deferred admission but also enrollment in another institution during this period. However, to avoid paying the application fees twice, hold off on applying to schools that don't meet this criteria. If you don't get in, or if you choose not to accept an admission offer, you'll apply to these schools (and others as well) next year. This means that while you're participating in your gap program, you will have to go through the whole application process all over again. And depending on how many credits you will earn from your program, you might have to reapply as a transfer student instead of as a freshman, which could have implications for financial aid.

6. *Defer enrollment (if applicable).* Once you've received your official acceptance or rejection letter from each school you applied to, accept the offer of admission from your favorite if you want to avoid having to reapply later. At the same time or shortly after, start the deferment

process. It varies from school to school, but most are fairly similar. You'll likely need to fill out a form or write a letter detailing your gap year plans and send the document to the admissions office. They'll review this paperwork and either accept or reject your request. If deferment is granted, you'll pay the tuition deposit typically by May 1. This payment will hold your spot and usually any merit-based scholarships you may have received as well. The school will not, however, hold your need-based awards. So while you won't have to reapply for admission, you will have to resubmit your FAFSA the following year. This is normal; all students wishing to receive federal aid must file a new FAFSA each year they are in college.

## PARTAKE IN THE PROGRAM

7. *Start the application process.* For each of your favorite programs, review the eligibility criteria. Some might set age and GPA restrictions, as well as require good physical and mental health. Next, read through the program expectations. Most will suspend or expel students who use drugs or alcohol (even if they're over 21) or display threatening or self-destructive behaviors. If you meet the standards and can commit to the rules, begin your application. In addition to completing a form, you might also need to answer essay questions, write a statement of purpose, request your high school transcript or a letter of good standing, obtain recommendation letters, face an interview, and pay an application fee or deposit.

8. *Submit your applications to one or more programs.* Applications for fall programs will either be due sometime in the spring prior (college-sponsored gap programs might have even earlier deadlines), or applicants may be accepted on a rolling basis until all of the spots are filled. Wait until you hear from all of the programs you applied to. Out of the ones that offer you admission, pick your absolute favorite and formally accept their offer. Confirm your decision with a deposit if you have yet to do so.

9. *Prepare for the program.* If you'll be traveling internationally for any part of the program, you'll at the very least need a passport and possibly one or more visas and vaccines or medicines. In addition to these necessities, you might also want to obtain an International Student Identity Card

(ISIC) or purchase travel insurance. While you won't need all of these items if you'll only be traveling domestically, you'll probably still have to book travel arrangements, and you'll definitely have to pack. For more detailed information on getting ready for the program, refer to Appendix E: Trip Preparations.

10. *Attend the program.* Upon arriving at your destination, you'll likely take part in an orientation with the staff and students in your group. You'll then jump right into the program, getting hands-on with whatever type of life-changing experience you signed up for. Toward the end of the program, you might meet with your group again to recap all of your experiences, and you might be assigned some written reflection. After this discussion, you'll once again pack your bags and board your flight, but this time, you'll head back home.

## RETURN TO SCHOOL

11. *Request an official transcript(s).* If you're planning to apply to colleges soon, you might need to request transcripts from your gap year program now and again after the program ends. If you're on deferred enrollment, you'll also need a transcript, but should wait until after the program ends. If you earned credits through a U.S. institution, you'll likely order each transcript from the registrar's office at that school. But if you earned credits through a foreign institution, you'll likely order each transcript from your program provider. They'll deal with the institution on your behalf. Have your transcript(s) sent in a sealed envelope to your home address or directly to the appropriate school(s).

12. *Apply to schools (if applicable).* If you didn't formally accept and defer admission to a college or university before beginning your gap year, apply or reapply to the top schools on your list. Depending on the number of credits you earned in your gap program and the school's policy, you'll be required to apply either as a freshman or as a transfer student. For freshman applicants, you'll likely submit a form, high school transcript, standardized test scores (SAT or ACT), essay, recommendation letters, and application fee. For transfer applicants, however, you might not need your high school transcript or test scores, but you'll definitely need your college transcript. Send all of the necessary paperwork to each school by its deadline.

13. ***Reaffirm your admission (if applicable).*** If you're on deferred enrollment, you'll need to state your intent to return to the college or university in the next term. Otherwise, you'll lose your spot and have to reapply. Sometime in the middle of your gap year, your school will likely send you a form to reconfirm enrollment. In addition to filling out this document, you might also have to describe your activities during the deferral period. Submit this paperwork before your school's deadline, and complete the FAFSA for need-based financial aid. If you don't hear from your institution or you have questions, contact the admissions office for further instructions.

---

||||||||||||||||||||||||| **DOUBLE-CHECK YOUR WORK** |||||||||||||||||||||||||

### DISCOVER POSSIBLE PROGRAMS
- ❏ Determine your must-haves
- ❏ Meet with your counselor
- ❏ Locate programs

### DEFER ADMISSION
- ❏ Investigate your top schools' deferment policies
- ❏ Apply to some or all of your top schools (if applicable)
- ❏ Defer enrollment (if applicable)

### PARTAKE IN THE PROGRAM
- ❏ Start the application process
- ❏ Submit your applications to one or more programs
- ❏ Prepare for the program
- ❏ Attend the program

### RETURN TO SCHOOL
- ❏ Request an official transcript(s)
- ❏ Apply to schools (if applicable)
- ❏ Reaffirm your admission (if applicable)

# FAST-TRACK OPPORTUNITY #17: INTERSESSION ABROAD

## When in Rome, Study as the Romans Study

- ✓ Start planning up to a year prior to the trip
- ✓ Complete during winter, spring, or summer break (typically winter or summer break)
- ✓ Spend approximately $$$
- ✓ Earn potentially + to ++ credits

I need a vacation from this vacation. Throughout my childhood, my family planned exhausting getaways. From sunup to sundown, we shuffled from place to place, barely stopping for food or beverage. While I appreciated my parents' effort, I desired a lower-key schedule—days spent poolside with a fruity drink in one hand and a tabloid in the other. Determined to turn my dreams into a reality, I made a vow after high school. I would never embark on another action-packed vacation ever again.

But I didn't keep my word. During my second year in college, the business department announced an upcoming study abroad trip. Students could choose a 10- or 20-day European excursion. When I first heard about the opportunity, I almost rushed straight home to pack my bags. However, my idealistic bubble soon burst. The purpose of this tour wasn't relaxation; it was education. Instead of enjoying the slowed-down European lifestyle, I'd experience the fast-paced business world.

Despite my second thoughts, I signed up for the trip. Only a few credits shy of my diploma, I needed the credit. And I preferred in-person tours to in-class texts. But after a taxing transatlantic flight, I foresaw a restless week. I was right. From dawn 'til dusk, our group strolled the cobblestone streets of London, Brussels, and Paris, visiting renowned establishments along the way. At the end of each day, I could barely remember my own name, let alone carry on a clear conversation. While I definitely needed a vacation after that vacation, I loved every single sleepless second. No beach retreat could compare. Sometimes promises are meant to be broken.

## The Basics

It's not exactly a small world after all. The surface area of the earth is over 195 million square miles, the land over 57 million. With this much planet to see and ground to cover, why wait to travel when you can start now? By participating in an intersession abroad trip, you'll go out of the country while still in college. During one of your school breaks, you'll step off campus and step onto foreign soil. So once you return home, you'll be a few miles down and only have a few million left to explore of this wide, wide world.

Many students think of study abroad as a semester or yearlong endeavor. You leave home for months, pay tens of thousands of dollars, and potentially delay graduation. However, there is another option. It's more affordable and less time-consuming. It'll even help reduce your overall time in school. What's this alternative? Intersession, or short-term study, abroad. During winter or summer break (or possibly spring break), visit and learn in at least one or more foreign countries for a few weeks. And at the end of your globe-trotting, add another couple of credits to your stockpile.

## The Benefits

- **_Learn a second language._** Besides Pig Latin, fluency won't happen overnight. You'll need practice, patience, and preferably, immersion. According to a 2012 study[11] by Ullman and Morgan-Short, students in immersion training acquired full native-like processing of grammar, unlike their classroom-taught peers. While you can always opt for

11.  Kara Morgan-Short, Ingrid Finger, Sarah Grey, and Michael T. Ullman. "Second Language Processing Shows Increased Native-Like Neural Responses after Months of No Exposure." *PLoS ONE* 7, no. 3 (2012): 16, accessed May 24, 2014, doi: 10.1371/journal.pone.0032974.

Spanish or French 101, you can't recreate or replace the real deal. You'll need to stay within the borders of a foreign country. And with intersession abroad, you'll have this opportunity even if only for a short while. So unless you want to communicate in Elvish or Klingon, close your instructional books and cross international borders.

- *Experience foreign cultures.* If a picture is worth a thousand words, how many words is an experience worth? Ten thousand? One million? Ten million? Instead of reading about distant lands, visit them through intersession abroad. Climb the Mayan ruins, walk the Great Wall of China, explore the Taj Mahal, or gaze upon the Sistine Chapel. At the end of your time away, you'll probably realize that no amount of words can truly capture any experience.

- *Leave the planning to the pros.* Airfare. Hotel. Car rental. Food. Excursions. Insurance. Grab your laptop and a couple aspirin; you're in for a long day of travel planning. Or maybe not. With many intersession abroad programs, you don't have to arrange any details. You just show up ready to learn and explore. No need to pop the pain pills— save them for an unavoidable headache.

- *Form real friendships.* What's on your mind? [Insert your name here] is lonely. Experts say that Americans are more socially isolated than ever before. Instead of face-to-face interactions, many people interact with others over the Internet instead. But this choice can leave them feeling very alone, even if they have 1,000 Facebook friends or 2,500 Twitter followers. By participating in an intersession abroad trip, you'll be forced to turn off your phone and other electronic devices (or pay a pretty penny on roaming charges) and communicate with those also on the trip the old-fashioned way. While you might not bond with everyone in the group, you'll probably click with at least a couple. So at the end of the trip, you won't come home with only dirty laundry and souvenirs, you'll come home with a few real friends, too. Ready to change your status? Just go offline and go abroad.

# The Bottom Line

Argent. Fedha. Penger. Dinero. Money. It's true in any language that the less you spend, the more you save. But for an international vacation, costs can add up quickly. With intersession abroad, however, you can keep extra euros, shillings, krones, pesos, or dollars in your pocket. Aware of students' limited budgets, schools and third-party providers minimize travel expenses by utilizing group discounts and subsidizing tuition fees. For example, Merrimack College offers a 10 day/9 night study abroad trip to London, England, for $2,975. This price includes two college credits, round-trip airfare, housing, ground transportation, tickets to class-related cultural activities and excursions, international travel insurance, and three meals a day. By taking a similar two-credit course at Merrimack College on campus during fall or spring semester and traveling to London on your own instead, you'd end up paying $5,680 ($2,680 for tuition and fees on a per-credit-hour basis plus around $3,000 for round-trip airfare, accommodations, ground transportation, excursions, insurance, and meals). *Short-term savings = $2,705.*

By traveling to London with Merrimack College instead of on your own:

> You could avoid $2,705 in credit card debt. You'll save **$1,156** in interest*, assuming the credit card has a 15% interest rate and takes 5 years to pay off.

OR

> You could invest $2,705 in retirement accounts. After 40 years, you'll earn **$16,338** in interest*, assuming each investment has a 5% interest rate, compounded annually.

*Numbers are rounded.*

# The Brief Questions

Ask yourself all of the following before starting this opportunity:

- *Do you want to visit another country?* To take a trip offering college credit, you don't have to journey across an ocean or even cross the border. If you'd prefer to stay in the United States, ask your school or third-party provider about trips for credit with domestic destinations. But if they inform you about an alternative break rather than an intersession abroad trip, go to FTO #18: Alternative Breaks (AB) instead.

## Answered "No"? **RED FLAG** or **DEALBREAKER**

- *Are you available during winter, spring, or summer break?* To avoid conflicting with students' schedules, schools and third-party providers arrange intersession abroad trips usually during January, June, July, August, and sometimes March and April. If your schedule is full throughout the next year, free up at least one or more weeks by eliminating a couple of currently booked activities or events from your calendar.

## Answered "No"? **RED FLAG**

- *Can you travel without feeling homesick?* To participate in an intersession abroad trip, you'll fly overseas or at least leave the States. If you often get lonely and nostalgic when away, communication from home can help. Research the time difference and schedule conversations with friends and family before you depart. Then, during the trip, contact your loved ones using an international calling card or SIM card, prepaid cell phone, Voice over Internet Protocol (VoIP), or Skype.

## Answered "No"? **RED FLAG**

- *Do you enjoy stepping outside of your comfort zone?* To make a long flight and jet lag worth your while, you'll need to love eyeing new places, embracing new people, and experiencing new cultures. If you have a passion for exploration and adventure and haven't responded with a "No" to any of the previous questions, strongly consider this opportunity.

## Answered "Yes"? **CLINCHER**

# The Blueprint

## FIND AND SELECT A PROGRAM

1. *Research programs.* Even though you're limited to short-term opportunities, you still have several intersession abroad options. First, search for programs offered by your school. Many institutions host faculty-led intersession abroad programs. Retrieve a list of upcoming trips during a general study abroad information session or from a study abroad advisor. Next, explore programs offered by other schools. Some institutions open their intersession abroad programs to nonmatriculated students (a.k.a. nondegree-seeking students). Find out about these trips by browsing the Internet or calling individual schools. Finally, look for programs offered by third-party providers. Companies such as AIFS, CIEE, GlobaLinks Learning Abroad, IES Abroad, and ISA all have intersession abroad programs (usually during January), and some even have condensed service, internship, and language-intensive programs as well. See details about these trips on each provider's website.

2. *Apply to one or more programs.* Compile all of your intersession abroad options and eliminate any for which you don't meet the eligibility criteria (such as a cumulative 3.0 GPA, a declared business major, and at least 60 credits already earned). Then, narrow down the remaining programs to your favorite three or four. Put these programs in order, with your absolute favorite at the top of the list. Unless two or more of the programs on your list have deadlines within weeks of each other, only apply to your absolute favorite program for now. In the event you aren't offered admission, apply to the next program on your list and so on. Since your top pick will likely offer you a spot, this strategy will save you time and money, as you won't have to fill out as many application forms or pay as much in application fees.

3. *Reserve your spot.* Once a program offers you admission, secure your spot. You might need to fill out a form and, if you haven't already, pay the deposit. After you have officially signed up, register for the intersession abroad course(s). If your program is offered by your school or another school, ask the study abroad office or the trip's faculty leader for instructions. You might register for the class just like you would

any other class. If your program is offered by a third-party provider, ask an employee of the organization for instructions. The company might handle registration for you.

## FINANCE THE PROGRAM

4. *Create a travel budget.* Create a new spreadsheet. List the program fee and any additional trip expenses. Some possible budgetary items include the following: tuition, transportation, accommodations, insurance, food, entertainment, souvenirs, passport, visa(s), luggage, student ID card, and vaccines. For food, entertainment, and souvenirs, research each country's exchange rate and then provide a rough estimate. After you've finished, calculate your total and save the document.

5. *Fund the program.* Unless you've hidden thousands under your mattress, you'll need to find the money elsewhere. Fortunately, you have several options: (1) File a FAFSA. If your program offers financial aid opportunities, grab last year's tax return and complete the forms online (fafsa .ed.gov). (2) Join the job force. Print out a few résumés and take on some shifts (www.monster.com and www.careerbuilder.com). (3) Search for scholarships. Request a list from the study abroad office and apply to one or more before their deadlines. (4) Fund-raise with friends. Gather other study abroad students and organize a car wash, auction, or bake sale (www.easy-fundraising-ideas.com and www.fundraising-ideas.org /DIY/), or simply ask family and friends for donations (www.gofundme .com and www.volunteerforever.com). (5) If all else fails, plead with your parents. Explain your reasons and request monetary assistance.

## EQUIP YOURSELF FOR THE PROGRAM

6. *Prepare for the program.* Since you'll be traveling internationally, you'll at the very least need a passport and possibly one or more visas and vaccines or medicines. In addition to these necessities, you might also want to obtain an International Student Identity Card (ISIC) or purchase travel insurance. But even if you already have a passport and don't need or want the other items, you'll probably still have to book travel arrangements, and you'll definitely have to pack. For more detailed information on getting ready for your trip, refer to Appendix E: Trip Preparations.

7. *Determine course requirements.* Obtain a syllabus for each intersession

abroad course. Read through the entire document, but pay close attention to the readings and assignments as well as to the schedule. Before the trip, you might have to attend class sessions or meetings and complete readings and assignments (such as forum posts). During the trip, you'll likely attend class lectures and visit local sites in the mornings and afternoons and complete readings and assignments (such as journal entries) in the evenings. After the trip, you might need to complete even more assignments (such as presentations and papers).

Don't bring your textbooks on the trip. The weight of your books might cause harm to your back and increase your baggage fees. To avoid this pain and cost, use ebooks while away or, if you only need a couple of chapters, photocopy the pages and pack them in your suitcase.

8. *Learn about your destination(s).* Pick up at least one travel guide and phrasebook. Read through the history of the area. Study the culture and customs. Locate key historical landmarks. Memorize commonly used phrases, greetings, and expressions. Determine correct pronunciation. Start your research a few weeks before the trip. Or if you're limited on time, put these materials in your carry-on and look through them on the plane.

## EXPERIENCE THE PROGRAM

9. *Explore each city.* When classes and homework aren't taking up your time, fully immerse yourself in the culture and enjoy this possibly once-in-a-lifetime experience. See the sites, eat the cuisine, and communicate with the locals. But all the while, put safety first. Before embarking on any excursion, grab a buddy, strap on your money belt, and carefully plan your route. During the outing, observe all laws and customs. Try to blend in. In the event of an emergency, seek help from the local authorities or the U.S. Embassy or Consulate.

10. *Transfer your credits (if applicable).* If you participated in an intersession abroad program through your school, your credits will appear on your transcript after you've completed the trip and all mandated assignments. However, if you participated in an intersession abroad program through another school or third-party provider, you might have to formally

request an official transcript. Since other schools won't automatically send them, you'll likely need to submit a request form electronically, by fax, or by mail. You might also have to pay a small processing fee. Many third-party providers, on the other hand, will automatically send your transcript to your school. But if they don't, you'll have to complete a process similar to the one required by schools. To ensure that your credits have transferred, check your unofficial transcript about once a week until the credits from your intersession abroad trip are listed. Contact the registrar's office at your institution if problems arise.

## DOUBLE-CHECK YOUR WORK

### FIND AND SELECT A PROGRAM
- ❏ Research programs
- ❏ Apply to one or more programs
- ❏ Reserve your spot

### FINANCE THE PROGRAM
- ❏ Create a travel budget
- ❏ Fund the program

### EQUIP YOURSELF FOR THE PROGRAM
- ❏ Prepare for the program
- ❏ Determine course requirements
- ❏ Learn about your destination(s)

### EXPERIENCE THE PROGRAM
- ❏ Explore each city
- ❏ Transfer your credits (if applicable)

# FAST-TRACK OPPORTUNITY #18:
## ALTERNATIVE BREAKS (AB)
### Break from Traditional Vacations

✓ Start planning up to a year prior to the trip
✓ Complete during fall, winter, spring, summer, or a weekend break (typically spring break)
✓ Spend approximately $ to $$$
✓ Earn potentially + credits

The Happiest Place on Earth. Throughout my life, I've had the privilege of visiting Disneyland several times. One of them was over Thanksgiving break my first year in college. During that week, my family and I strolled down Main Street, U.S.A., rode Splash Mountain, ate Dole Whips, and watched the Electrical Parade. Those days were meaningful, memorable, and magical. Even so, I wouldn't say I was at my happiest. I'd reserve that honor for a few experiences that were much less glamorous.

Like when I handed out blankets and sandwiches to the homeless. Or sang for seniors in a nursing home. Or—one of my favorite experiences— taught school-aged children at a facility for single mothers with unplanned pregnancies. Halfway through my second year of college, I came across a flyer looking for an unpaid tutor at a local nonprofit. Drawn to the position, I contacted the organization and signed up for one evening a week. Some of those nights weren't easy. I left exhausted and overwhelmed. However, when my instruction helped a kid understand a difficult concept, the tough parts disappeared. And all that remained was pure joy.

I didn't want those moments to end. But since my commitment was only a few hours every Monday, they didn't last long enough. I wanted more time. Alternative break trips would have provided me that opportunity. If my school had offered them, I would have gladly traded a week going to Disney for a week giving back somewhere. Because while eating churros and touring Sleeping Beauty Castle made me happy, serving others would have made me happier. Maybe one of the happiest gals on Earth. Sorry, Walt, even your theme park can't beat that.

## The Basics

Would you rather acquire an incurable STD or an invaluable job skill? Make enemies at the police station or friends with other students? Improve your tolerance of alcohol or the lives of others? Leave with a feeling of shame or a sense of accomplishment? Instead of wasting a week partying in Daytona Beach or Cancun, spend this time volunteering on an alternative break (AB) trip. While your classmates kill their brain cells, you'll stimulate yours through service learning.

Alternative breaks are the antithesis to traditional breaks. They aren't about drugs and alcohol; they're about volunteerism and community service. Often led by one or two students, groups of around 10 to 20 undergraduates travel domestically or internationally to complete projects focused on a particular social issue. And while these trips are typically held over the week of spring break, they can also last for just a couple of days or for a couple of weeks and take place during fall, winter, summer, or even weekend breaks.

## The Benefits

- *Make a difference in the world.* Nelson Mandela, Mother Teresa, Martin Luther King Jr., Helen Keller—these people devoted their lives to a particular cause, and by doing so, they each left a mark on society. But you don't have to commit to a lifetime of service to do the same. You can simply go on an alternative break trip. And while your time away may be short and your number of tasks may be small, you'll still make a pretty large impact. As the saying goes, "I alone cannot change the world, but I can cast a stone across the waters to create many ripples."

- *Gain a deeper understanding of a current social issue.* Being *Clueless* is so 1995. These days, it's cool to know what's going on in the world. Ignorance is out; informed is in. But how do you really grasp social issues like racial profiling, homelessness, and drug abuse? Participate in an alternative break. Unlike with the news, an AB provides you with the opportunity to learn about a social problem firsthand. Which means after you've finished the trip, you'll not only comprehend the issue but also be able to spread awareness about it with others. Being clued in is so this millennium.

- *Get involved on your campus.* You almost have a permanent place on the sidelines. You want to participate in college clubs and events, but you watch your peers take part instead. Unsure how to become a more active student, you attend school for the academics and nothing else. But by signing up for an alternative break, you can stop missing out. In addition to the trip, you'll engage in campus activities like service days, weekend retreats, fund-raisers, and socials with other civic-minded undergrads. So in only a matter of months, you'll go from warming the bench to playing in the game.

- *Develop an attitude of gratitude.* #firstworldproblems. If you're on Twitter, Instagram, or Facebook (and who isn't?), you've probably come across this satirical hashtag. It's often preceded by a "complaint," such as a chipped freshly painted nail, cracked cell phone screen, or spilled iced vanilla latte. And while some Americans see these as issues, many (especially those in Third World countries) don't view them as such. Through an alternative break, your outlook on life might drastically change. You'll encounter real struggles like poverty, hunger, disease, and war. So when you return from your trip, you'll have a deeper appreciation for all you have. #thankfulness.

## The Bottom Line

An alternative break trip isn't just an alternative to a "break-the-law" vacation; it's also an alternative to a "break-the-bank" vacation. Even if you don't fly first class, stay at the Ritz, or eat filet mignon, a weeklong getaway in the states can cost a couple thousand dollars. An AB trip, on the other hand, will likely be much less expensive. While most are around a few hundred (excluding tuition), some are even cheaper. At Ivy Tech Community College, the tuition for the two-credit alternative break course ($262.30 for in-state students) covers the entire cost of the AB trip to Antigua, Guatemala. If you took a similar two-credit class at Ivy Tech Community College and traveled to Guatemala for 8 days/7 nights on your own instead, you'd fork over $1,492.30 ($262.30 for tuition on a per-credit-hour basis plus around $1,230 for round-trip airfare, accommodations, ground transportation, and meals. *Short-term savings = $1,230.*

By taking an alternative break through Ivy Tech Community College instead of a traditional break:

> You could avoid $1,230 in credit card debt. You'll save **$526** in interest*, assuming the credit card has a 15% interest rate and takes 5 years to pay off.

OR

> You could invest $1,230 in retirement accounts. After 40 years, you'll earn **$7,429** in interest*, assuming each investment has a 5% interest rate, compounded annually.

*Numbers are rounded.*

# The Brief Questions

Ask yourself all of the following before starting this opportunity:

- *Does your school host alternative breaks for college credit?* To find out, ask a staff member in the community service office on your campus. If your school doesn't offer any AB trips, research trips offered by third-party providers (Step #1 in The Blueprint that follows) or consider creating one yourself (skip Step #1, but work through Steps #2 and #3). Since alternative breaks hosted by colleges and universities are typically reserved for matriculated students (a.k.a. degree-seeking students) and require pre-trip meetings and activities, you likely can't participate in an AB trip organized by another institution. If your school offers AB trips but refuses to grant credit for them, participate for other reasons or don't complete this opportunity. In either case, you should also look for other ways to earn credit for service learning.

## Answered "No"? **RED FLAG** or **DEALBREAKER**

- *Can you attend all of the AB meetings and activities?* To go on an AB trip, you'll need to commit to more than just a week or weekend. You'll also likely be required to show up to several pre- and post-trip meetings and events. If your schedule is extremely busy (e.g., taking a full course load and working full-time) or you can't be on campus during scheduled activities, participate in AB at a later point or don't complete this opportunity.

## Answered "No"? **RED FLAG** or **DEALBREAKER**

- *Are you passionate about a particular cause?* To address a variety of societal needs, most alternative break trips focus on a problem plaguing today's world (e.g., global warming, social injustice, animal cruelty, substance abuse). If you care deeply about one or more social issues and haven't responded with a "No" to any of the previous questions, strongly consider completing this opportunity.

## Answered "Yes"? **CLINCHER**

- *Do you prefer to put the needs of others above your own?* To give up your break and work for free, you'll need to have a fairly selfless heart. If the previous statement describes you (forget humility this once and be completely honest) and you haven't responded with a "No" to any of the previous RED FLAG or DEALBREAKER questions, strongly consider completing this opportunity.

## Answered "Yes"? **CLINCHER**

# The Blueprint

## CHOOSE OR CREATE A TRIP

1.  *Select your favorite trips.* If your school offers alternative breaks, obtain a list of all of the upcoming trips for credit in its community service office or on its website. These trips will be planned for you and be linked to a course awarding college credit. If your school doesn't offer alternative breaks, look for trips organized by third-party providers like i-to-i, Cross-Cultural Solutions, and Projects Abroad. These trips will also be planned for you, but probably won't award any college credit. You'll need to speak to your advisor about earning credit for this service-learning opportunity from your school, possibly through an independent study course. Once you've discovered your AB options, review each possibility carefully. Based on the trip's focus, dates, location, and cost, pick out your favorites and rank them in order. If none of them interest you or every one of them conflicts with a prior commitment, put together your own AB (see Steps #2 and #3).

My school didn't have a community service office. If I wanted to find out about an outreach opportunity, I had to visit the campus ministries department. This is common at religious institutions.

2.  *Plan an alternative break trip (if applicable).* Depending on your school's policies, you might be able to organize and lead an AB. First, select your cause and a community service organization that supports this cause. Ask around or search the Web for organizations. Some good options are Habitat for Humanity, United Way, American Red Cross, and Boys & Girls Clubs of America. Next, determine the logistics, including dates, location, transportation, budget, and academic credit. You'll need to know these details for your site leader proposal. Finally, choose your faculty advisor and coleader, if required. They'll help with coordination as well as supervision during the trip.

## BREAK AWAY

Break Away is a national nonprofit providing colleges and universities the tools needed to create and run alternative breaks. If your college is one of the more than 160 Break Away Chapter schools, you'll have access to the Break Away database (SiteBank) with more than 500 community organizations, templates through the Sample Documents Library, and more. If your college is not yet a Break Away Chapter school, ask a staff member in the community service office about joining. The cost is $350 per year (Associate Chapter) or $700 per year (Advantage Chapter).

## SUBMIT THE TRIP APPLICATION

3. *Apply to be a site leader (if applicable).* Now that you've put together an initial plan, you can complete the application to lead the alternative break. You'll likely need to attend an information session and create a proposal. In this document, you'll detail your service-learning idea and all of the trip logistics. Return the proposal to the appropriate campus office by the deadline (typically the fall for alternative spring breaks and the spring or summer for alternative fall breaks and alternative winter breaks). After submission, you may or may not be finished. If the application process is quite competitive, your school might further evaluate candidates through formal presentations or face-to-face interviews.

4. *Apply to be a participant (if applicable).* Begin by reading through the trip's eligibility criteria (such as minimum GPA, no record of disciplinary action, and at least part-time enrollment status) and expectations (such as no drugs or alcohol, respectful behavior, perfect attendance, and modest dress). If you meet the qualifications and can commit to the rules, fill out the application form and answer

Leading an AB won't just provide you with leadership practice and enhance your résumé—it might also be financially beneficial. Many schools give discounts to trip leaders for taking on this responsibility.

the essay questions. These questions might range from "Why did you choose an alternative break?" to "Which social issues are most important to you?" to "What are your previous community service projects?" Turn in this paperwork along with any other necessary material (such as recommendation letters, college transcript, cover letter, and résumé) by the deadline. The deadline might be very specific—not just a date, but also a time. Once submitted, await acceptance. They'll likely notify you through email.

If you're concerned about funding your AB trip, apply to any need-based scholarships or grants offered by your school for AB. Most colleges and universities want to make AB available to all interested students regardless of their financial situation.

Even though I could generally use a credit card, sometimes I needed another form of payment for a deposit. Therefore, I always had checks on hand.

5. ***Pay for the trip.*** You'll likely pay in two installments. The first installment will be due several months prior to departure. Once you've been offered a spot, you'll have to hand over around $50 to $100 for the nonrefundable deposit. Although you can withdraw from the trip at a later date, you won't get this money back. The second installment will be due within a few weeks of departure. Since this amount will cover the remaining balance, you might have to cough up a large sum. Fortunately, it won't all come out of your pocket. Your site leader will probably run at least one team fund-raiser and encourage individual fund-raising.

## COMPLETE TRIP REQUIREMENTS

6. ***Prepare for the trip.*** If you'll be traveling internationally, you'll at the very least need a passport and possibly one or more visas and vaccines or medicines. In addition to these necessities, you might also want to obtain an International Student Identity Card (ISIC) or purchase travel insurance. While you won't need all of these items if you'll only be traveling domestically, you might have to book travel arrangements if the program hasn't prearranged them, and you'll definitely have to pack.

For more detailed information on getting ready for your trip, refer to Appendix E: Trip Preparations.

7. ***Attend pre-trip meetings.*** Led by your site leader(s) and/or faculty advisor, these obligatory meetings will help prepare you for the AB. Your school will determine the total number of sessions. Maybe four, maybe 15, or maybe something else. These meetings will help with team building among the participants through group activities and games; teach about the history and culture of the destination as well as the social issue(s) at hand; and provide an overview of the trip, including the agenda.

8. ***Register to receive academic credit.*** Simply going on an alternative break trip won't earn you credit; you'll also need to sign up for a course related to the experience. Start by finding out the exact course number and title. It might be a traditional or an independent study course. Either way, it'll likely range from one to three credits and might be graded as a P (pass) or F (fail). Next, register for the course in the appropriate term and pay the tuition costs. Even if your trip is in March, the class might be offered during the fall semester. Finally, determine the course assignments and complete all of them. If you're in a traditional course, you'll do some assignments in class and some on your own. But if you're in an independent study course, you'll do all of the assignments on your own.

9. ***Go on the trip.*** Weeklong alternative breaks tend to follow a fairly similar itinerary. (Weekend alternative breaks involve less travel and a more condensed schedule.) On the first day, you and your group will travel to your destination and settle into your sleeping quarters. There might be an orientation and training or it might take place the following morning. Over the next several days, you'll complete community service projects at one or more sites during typical business hours. In the evenings, you'll debrief, sightsee, play games, watch movies, experience the local nightlife, or share in some other activity with your team. You might also have to move to another location. On the final day, you'll pack up your belongings and head home.

# |||||||||||||||||||||||||| DOUBLE-CHECK YOUR WORK ||||||||||||||||||||||||||

## CHOOSE OR CREATE A TRIP
- ❏ Select your favorite trips
- ❏ Plan an alternative break trip (if applicable)

## SUBMIT THE TRIP APPLICATION
- ❏ Apply to be a site leader (if applicable)
- ❏ Apply to be a participant (if applicable)
- ❏ Pay for the trip

## COMPLETE TRIP REQUIREMENTS
- ❏ Prepare for the trip
- ❏ Attend pre-trip meetings
- ❏ Register to receive academic credit
- ❏ Go on the trip

# FAST-TRACK OPPORTUNITY #19: INTERNSHIP

## The Proof of Your Education Is in an Internship

✓ Start planning several months prior to the desired internship start date

✓ Complete any year in college (typically junior or senior year)

✓ Make approximately $0 to $$$

✓ Earn potentially + to ++ credits

Once upon a time, I was offered a coveted spot in Google's internship program. But even with my best bud in tow, my lack of technical prowess didn't help me win friends or influence people. I was ostracized by most of my peers and even taunted by a few. But as the weeks progressed, I began to stand out from the crowd with my advancing computer skills and magnetic personality. And by the end of the program, I landed not only my dream job but also my dream mate. From that day forward, I lived happily ever after.

All right, you've caught me. This account isn't my story—it's actually the premise of *The Internship* starring Vince Vaughn and Owen Wilson. My internship experience wasn't nearly as riveting. Thumbing through a big book of internships at my school, I came across an intriguing opportunity: promotions intern at a local radio station. After an email exchange and a brief interview, I was hired. But unlike the movie, I didn't receive a creative workspace with unlimited free food. Instead, I sat at a makeshift desk in the hallway and brought Lean Cuisines for lunch.

The work wasn't as innovative either. I didn't build any new apps, but I did help prep and run a booth at several music events. While some would refer to these tasks as mundane, I thoroughly enjoyed them. And at the end of the summer, my signed concert T-shirts weren't my only souvenirs from the internship. I also improved my organizational skills, interpersonal abilities, and self-confidence. A few years later, I received a job offer from the company. I declined the request, since I was in graduate school, but I was honored nonetheless. I guess happy endings aren't just reserved for movies; they exist in real life as well.

## The Basics

The interns are typically the low rungs on the ladder. They're below virtually everyone in the organization. Nevertheless, being an intern isn't a bad position. Although you might have to pour a few cups of coffee, run a few errands, and make a few phone calls, you'll probably still receive an immensely valuable experience and education. Even more, your "low rank" might come with some serious perks. Who wouldn't like to get complimentary theme park admission? Or meet new and upcoming artists? Or fly free to hundreds of destinations? So while you won't actually be the top dog, you might still feel like it.

An internship is a type of paid or unpaid work experience. While similar in many aspects to a temporary job, its primary focus is on learning. During the school year or over the summer, college students (most often juniors and seniors) apply to internships to gain knowledge and skills relevant to their academic disciplines. But internships can provide more than just on-the-job training. By registering for an internship course through your school and then actively participating in your selected internship and completing all of the required assignments listed in the course syllabus, you can earn college credit. Your school might charge a special fee for this credit, or more likely, treat internship credit the same as regular course credit. Therefore, if your school charges a flat fee for a varying amount of credit (e.g., 12 to 18) and you have yet to reach the maximum number of credits allowed without a tuition increase (e.g., 15), your internship credit might not cost you anything extra.

## The Benefits

- *Explore your field of study.* Reading about psychology is much different from actually being a psychologist. To reveal your true feelings about a particular job, you can't stay locked up in the library; you'll need to experience the work firsthand. An internship can provide you with this opportunity—all while you're still in school. Which means if you end up hating the work or discovering that you're not really interested, you can change your career plans before even graduating. On the other hand, if you end up loving it, you'll obtain knowledge and skills in the field that you can use later. Ultimately, an internship will help you determine whether a profession is only good on paper or in practice as well.

- *Apply your classroom knowledge.* In college, you're like a sponge. You absorb countless pieces of information, from techniques to terms to theories. But by not applying this knowledge outside of school, you might not fully grasp the material and may even question its worth. An internship allows you to put what you've learned on campus into practice off campus. It'll strengthen your comprehension as well as reignite your passion for your area of study. So once you're back in the classroom, you'll be better equipped and more eager to soak everything up.

- *Gain work experience.* Many recent grads face a similar dilemma. They can't get a job without experience, but they can't get experience without a job. These highly educated young people are stuck in limbo, no longer students but not able to become employees either. Fortunately, you can escape this catch-22 by completing an internship. Unlike typical jobs, internships are designed for those with little to no prior work history. They provide you with much-needed work experience, but with significantly easier requirements for entry. Problem solved.

- *Network with industry professionals.* To get your foot in the door at many companies, you'll need to have the right contacts. As you've probably heard, it's often less about *what* you know and more about *who* you know. Case in point: children with famous folks have a better chance of becoming famous themselves (e.g., Kiefer Sutherland, Miley Cyrus, Charlie Sheen, and Kate Hudson). But if you aren't on the same career path as your mom or dad, you aren't out of luck. During an internship, you'll establish relationships and build trust with multiple people in your chosen field, which could result in steady employment soon after graduation. Most likely, your internship employer will offer you a job. According to a survey by the National Association of

Colleges and Employers (NACE),[12] almost 65 percent of interns were made full-time offers by their employers in 2013. Less likely but still possible, someone else you meet while interning will give you an offer. Either way, a great position should be within arm's reach.

# The Bottom Line

Want fries and a shake with your order? Ditch the fast-food lingo and adopt a more professional vocabulary. Completing an internship rather than working at a minimum-wage job will leave you with a heftier piggy bank in the long run. For example, by choosing a minimum-wage job, you could make $7.25 an hour. That means, over the course of a year in college, you'd bring in $2,175 ($7.25 an hour x 10 hours a week x 30 weeks). On the other hand, by selecting a 12-credit, paid internship instead, you could make $16.35 an hour, the average for interns at the bachelor's degree level according to a survey by the National Association of Colleges and Employers (NACE).[13] With this option, over the course of the same year in college, you'd bring in $4,905 ($16.35 an hour x 10 hours a week x 30 weeks). Additionally, you would graduate up to a semester early. So while your classmates are still finishing their senior year, you could start work at a well-compensated job. ***Extra short-term earnings = $2,730.***

By interning instead of working:

> You could invest $2,730 in retirement accounts. After 40 years, you'll earn **$16,489 in interest***, assuming each investment has a 5% interest rate, compounded annually.

*Numbers are rounded.*

12.   National Association of Colleges and Employers, *2014 Internship & Co-op Survey: Executive Summary*, accessed November 11, 2014, http://www.naceweb.org/uploadedFiles/Content/static-assets/downloads/executive-sum mary/2014-internship-co-op-survey-executive-summary.pdf.
13.   Ibid.

# The Brief Questions

Ask yourself all of the following before starting this opportunity:

- *Does your school award credit for an internship in your field of study?* To discover the answer, ask your academic advisor or department chair. If you have yet to declare a major or your department doesn't offer internship credit, contact the career services or internship program office. You might be able to complete an internship not directly related to your academic discipline. But if that option isn't a possibility, don't complete this opportunity.

## Answered "No"? **RED FLAG** or **DEALBREAKER**

- *Can you take on full-time work?* To add an internship to your schedule, you'll need a fixed number of available hours. If you're already busy with a heavy course load, job, or extracurricular activity, only search and apply for part-time positions. Or wait until you have a school break and complete a condensed internship (40 or more hours a week for around a month).

## Answered "No"? **RED FLAG**

- *Are you unsure about your career path?* To determine whether a career's right for you, you probably need to actually experience the job by performing the day-to-day duties and tasks. If you haven't selected a career yet or have doubts about the one you have selected, and if you haven't responded with a "No" to any of the previous questions, strongly consider completing this opportunity.

## Answered "Yes"? **CLINCHER**

- *Are you eager to start your career?* To even be given an interview for something other than a dead-end job, you'll probably need at least a bachelor's degree. Which means as a college student, you're likely to get stuck working in food service or retail. If you're not a future chef or fashion designer and want a job that could possibly progress and advance into a higher position, and if you haven't responded with a "No" to any of the previous RED FLAG or DEALBREAKER questions, strongly consider completing this opportunity.

Answered "Yes"? CLINCHER

# The Blueprint

## DETERMINE INTERNSHIP SPECIFICATIONS AND REQUIREMENTS

1. *Identify your ideal internship.* Figure out this information by asking yourself all of the following questions:

   - *What type of work?* Even if you have to pick an internship related to your field of study, you'll still have many options. For example, if you're a psychology major, you could intern at a hospital, prison, women's shelter, drug addiction treatment facility, or group home.

   - *Where's the location?* You could stay close to home or school or travel to another U.S. or international city. If you pick the latter, consider the extra expenses of housing and transportation.

   - *What time of year?* During the school year, you'll have to balance an internship and homework. Over the summer, you'll have more free time and possibly more internship choices; however, you might have to pay tuition for the internship on a per-credit-hour basis. If you opt for summer, ask your college about rolling the credit from your internship into the fall to potentially avoid this added cost.

   - *How much is the pay?* Review your budget to determine how much you need to cover your bills. Paid internships might give an hourly wage, salary, or stipend (a typically small, fixed sum of money intended to cover basic living expenses) and may or may not also provide other benefits, like housing, transportation, and food. If you don't require a steady income to live (e.g., your parents send you money each month or you have a good amount stashed away in savings), consider unpaid internships as well as paid ones. This decision will open up many more internship opportunities for you.

2. ***Obtain details on earning credit for an internship.*** Make an appointment to meet with a staff member from the career services office or internship program office or a faculty member from your department. Ask about internship registration as well as required assignments. In addition to recording your hours, you might also need to keep a journal, write a paper, conduct research, create a portfolio, or do something else entirely. Toward the end of the meeting, request the staff or faculty member's contact information in case further questions or issues arise.

## LOCATE INTERNSHIPS

3. ***Utilize your school's resources.*** Head to the career services office or internship program office. Look over a list of the most current internship opportunities for college credit and, if available, read through the feedback on these internships from students who've previously completed them. Next, if your school has one, visit the alumni office. Obtain the contact information for any alums who would be willing to sponsor an intern at their organization or company.

4. ***Explore one or more websites.*** Start with www.internships.com. Not only can you search a comprehensive database of internship opportunities, but you can also read articles in the student resources section and take the Internship Predictor assessment test. If you want other options, try www.internmatch.com, www.college.monster.com, www.experience.com, and www.idealist.org (for nonprofits). If you already have some specific companies or organizations in mind, go directly to their websites and see if they have any information posted about internship opportunities.

5. ***Attend an internship or career fair.*** At these events, students can connect with recruiters and potential employers to gain information about their companies and available positions. But don't just show up and expect to be hired. First, register for the fair. Then, review the list of attending companies and research any companies offering an internship that matches your skills and interests. Finally, write a one-minute "elevator speech" introducing yourself, including your passions, abilities, experience, and motivation. Only after all of this preparation should you make an appearance.

6. ***Network with your family, friends, strangers, and everyone in between.*** Ask around for any internship openings. While it may feel awkward, even try your mail carrier, hygienist, or yoga instructor. You might discover the perfect opportunity through your doctor's niece's best friend's cousin's brother.

7. ***Cold-call a few companies.*** Searched multiple avenues for internships but still coming up empty-handed? Interested in one particular business but unsure if it offers internships? Contact the organization directly and ask about any student positions. But only try this option as a last resort. It's time-consuming for the company's employees to respond to such inquiries and could disrupt or potentially annoy them.

8. ***Narrow down your list of internships to between three and five.*** Then, compare your choices based on several criteria, including location, duration, pay, benefits, duties, and interest level on a scale of 1 (least) to 5 (most). Lastly, if applicable, note the deadline for the internship application. Some competitive summer internships may have deadlines as early as October of the year prior. Consider creating a spreadsheet similar to the example below. Include additional categories if desired.

| COLLEGE | LOCATION | DURATION | PAY | BENEFITS | DUTIES | INTEREST | DEADLINE |
|---------|----------|----------|-----|----------|--------|----------|----------|
|         |          |          |     |          |        |          |          |
|         |          |          |     |          |        |          |          |
|         |          |          |     |          |        |          |          |
|         |          |          |     |          |        |          |          |
|         |          |          |     |          |        |          |          |

## ASSEMBLE INTERNSHIP APPLICATIONS

9. ***Build an internship résumé.*** You can edit a previously constructed one or start from scratch. Include your name, address, phone number, and

email at the top of the page. Then, write a one- to two-sentence objective statement and list your education and any awards. Finally, detail your professional experience with the most recent position first. For examples and more detailed instructions, check out résumé guidelines and templates at internships.about.com.

10. ***Write a cover letter specific to each internship.*** These types of letters follow a particular format. In the heading, type your contact information, the date, and your potential employer's contact information. Next, address the employer directly and briefly explain how you heard about the position. Take a few more paragraphs to describe why you're the best candidate for the position based on your skills, education, and experience. In the closing, mention your phone number and email once more and thank the employer. Lastly, sign and type your name.

Don't address your cover letter with "To Whom It May Concern." You're practically saying, "To the Individual Whose Name I'm Too Lazy To Figure Out." Instead, search the company's website or call the company and ask for the name of the internship hiring manager.

11. ***Obtain references.*** Compile a list of your current and previous employers, coworkers, and professors. If you're struggling, write down any respected individuals who know your character and skills. Pick three to four who will likely provide a glowing recommendation (e.g., not your Biology 101 professor who doesn't know you from the other 300 students in your class). Ask your chosen few for their permission to be a reference. For those who agree, verify the correct spelling of their full name, job title, phone number, and email address.

To stand out from the other applicants, I didn't follow the typical cover letter format. Instead of body paragraphs, I created two columns with bulleted lists. In the left-hand column, I wrote the duties and responsibilities according to the internship description. In the right-hand column, I explained how I could fulfill each of them based on my qualifications.

Type up this information and save the document as a readily accessible computer file.

## APPLY TO INTERNSHIPS

12. *Send in your applications.* Remember to meet the deadlines and include all necessary paperwork. If you're using the U.S. Postal Service, consider purchasing delivery confirmation. This extra service provides you with the date and time of package delivery, but doesn't require a signature from the recipient.

13. *Prepare for your interviews.* A day or two prior to each interview, spend a few hours researching the company, constructing a list of specific questions for your potential employer, and partaking in a mock interview with a family member or friend. Then, the night before the interview, print out a few extra copies of your résumé. Map out directions to the interview site and select the appropriate attire (for example, business professional for an established finance company or business casual for an Internet start-up).

14. *Interview at each company.* Don't eliminate your chances of getting the perfect internship within the first few moments. Instead, make an excellent impression by arriving 15 minutes early, dressed for success. Greet your interviewer with a smile, good eye contact, and, if offered, a firm handshake. During the interview, answer the questions thoroughly and request clarification if needed. Toward the end, bring up any of your own inquiries and find out when you'll hear back about the internship.

Even if I had already emailed my résumé and cover letter to the hiring manager, I still brought hard copies of both to the interview. More often than not, the hiring manager or another employee wouldn't have had time to print them and would need a refresher of my education and experience.

15. *Express your appreciation.* Follow up right away with a typed or handwritten note (emailing thank-you notes is discouraged). Start off the letter with a thank-you for the interviewer's time and consideration. In the next couple of paragraphs, express your increased interest in the position, how your skills match the position's requirements, and any information left out during the interview. Close

the letter by reiterating your gratitude and mentioning that you'll follow up within a specified period of time. Then, sign, seal, and mail it as soon as possible.

16. ***Wait for news.*** Some companies will inform you about the position within a matter of hours or days, while others will take weeks or even longer. During this stretch, keep your phone close by but your mind distracted. Reach out to your contact if you don't hear back within your previously identified time frame. If you receive a rejection, kindly ask for a reason. Use any feedback you get to improve upon weak areas in your next interview.

## COMPLETE THE INTERNSHIP

17. ***Select an internship.*** If you receive multiple offers, weigh your options with or without assistance from family and friends. To help make your decision even clearer, consider contacting each company and asking for more information about the position. Once you've settled on an internship, officially accept the offer but hold off on rejecting the other ones for now. In case your school doesn't approve your selected internship (Step #18), you might be able to go with one of these backups instead.

18. ***Start the internship approval process.*** In order to register for an internship course and earn college credit, a staff member from the career services office or internship program office or a faculty member from your department will probably need to approve your selected internship. Submit the internship approval form, if applicable, or send detailed information about the internship. Your internship supervisor or manager might also need to provide documentation and a signature. If the staff or faculty member reviews and approves the internship, he or she will provide you with authorization to add an internship course to your schedule.

19. ***Demonstrate model intern behavior.*** Start with the basics: act and dress professionally. Don't use Internet slangs (OMG, LOL, TTYL) in an email, show up late to a meeting, or wear flip-flops at the office. But to really shine in your internship, you'll have to do more than just adhere to workplace standards. You'll need to observe, experience, and imitate. During the first few weeks of your internship, take in any and all information. Ask questions and jot down notes for later reference. After the initial training phase ends, apply this knowledge to your position.

Whether you're filing paperwork or running a meeting, perform to the best of your ability with a good attitude. Go above and beyond expectations by volunteering to help with extra projects that haven't been assigned to you. In the final stage of your internship, shift your focus once again toward watching and emulating successful individuals at the company. By using these internship strategies, you'll attract the right kind of attention from the right kind of people.

20. ***Complete your homework.*** Over the course of your internship, work on the assignments required by your school to earn credits for the experience. If you need to log your hours, leave a notepad on your desk or in your bag and write your time in and out every day. Once the internship concludes, turn in all of your assignments and ensure you've satisfied the rest of the requirements. After a few weeks, verify you've received college credit on your unofficial transcript.

21. ***Keep in contact with your manager.*** Immediately following the internship, write a detailed thank-you letter. While you're still in school, offer your assistance on projects or events for the company. Near graduation, reach out and mention that you're seeking employment and would love a position. If no opening exists, send your résumé to the hiring manager to keep on file for future opportunities.

---

## ‖‖‖‖‖‖‖‖‖‖‖‖‖‖ DOUBLE-CHECK YOUR WORK ‖‖‖‖‖‖‖‖‖‖‖‖‖‖

### DETERMINE INTERNSHIP SPECIFICATIONS AND REQUIREMENTS
- ❐ Identify your ideal internship
- ❐ Obtain details on earning credit for an internship

### LOCATE INTERNSHIPS
- ❐ Utilize your school's resources
- ❐ Explore one or more websites
- ❐ Attend an internship or career fair
- ❐ Network with your family, friends, strangers, and everyone in between

❑ Cold-call a few companies
❑ Narrow down your list of internships to between three and five

## ASSEMBLE INTERNSHIP APPLICATIONS

❑ Build an internship résumé
❑ Write a cover letter specific to each internship
❑ Obtain references

## APPLY TO INTERNSHIPS

❑ Send in your applications
❑ Prepare for your interviews
❑ Interview at each company
❑ Express your appreciation
❑ Wait for news

## COMPLETE THE INTERNSHIP

❑ Select an internship
❑ Start the internship approval process
❑ Demonstrate model intern behavior
❑ Complete your homework
❑ Keep in contact with your manager

# BONUS FTO #20:
## Extracurricular Activities

You can put away your textbooks and pick up an easel, camera, or script instead. For your involvement in on-campus activities like the school play, soccer team, marching band, or student government, your college or university might award you credit. As it doesn't occur automatically, you'll first need to obtain approval from a faculty member and then register for a particular course before each semester. But don't bank on this type of credit forever; there might be a cap on the total number you can earn. For your involvement in off-campus activities like dance, photography, rock climbing, and woodworking, another accredited college or university might grant you credit. Some organizations partner with schools to offer a college credit option for participants in their classes. Examples include Boulder Jazz Dance Workshop, Santa Fe Photographic Workshops, National Outdoor Leadership School, and Arrowmont School of Arts and Crafts. You sign up, take the classes, complete any assignments, and once finished, transfer the credits from the partner school to your current school.

# CAPITALIZE ON NONTRADITIONAL OPPORTUNITIES

I was what you'd call a "traditional student." I went straight from high school to college, with only a couple of summer months in between. Which meant when I started my undergrad, I was still in my late teens without a spouse or a home or a career. My husband was the exact opposite. He's what you'd call a "nontraditional student." He went from high school to an arts conservatory to the workforce and then to college. Which meant when he finally started his undergrad, he was well into his 30s with a wife and a house and a job. Since he had to juggle all these responsibilities and school, he initially felt envious of the substantial downtime I had enjoyed in college. However, had he attended school as a traditional student like me, it may have been less chaotic but also possibly less rewarding. Because of his years of experience and education outside the traditional classroom, my husband acquired college-level learning that translated into nontraditional college credit. It counted just as much as all the other types of credit, and it was the easiest and cheapest credit he ever earned. So while his jealousy of my college experience faded, the green-eyed monster ended up taking hold of me.

Even if you're a traditional student, but especially if you're a nontraditional student, you can capitalize on nontraditional opportunities. Whether you can complete one or more of the next three FTOs depends on your prior life experiences. Try FTO #21: Noncollegiate Learning if you've taken nondegree courses or professional training (or are willing to do so now). Or try FTO #22: Prior Learning Portfolio if you worked, volunteered, served in the military, traveled, or participated in some other activity outside of school for an extended period of time. Or try FTO #23: Military Transcript if you've served in any branch of the U.S. military. Whichever you choose, make sure your school accepts nontraditional credit. Colleges with adult or evening programs generally award this type of credit, and many traditional colleges and universities with younger demographics do as well.

Do you currently have a professional license or certification? Explore the mini fast-track opportunity (*Bonus FTO #24:* Professional Licenses and Certifications) at the end of this section.

# FAST-TRACK OPPORTUNITY #21: NONCOLLEGIATE LEARNING
## Where There's a Course, There's a Credit

- ✓ Start planning as early as summer before freshman year in college
- ✓ Complete any year in college (typically freshman or sophomore year)
- ✓ Spend approximately $ to $$$ (per course or exam)
- ✓ Earn potentially + to ++ credits (per course or exam)

Shortly before tying the knot, my husband and I started receiving throngs of marital advice. Whether wedded or widowed, dating or divorced, couples and singles offered us their pearls of wisdom. "A happy wife is a happy life." "Don't go to bed angry." And one of my favorites, "Agree to disagree." While I saw eye-to-eye with my spouse on the majority of issues, we weren't on the same page about noncollegiate learning. Since courses taken outside a traditional degree program don't normally provide credit (or so I thought), I regarded them as more or less worthless.

My husband, however, didn't share my viewpoint. To him, noncollegiate instruction most certainly had merit. It offered the same quality of education, but often with less time commitment and at a lower cost than a regular college class. So when faced with the choice, he elected to enroll in noncredit business courses. After completing several, he sat for the Project Management Professional (PMP) exam and passed with flying colors. But even though this schooling positively impacted his job performance, he still desired greater advancement within his company.

To stand out from his peers, he needed an achievement larger than his PMP certification. He needed a college diploma. After researching a few schools, he settled on my alma mater. Once he'd been accepted and enrolled, the university reviewed his past work and education history. Most of his credits from previous schools transferred. But to my surprise, he also received seven college credits for his noncollegiate learning courses. These classes not only helped my husband's actual career, but also his college career. In that moment, I saw the error in my thinking. My husband had it right all along. All I could do was agree to agree.

## The Basics

A noncredit, credit-earning course. Quite an oxymoron, right? Just like silent alarms and black lights, these types of classes actually exist. And you might have already completed a few without even realizing it. Maybe at your work five years ago. Or at a school six months ago. Or online two weeks ago. But even if you haven't taken any noncollegiate learning courses, you can now and put yourself one step closer to an early graduation. What an awfully good way to earn college credit.

Noncollegiate learning includes nondegree courses and professional training that is typically intended to provide intellectual or personal stimulation and growth. However, if you attend a school that acknowledges prior learning and complete a course or exam recognized by the American Council on Education (ACE) or the National College Credit Recommendation Service (NCCRS), you could also earn a few college credits. But even if the course or exam isn't approved by the ACE or NCCRS, don't throw in the towel. Your school might make an exception. And if that fails, you can try earning credit by detailing your noncollegiate learning in the next fast-track opportunity, FTO #22: Prior Learning Portfolio.

## The Benefits

- *Increase your marketability.* A résumé is similar to an online dating profile. While the content is obviously different, the ultimate goal is the same: showcase your best self in less than a few hundred words. In a résumé, you do this by describing your work experience, education, and awards. And just like with a potential mate, employers desire the total package. Spelling errors? Grammar mistakes? Lack of content? All turnoffs. But by completing a few noncollegiate learning courses, you'll not only fill a gap in your résumé, but also reveal your passion for lifelong learning. So even though you might still have to wait the typical three days for a date to call, employers will want to snatch you up right away.

- *Develop valuable job-related skills.* You might have heard this quote by Vernon Sanders Law: "Experience is a hard teacher because she gives the test first, the lesson afterward." But even though she's tough, she's also a darn good instructor. You won't sleep through a meeting or write an angry work email twice. But you can't master everything through experience alone. You'll need formal training as well. With noncollegiate learning, you can address and improve your weaknesses. If you don't know how to use Facebook or Twitter for more than personal communication with friends, take a social media seminar. If you don't know how to balance the books, attend an accounting workshop. You won't need to take the exam first every time.

- *Meet other working professionals.* Most noncollegiate learning classes cater to adult learners. These students may be newcomers to the industry or seasoned pros. If you're in the first group, ask the pros about their experience and expertise. And if interested, see if they know of any job openings at their company. If you're in the second group, seek out the opinions of amateurs about a work issue. They might offer a fresh perspective. But even if you don't find a mentor or mentee, at least you won't hear "OMG. YOLO. Time for a selfie," from another classmate.

- *Receive a promotion.* First the guy a few doors down, then the woman on the second floor, and now your office mate. When will you move up the ranks? Stop twiddling your thumbs and waiting for the perfect opportunity to drop into your lap. Instead, take matters into your own hands by enrolling in noncollegiate learning courses. You'll display a thirst and enthusiasm for knowledge, capture the attention of your manager, and hopefully catapult up the corporate ladder.

# The Bottom Line

Continuing education or continuing student loans? While it might seem a bit mind-boggling, this question isn't a trick. Unlike credit-earning courses, some continuing education classes cost little to nothing. And even though it won't happen immediately, you'll still receive credit just like you would for the more expensive alternative. The ACE-approved courses offered through StraighterLine are just one great example. You simply pay a $99 membership fee each month (you can cancel at any time) and can sign up for any of their courses for as low as $49 a course. If you spend two months taking four 3-credit courses at $49 each, you could accumulate 12 semester credits at Marian University for $394 ($198 in membership fees plus $196 in course costs). The same number of credits during a regular semester at this school would set a student back $14,700 in tuition and fees. *Short-term savings = $14,306.*

By registering for four courses through StraighterLine instead of 12 semester credits through Marian University:

> You could avoid $14,306 in student loans. You'll save **$3,902** in interest*, assuming each loan is subsidized and has a 5% interest rate and a term of 10 years.

OR

> You could invest $14,306 in retirement accounts. After 40 years, you'll earn **$86,408** in interest*, assuming each investment has a 5% interest rate, compounded annually.

*Numbers are rounded.

# The Brief Questions

Ask yourself all of the following before starting this opportunity:

- ***Does your school award credit for noncollegiate learning without approval from the ACE or NCCRS?*** To have a place in either the ACE or NCCRS database, a course or exam must have been officially evaluated by the organization. If your school requires an ACE or NCCRS credit recommendation for all noncollegiate learning, only sign up for a course or exam listed in the ACE National Guide to College Credit for Workforce Training or the CCRS Online Directory.

Answered "No"? **RED FLAG**

- *Have you taken a course or exam through a business, union, or government agency?* To receive credit for noncollegiate learning, you must take a course or exam that offers college-level learning and that also has possibly been officially approved by the ACE or NCCRS. If you haven't, or if you took a course or test but didn't pass it, work through Step #1 in The Blueprint that follows. But if you passed and haven't responded with a "No" to the previous question, strongly consider completing this opportunity.

Answered "No"? **RED FLAG**

Answered "Yes"? **CLINCHER**

# The Blueprint

## DETERMINE CREDIT RECOMMENDATION

1. *Take a noncollegiate learning course or exam (if desired).* If you haven't already taken one or want to take another, register for a noncollegiate learning course or exam. As you might guess, not all noncollegiate instruction is at the college level. Therefore, you shouldn't sign up for just any course or exam and expect college credit. Your safest bet is to select one that is listed in the ACE National Guide to College Credit for Workforce Training (www.acenet .edu/credit) or the CCRS Online Directory (www.nationalccrs.org/ccr). If you're overwhelmed by the choices in these databases, check out the online courses offered by StraighterLine, ALIGN Degree Services, Penn Foster College, Propero, Coursera, ALEKS, and/or Sophia Learning.

The Saylor Foundation, the Emergency Management Institute (EMI), the National Fire Academy (NFA), and the Texas Engineering Extension Service (TEEX) all offer either ACE- or NCCRS-approved classes at no cost. But since not every course is ACE- or NCCRS-approved, make sure the one you choose is listed in the ACE National Guide or CCRS Online Directory before registering for it.

I wish I had spent more time looking through the ACE and NCCRS databases. If I didn't immediately find the organization I was searching for, I assumed that it didn't have a credit recommendation. Many times, however, the organization was simply listed under a slightly different name. I could have also contacted the organization directly to double-check whether its courses were approved.

2. ***Recall all previous noncollegiate learning.*** Include any from the previous step. Write down the name, number (if applicable), and a brief description of all courses or exams you've taken through businesses, unions, or government agencies. If you can't remember some of these details, contact the organization directly for specifics.

3. ***Add up your potential credits.*** The ACE and NCCRS provide credit recommendations for thousands of courses and exams. You can search for a specific class or test on the ACE and NCCRS websites (see URLs listed in Step #1). Once located, skim through the description, paying close attention to the recommended number of semester hours as well as the category (vocational certificate, lower-division baccalaureate/associate's degree, upper-division baccalaureate degree, or graduate degree). After you've gathered this information for all of your noncollegiate learning, total the number of credits. If you can't find the course or exam or your school doesn't accept ACE or NCCRS recommendations, ask your academic advisor or a transfer counselor for further instructions.

## REQUEST A TRANSCRIPT

4. ***Obtain a transcript.*** If your course or exam is listed in the ACE National Guide, you can request a transcript directly from ACE. The cost is $45 for the first transcript and $15 for any

additional ones. If your course or exam is listed in the CCRS Online Directory or if it's not found in either database, you'll need to order a transcript from the organization that offered it. You may or may not pay a fee for this service.

5. *Resolve any issues.* You might have questions during the transcript process. You can find most answers in the "FAQs" sections on the ACE and NCCRS websites. But if you're still confused, call or email the company. Following is the contact information for both.

ACE
Phone: (866) 205-6267
Email: credit@acenet.edu
Address: College Credit Recommendation and Transcript Service (ACE CREDIT)
American Council on Education
One Dupont Circle NW, Suite 250
Washington, DC 20036

NCCRS
Phone: (518) 486-2070
Email: nccrs@mail.nysed.gov
Address: NCCRS
New York State Education Building
89 Washington Avenue
Education Building Addition, Room 960A
Albany, NY 12234

Don't expect your school to accept Continuing Education Units (CEUs) for college credit. In order to renew a license or certification, many professionals must acquire a certain number of CEUs within a specified time frame. One CEU is often equivalent to 10 contact hours (1 contact hour = 50 to 60 minutes of participation in an organized continuing education experience). You can earn contact hours through workshops, conferences, seminars, courses, and so on. While these hours will likely benefit your work, it's unlikely that you'll earn any credit for them. Still, it's worth a shot to ask your school to evaluate the course.

---

||||||||||||||||| **ADULT LEARNER OF THE YEAR AWARD** |||||||||||||||||

If you have received credit for workforce or military training based on an ACE recommendation, you may be eligible for the Adult Learner of the Year Award. This accolade honors one outstanding individual for successfully balancing career, family, and education with a $500 scholarship and recognition at the ACE Annual Meeting. If interested, write a 300-word essay on why you should be recognized as an outstanding adult learner and obtain a letter of support from a faculty member, academic advisor, or employer. On the online ACE Student of the Year Nomination Form, attach both documents and enter your contact information and the nominating individual's contact information. Submit the form by the stated deadline (typically late fall).

---

## HANDLE EITHER OUTCOME

6. *Hear news.* After you've ordered a transcript, a staff member from your school should contact you within a few weeks. He or she will reference your petition to earn credit for your noncollegiate learning and likely say one of two statements: your request was accepted and course credit or advanced placement was granted (go to Step #7) or your request was denied and credit or advanced placement was not granted (go to Step #8).

7. *Celebrate any success (if applicable).* Although the ACE and NCCRS provide credit recommendations, your school doesn't have to follow them. It might award you two instead of three credits. Or it might apply the credits to an elective instead of an advanced course. Or it might waive a prerequisite or course instead of granting credit (see page 21 for the difference between advanced placement and course credit). Whatever the case, accept your school's decision with a positive attitude. Even advanced placement is better than nothing.

8. *Fight a rejection (if applicable).* Even after all of your hard work, your school might not award you anything for your noncollegiate learning. But don't give up so fast. Talk with your academic advisor or a transfer counselor. Ask for a list of reasons. It might be as simple as a missed signature. Don't agree with the explanation? Appeal the decision. You

might need to fill out a specific form or write your own statement. If the ACE or NCCRS approved the course or exam, it'll advocate on your behalf. For ACE's assistance, call, email, or mail them; for NCCRS's help, submit an online form or email them (see contact information for both in Step #5).

Don't assume no news means good news. Sometimes no news actually means no news. Especially at large or understaffed schools, incoming transcripts may take a while to process. However, after a month without word, email or visit the registrar's office. If they're backed up, wait a few more weeks. But if they're on top of paperwork and they haven't received your transcript, consider it lost and order a new one.

---

## ⫼⫼⫼⫼⫼⫼⫼⫼ DOUBLE-CHECK YOUR WORK ⫼⫼⫼⫼⫼⫼⫼⫼

### DETERMINE CREDIT RECOMMENDATION
- ❐ Take a noncollegiate learning course or exam (if desired)
- ❐ Recall all previous noncollegiate learning
- ❐ Add up your potential credits

### REQUEST A TRANSCRIPT
- ❐ Obtain a transcript
- ❐ Resolve any issues

### HANDLE EITHER OUTCOME
- ❐ Hear news
- ❐ Celebrate any success (if applicable)
- ❐ Fight a rejection (if applicable)

# FAST-TRACK OPPORTUNITY #22:
# PRIOR LEARNING PORTFOLIO
## Experience Is the Best Teacher

- ✓ Start planning several months prior to the portfolio submission deadline
- ✓ Complete any year in college (typically freshman or sophomore year)
- ✓ Spend approximately $ to $$$
- ✓ Earn potentially + to +++ credits

With only seconds remaining, the countdown started. Ten, nine, eight, seven, six, five, four, three, two, one. After uttering the final number, the entire room erupted in cheer. But the excitement wasn't triggered by the dropping of the New Year's Eve Ball at Times Square or followed by an a cappella version of "Auld Lang Syne." Because it wasn't the first day of the New Year—it was the last day of the school year. And even though this occasion was also about beginnings, it was much more important to me than New Year's Eve. It stood for the beginning of summer. A time free from lectures, lessons, and especially learning.

But I didn't actually want to escape learning; what I really wanted was liberation from classroom curriculum. Because from June to August each year, I actually gained many academic skills. I learned spelling by writing on the sidewalk with sidewalk chalk. I learned addition by totaling the miles driven on our family vacations. And I learned measurement by jumping off the low and high diving boards. As I entered young adulthood, I acquired even more advanced knowledge. I learned family dynamics by babysitting the neighbor's kids. I learned acting theory by performing in a theater production. And I learned accounting by ringing up customers' orders. While these experiences resulted in continuous education, I didn't mind getting schooled this way. Or perhaps more accurately, I didn't really notice that I was learning. It just happened.

After enrolling in college, the way I thought about my everyday experiences changed. Late in my first year, I found out that by documenting my experiential learning, I could potentially receive a large amount of credit. Since I had already accumulated 30 credits through exams and thus reached the maximum number allowed by my school for prior learning, I unfortunately couldn't pursue credit along this avenue. But this discovery wasn't all in vain. I no longer viewed learning as a burden but as a blessing. I even started to really love it, whether I was attaining it outside *or* inside the classroom. Now that's a real reason to bring out the party horns and celebrate.

# The Basics

Instead of enrolling in college immediately after graduation, you went to the "University of Life." You spent a few years working as a sales associate, volunteering at a soup kitchen, serving in the armed forces, or traveling across Asia. Or maybe you did go straight to college, but you went to the "University of Life" while in high school. You worked as a cashier on weeknights, volunteered at a community center on weekends, or independently studied environmental science over the summer. Although you weren't studying on a college campus, you did acquire college-level learning through your work, volunteer, military, travel, hobby, and independent study experiences. And with a bit of effort now, you can potentially earn college credit for this learning. You probably won't even have to take a test, exam, or quiz. Just one of the many benefits of being a "U of Life" alum.

Prior learning (or experiential learning) takes place outside the traditional academic environment. Rather than learning by studying on campus, you learn by experiencing off campus. But you won't automatically earn college credit for working at a grocery store or volunteering at a homeless shelter. You'll have to prove college-level learning occurred in these positions. To accomplish this goal, you'll construct a portfolio on your own or with help from an instructor in a portfolio development course. Upon completion, you'll submit the portfolio to your school or LearningCounts for evaluation and, after a thorough review, possibly be awarded credit. Throughout this portfolio process, you might also be required to pay course tuition and several fees, including but not limited to an evaluation fee and a fee per awarded credit. But while the costs can quickly add up, prior learning portfolios can still result in major savings in the long run, especially if your learning can be applied to several different college courses.

# The Benefits

- *Prevent duplication of learning.* Although engaged couples often create wedding registries, not all invited guests review them. Consequently, many newlyweds receive two of the same item. They only need one coffeemaker, toaster, or iron, so the extra sabotages space and collects dust. Similarly, learning the same material twice takes up precious brain capacity. By crafting a prior learning portfolio, you won't have to listen to lectures on topics you already understand thoroughly. You can earn credit for your prior learning and move to more advanced courses. While you can easily return a crockpot, you can't get back the time you spent in a superfluous semester of English 101.
- *Validate previous experiences.* You spent five years waiting tables. Now you want to be a lawyer. It's easy to think that it was all a waste. But unlike old Styrofoam cups or plastic wrap, old experiences aren't garbage. You can use the learning acquired through this past job—like interpersonal skills—not only to win a trial in the future, but to earn prior learning credit now. Turns out your past experiences aren't trash but treasure.
- *Showcase your knowledge.* In many homes and offices, diplomas and certificates line the walls, outlined by exquisite frames. But how do you proudly display your learning outside the classroom? By constructing a portfolio, you'll have a detailed catalog of all your college-level learning. Share it with your boss. Give it to your parents. Or keep it to yourself. While you probably won't hang it above your mantel, it will still serve as a continual reminder of the value of lifelong education.
- *Sharpen your writing skills.* Writing, like swimming and playing the

piano, is a skill. And similar to any other skill, it isn't mastered overnight. It takes practice—lots and lots of practice. One way to practice your writing is to craft a prior learning portfolio. You'll have to compose around 10 or more pages describing yourself, your past experiences, and your college-level learning through these past experiences. If you're in a portfolio development class, you'll also have your work critiqued by your teacher and possibly your peers, who will point out its strengths and weaknesses. So by the time you submit your portfolio for the formal evaluation, all that practice will have made perfect (or pretty darn close).

# The Bottom Line

Hard hat: $26. Work gloves: $14. Hammer: $9. Gas to and from the construction site: $45. Building homes for low-income families: priceless—or at least that's what the old MasterCard commercials used to say. In actuality, your life experiences (whether you receive wages from them or not) might have indirect monetary value. By documenting in a portfolio your college-level learning acquired through your prior experiences, you can earn credit at a cost typically much less than regular college tuition. Instead of spending $3,990 for 15 credits as an in-state student at University of Maryland University College, you'd only pay $2,158 for the same number of credits earned through the prior learning portfolio process. This figure includes $30 for the prior learning enrollment fee, $798 for the three-credit portfolio development course, $250 for the portfolio evaluation fee, and $1,080 for the posting fee (12 credits awarded × $90 per credit). ***Short-term savings = $1,832.***

By completing a prior learning portfolio instead of 15 semester credits at University of Maryland University College:

> You could avoid $1,832 in student loans. You'll save $500 in interest*, assuming each loan is subsidized and has a 5% interest rate and a term of 10 years.

> OR
>
> › You could invest $1,832 in retirement accounts. After 40 years, you'll
> earn **$11,065** in interest\*, assuming each investment has a 5% interest
> rate, compounded annually.
>
> *\*Numbers are rounded.*

# The Brief Questions

Ask yourself all of the following before starting this opportunity:

- *Do you meet the eligibility qualifications?* To submit a prior learning
  portfolio, you might need to fulfill several stipulations established by
  your school, such as a certain GPA, enrollment status, and class standing.
  Some colleges and universities also only accept prior learning portfolios
  from adult learners, requiring students have a minimum number of
  years of prior learning experience beyond high school. If your school
  doesn't welcome prior learning portfolios from all students and you
  don't satisfy every one of its criteria, don't complete this opportunity.

Answered "No"? **DEALBREAKER**

- *Can you afford the tuition and fees?* To cover all of the costs associated
  with a prior learning portfolio, you may need up to a few thousand
  dollars. And even though you can likely use financial aid for the portfolio development course, the same rules don't apply for the one-time
  evaluation fee and fee per credit awarded. If you don't have enough
  funds for these expenses, borrow money from an individual or organization. But if you can't get a loan with a reasonable interest rate, don't
  complete this opportunity.

Answered "No"? **RED FLAG** or **DEALBREAKER**

- *Can you clearly and concisely express your thoughts in writing?* To
  make a prior learning portfolio, you'll need to write multiple pages

about your previous experiences and past learning. Your portfolio development course will teach you the expectations for structure, content, and tone, but if you have difficulty communicating your ideas in writing, you'll need to seek additional help. Ask an English teacher or a student from the writing lab to help you create a detailed outline before starting your portfolio. Once your first draft is finished, have the same person edit your document for spelling and grammatical errors.

Answered "No"? **RED FLAG**

- *Have you invested significant time in activities outside of school?* To acquire experiential learning, you'll need to spend at least several months, but more likely several years, engaging in activities like work, military service, volunteerism, travel, hobbies, and independent study. If you participated in one or more of these activities for a substantial length of time and gained skills or knowledge from them, and if you haven't responded with a "No" to any of the previous questions, strongly consider completing this opportunity.

Answered "Yes"? **CLINCHER**

# The Blueprint

## UNCOVER YOUR PRIOR LEARNING

1. *Review your past.* Think beyond your formal education and focus on other life experiences. Write down previous employment, volunteer projects, military service, employer-sponsored training, self-directed study, travel, and recreational activities. If needed, review your résumé to refresh your memory. Next to each item, list the college-level learning acquired through the experience. For example, maybe you gained knowledge of biology through a lab assistant job, business management through a PTA position, and psychology through an OpenCourseWare (OCW) class.

2. *Match your prior learning with actual college courses.* Get a current course catalog from the registrar's office or on your school's website. Open the catalog and skim through the course descriptions. If you acquired public speaking skills, look for a class in communication. Or if you gained computer skills, search for a class in computer science or technology. Once you locate the right course, note the department, name, course number, and title. Then, get a syllabus for each course. Make sure your prior learning satisfies all of the course objectives. Also note that the course you're attempting to get credit for (which is sometimes referred to as "challenging a course") cannot duplicate any previous credit you've already earned.

## GATHER INFORMATION ON THE PORTFOLIO PROCESS

3. *Meet with your academic advisor.* Discuss your school's policy on prior learning portfolios. If time allows, ask all of the questions below.

   - *How many credits can I earn?* Your school may limit the number of credits awarded for a portfolio or for all types of prior learning assessments (including prior learning portfolios, standardized exams, noncollegiate learning, and military training and experience).

   - *Which courses can I challenge for credit?* Your school may grant credit only for specific classes or for any class listed in its current course catalog.

   - *How much will this process cost?* Your school will likely charge an evaluation fee as well as a fee per credit awarded. Additionally, you may need to pay tuition for a course in portfolio development.

   - *When must I submit my portfolio?* Your school may set a strict deadline, or it may accept your portfolio at any time.

   - *How long will the evaluation last?* Your school may finish its evaluation within a few weeks, or it may take as long as several months.

4. *Apply for prior learning credit.* Obtain an assessment form. Fill out all of the required information and then get approval signatures from the appropriate staff or faculty members. Although some schools want this document submitted at the same time as your portfolio, many request the form and one-time evaluation fee early. By completing these two actions, you'll be allowed to either enroll in a portfolio development course or start creating the portfolio on your own.

5. *Take a portfolio development class (if applicable).* Your school may mandate completion of a course on how to construct a prior learning portfolio. Your school may offer the class on its campus or defer responsibility to the Council for Adult and Experiential Learning (CAEL). With the former, simply visit the registrar's office, sign up for the class, and pay the regular tuition costs. In the end, you'll earn one or more credits. With the latter, the process is just as easy. Go to learningcounts.org and enroll in CAEL 100. Choose either the Instructor-Led or Do-It-Yourself option. A new Instructor-Led course starts every two weeks, lasts for six weeks, costs $895, and includes an evaluation of your first portfolio. The Do-It-Yourself course starts anytime, is self-paced, costs $149, and doesn't include an evaluation. In the end, you'll earn either three credits (Instructor-Led) or none (Do-It-Yourself).

## BUILD YOUR PORTFOLIO

6. *View sample portfolios.* Even if you understand the basic structure, you might still have difficulty picturing the final product. Fortunately, you can solve this dilemma fairly easily. Ask your school or search the Web for examples of prior learning portfolios. For comparison, obtain a well-written *and* a poorly written sample. Pay attention to not just the content, but the format as well. Frequently reference the well-written sample while you construct your portfolio—but be sure that your portfolio is entirely your own, original work.

Don't plagiarize. Stealing someone else's words is so elementary school. "Give it back!" "Give it back." "Leave me alone!" "Leave me alone." "Stop copying me!" "Stop copying me." You're an adult now—act like one.

7. *Use the correct formatting.* Your school's exact specifications may vary; it will disclose this information either in its portfolio development course or its prior learning handbook. But often, the following guidelines are required:
   - Times New Roman or Arial font
   - 12-pt. type size

- Double-spaced
- One-inch margins on all sides
- Headings for each section
- Numbered pages starting after the table of contents

If you have any questions, ask your course instructor or refer to the Modern Language Association (MLA) or the American Psychological Association (APA) manual. Your school will likely choose between one of these two style guides. Buy or borrow the newest edition and keep it readily accessible. In it, you'll find rules about organization, grammar, and in-text and end-of-text citations.

If I didn't have my style manuals with me, I would visit the Online Writing Lab (OWL) at Purdue University (owl.english.purdue.edu/owl). While it wasn't ever as comprehensive as my official MLA and APA style manuals, the website usually contained the formatting or citation guideline I was looking for.

8. **Create your portfolio.** Your school may require one large portfolio in which you challenge numerous courses or several smaller portfolios, each of which challenges just one course. Regardless, each prior learning portfolio must contain multiple sections. And just like formatting, the specific section requirements differ from school to school. But in general, they tend to be pretty similar. Following is a brief outline of the most common sections (arranged in order). Since this outline is far from thorough, consult with your portfolio development course instructor or your school's prior learning handbook for more details.

a. *Cover page:* Highlight at least your title, name, and institution.
b. *Table of contents:* List the remaining sections and their respective page numbers.
c. *Autobiography:* Share your prior life experiences and future goals.
d. *Résumé:* Detail your education and work history, as well as any formal training, volunteer service, and recreational activities.
e. *Narrative:* Describe the skills and knowledge gained through your life experiences. Then, pair this college-level learning with an actual course. Finally, explain how this prior learning meets the course objectives.
f. *Documentation:* Show proof of your college-level learning.

Examples in-clude job descriptions, performance reviews, transcripts, and certificates.

g.  *Bibliography:* Reference in-text citations in MLA or APA format.

## ASSEMBLE YOUR PORTFOLIO

9.  *Buy portfolio materials (if applicable).* You may be able to submit your portfolio electronically, but if not, you'll need some supplies. Before opening your wallet, request a list of needed materials from your school. Then, head to a local office supply store and fill up your shopping cart with the items. Likely, you'll need a 3-ring view binder (with a front cover pocket), dividers, and plastic protective covers. Purchase the materials and save your receipt. If you don't use all of the items, you can return them later and get your money back.

10. *Put together your portfolio (if applicable).* Unless you're submitting electron-ically, you'll need to assemble your portfolio. First, print out your written work and place each page in a protective cover. Next, order the pages correctly and separate the sections with labeled dividers. Finally, slip your cover page in the outside clear pocket and secure the remaining protected pages inside the 3-ring binder. Once your portfolio is polished and present-able, give it to the appropriate school office—usually the registrar's office, or if available, the Prior Learning Assessment (PLA) office.

## OBTAIN CREDIT FOR YOUR PORTFOLIO

11. *Receive your portfolio assessment.* One or more faculty members will evaluate your prior learning portfolio. While this process generally takes up to a few months, it may last longer if additional information is required. Once your evaluation is finally complete, you'll be notified about the number of credits awarded for each challenged course. Review this amount and read any comments. Since this credit is often graded as P (pass) or F (fail), it won't affect your GPA.

I stocked up on all my school supplies for the entire year between the end of July and the middle of August. Since most retailers have back-to-school sales with drastically reduced prices, I could find many items for around a dollar or two, and some for even $0.50 or less.

Don't wait to pay your fees for the PLA credits you've received. Otherwise, a hold might be placed on your account. This hold could prevent you from receiving your financial aid disbursement, registering for classes, or requesting a transcript.

12.   *Pay for the credits (if applicable).* Your prior learning credits won't automatically appear on your school transcript. You'll have to cover the fee for each awarded credit first. While this amount ranges, it generally won't exceed $100 per credit. Therefore, even if the fee is $80, it will only cost $1,200 for 15 credits—much less than five courses at regular tuition prices.

## REQUEST A TRANSCRIPT

13.   *Procure a transcript (if applicable).* Through LearningCounts, you might have earned credit by completing the Instructor-Led CAEL 100 course and/or receiving a credit recommendation for your portfolio. At some schools, credit for just the course or the course and the portfolio are directly transferred to the registrar's office. (View the list of participating schools on the "FAQ" page on the LearningCounts website.) But at most schools, your credit won't just magically appear on the registrar's desk. You'll need to request a transcript through the National College Credit Recommendation Service (NCCRS). While the NCCRS doesn't normally provide transcripts, it makes an exception for LearningCounts. To order one, follow the instructions provided at the end of the Instructor-Led course and pay the $15 fee.

14. *Review your transcript.* Log in to your student account online to access your unofficial transcript. Scan for prior learning credits. Not transcribed? Contact the registrar's office and ask for a status update. They may just be backed up with paperwork. Or, if you requested a transcript from LearningCounts, they might not have received the document. With either scenario, wait a few weeks and then check your unofficial transcript again. Still not transcribed? Visit the registrar's office and resolve the issue. If they haven't yet received your LearningCounts transcript, email studenthelp@learningcounts.org and inquire about the missing document.

## ⅢⅢⅢⅢⅢⅢⅢⅢ DOUBLE-CHECK YOUR WORK ⅢⅢⅢⅢⅢⅢⅢⅢ

### UNCOVER YOUR PRIOR LEARNING
- ❒ Review your past
- ❒ Match your prior learning with actual college courses

### GATHER INFORMATION ON THE PORTFOLIO PROCESS
- ❒ Meet with your academic advisor
- ❒ Apply for prior learning credit
- ❒ Take a portfolio development class (if applicable)

### BUILD YOUR PORTFOLIO
- ❒ View sample portfolios
- ❒ Use the correct formatting
- ❒ Create your portfolio

### ASSEMBLE YOUR PORTFOLIO
- ❒ Buy portfolio materials (if applicable)
- ❒ Put together your portfolio (if applicable)

### OBTAIN CREDIT FOR YOUR PORTFOLIO
- ❒ Receive your portfolio assessment
- ❒ Pay for the credits (if applicable)

### REQUEST A TRANSCRIPT
- ❒ Procure a transcript (if applicable)
- ❒ Review your transcript

# FAST-TRACK OPPORTUNITY #23: MILITARY TRANSCRIPT
## Awarded Beyond the Call of Duty

- ✓ Start planning as early as right before your freshman year in college
- ✓ Complete any year in college (typically freshman or sophomore year)
- ✓ Spend approximately $ to $$$
- ✓ Earn potentially + to +++ credits

Formerly a recruiting slogan for the U.S. Air Force, the call to action "Aim High" now exists as a part of its motto. And my grandfather, a veteran of this branch, did just that not only in the military but in his civilian life as well. He started as a farm boy in a small town and ended up a store manager in a big city. But even though he accomplished many of his dreams, he wasn't able to completely take off. Throughout his adult life, he felt held back. Because unlike several of his peers, he never earned a bachelor's degree.

Although my grandfather traveled straight from high school to the Air Force, his ultimate destination was college. But when he finally left the military at age 25, he had precious cargo to support—a wife, a one-year-old, and a baby on the way. He couldn't simply stop working to start school. So like many other adult learners, he tried the next best thing. He enrolled in night classes. He labored during the day and learned in the evening. But after a mere six months, his exhausting schedule proved too demanding, and he gave up on his goal of an undergraduate education. He departed school and never returned.

While he still regrets this decision, at the time, he felt he had no other choice. Two or three years in school may have been feasible, but four years would have caused too much turbulence at home. He would have had to sacrifice his roles as husband and father to satisfy his desire for the role of student. If he had faced this same dilemma today, however, he could have taken a different path, one that wouldn't make him feel like he was abandoning his family. He could earn credit for his military training and experience, graduating much faster than the typical ETA of a four-year degree. And with a diploma and newfound confidence, he'd still aim high, but this time, he'd hit every target he set his sights on.

# The Basics

"It's better to give than to receive." While this statement may often be true, it fails to mention the best-case scenario: "It's best to give and receive." As a past or present member of the military, you've already done the first part; now you can enjoy the second. Since you've given years of service to the good ol' U.S. of A., you're now eligible to receive college credit for your military training and experience. So get ready to unwrap your reward and discover the perks of giving *and* receiving.

Earning college credit by requesting a military transcript has never been easier. Until recently, almost every branch of the military had its own transcript. Fortunately, this is no longer the case. Only two military transcripts exist today: the Joint Services Transcript (JST) and the Community College of the Air Force (CCAF) transcript. If you're a service member or veteran of the Army, Navy, Marine Corps, or Coast Guard, you'll order a JST. This transcript replaced the Army/American Council on Education Registry Transcript System (AARTS), the Sailor/Marine American Council on Education Registry Transcript (SMART), and the Coast Guard Institute Transcript. But if you're a service member or veteran of the Air Force, you'll order a CCAF transcript.

# The Benefits

- ***Earn credit without much additional effort.*** You can breathe a sigh of relief; the hard part's over. You've already invested significant time in the military and gained valuable skills and knowledge through your training and experience. Putting in just a bit more work now could even earn you credit for this college-level learning. All you have to do is request your military transcript and have it reviewed by your institution. Compared to your previous military duties and responsibilities, completing the six steps in The Blueprint that follows will seem like nothing. It'll be as easy as pie.

- ***Avoid a negative impact to your GPA.*** You can run, but you can't hide them—your college transcripts will be seen. Which means a few low grades or an off semester can really impact your GPA and possibly translate into a rejection from a grad school admissions officer or future employer. Military transcripts, on the other hand, don't contain letter grades and thus don't affect GPAs. Whether you barely passed a military course with a 70 percent (C−) or received top marks with a 100 percent (A+), your transcript will look the same. So if you haven't always been the strongest student, you won't mind having this academic record viewed. You might even want to show it off.

- ***Narrow down your options for a college major.*** Choice is good, but too much choice can actually be bad. Having dozens if not hundreds of college major choices might leave you feeling overwhelmed and confused. How do you pick just one out of such a large pool of possibilities? In addition to following the strategies presented in FTO #11: One Major, No Minor, you can reduce your options by reviewing your military transcript. This transcript can help you discover a few majors more suitable to your skill set and provide you with a clearer sense of direction. So while you don't have to limit yourself to programs related to your military training, using your military transcript is not a bad way to find a good major.

- ***Construct a more accurate résumé.*** Even though your memory's sharp, to err is human. While crafting your résumé, you might unknowingly make small mistakes. Maybe you are slightly off on a date or mix up two locations. It can be quite a challenge recalling all of the minute details about your previous military courses and occupations. Fortunately, you don't have to rely solely on your own capabilities. Although you should check it for correctness, your military transcript can provide you with specific information about your military training and experience. Which means by using this handy tool instead of just going off of memory, you can guarantee a much more accurate résumé and leave much less room for human error.

# The Bottom Line

Even if you haven't spent a day on the battlefield, you've spent years fighting for the freedom of millions of Americans. Freedom of religion, speech, press, assembly, and petition. But your time in the military wasn't just spent protecting the freedom of others. You were also helping to secure your own type of freedom—freedom from student loan debt. In addition to benefitting from Tuition Assistance (TA), GI Bills, the Reserve Education Assistance Program (REAP), the Veterans Educational Assistance Program (VEAP), and the College Loan Repayment Program (CLRP), you can reduce your education costs by earning college credit for your military courses and occupations. While you may have to pay a small fee per credit awarded, many schools give you the credit for free. For example, you can receive up to 21 credits for your military experience and training for $0 at Columbus State University in Georgia. A nonmilitary, out-of-state student would have to fork over $14,395.80 in tuition and fees (cost for tuition on a per-credit-hour basis) for the same number. ***Short-term savings = $14,395.80.***

By receiving 21 semester credits for military training and experience instead of for coursework at Columbus State University:

> You could avoid $14,395.80 in student loans. You'll save **$3,927** in interest*, assuming each loan is subsidized and has a 5% interest rate and a term of 10 years.

OR

> › You could invest $14,395.80 in retirement accounts. After 40 years, you'll earn **$86,951** in interest*, assuming each investment has a 5% interest rate, compounded annually.

*Numbers are rounded.*

# The Brief Questions

Ask yourself all of the following before starting this opportunity:

- ***Are you a freshman or sophomore in college?*** To prevent a duplication of credit, your school won't accept any military training or experience that matches up with a course you've already taken and received credit for. Military credit typically fulfills general education and elective requirements (mostly lower level), which most juniors and seniors have already completed. If you're an upperclassman, have the registrar's office review your unofficial military transcript before requesting the official version. If based on their initial evaluation they inform you that they won't award you credit, don't continue with this opportunity.

### Answered "No"? **RED FLAG** or **DEALBREAKER**

- ***Do you have an extensive history in the military?*** To potentially earn a large amount of credit for your time in the service, you'll need to have taken several military courses and/or held several military occupations. The more courses and occupations, the more credit the ACE will recommend you receive. If you have significant military training and experience and you haven't responded with a "No" to the previous question, strongly consider completing this opportunity.

### Answered "Yes"? **CLINCHER**

# The Blueprint

## EXAMINE YOUR UNOFFICIAL TRANSCRIPT

1. *Register for an account (if applicable).* To view an unofficial JST or order an official JST, you'll need to log in to the JST website. If you're currently on active duty or were formerly enlisted and have a Common Access Card (CAC), you can log in with your CAC. But if you don't have access to a CAC or CAC reader, you'll need to register for a JST account. Go to the JST System at jst.doded.mil (provided for USG-authorized use only), complete the online registration form, and submit your information for verification. To view an unofficial CCAF transcript, you'll need to log in to the Air Force Portal. If you currently have a CAC, you can create an Air Force Portal account immediately. But if you don't have a CAC, first acquire the card by following the local procedures of your servicing Military Personnel Flight (MPF), and then create your account 48 hours after your card is issued to you. Go to my.af.mil (also provided for USG-authorized use only), complete the online registration form, and submit your information for verification. Within 24 hours, you'll receive an email with login instructions.

2. *View your unofficial transcript (if applicable).* Glance over your military training and experience. If some or all of your courses and occupations have been evaluated and approved by the American Council on Education (ACE), they will have been given a credit recommendation. However, since these are only suggestions, your school doesn't have to follow them. The actual amount of credit that transfers could vary widely, depending on your school's transfer credit policy and your selected program of study. To receive an informal review of your military training and experience, print out and give your unofficial transcript to your college or university. But keep in mind that since it will still likely require an

Don't assume you'll be able to see your unofficial military transcript. Active duty, Reserve, National Guard, and Veteran personnel can see their unofficial JST, while only active duty Air Force members can see their unofficial CCAF transcript.

I frequently visited the "College Credit for Military Service" portion of the ACE website (www .acenet.edu/news-room/Pages /Military-Guide-Online.aspx). It not only offers a military transfer guide, but also FAQs, sample transcripts, direct links to the JST portal and the CCAF website, and much more.

If some training or experience is missing from your military transcript, don't automatically assume it's a blunder. Not all military courses and occupations are evaluated and approved by the ACE. To see if yours has an ACE credit recommendation, look in the Military Guide on the ACE website. You can search by ACE identification number, military course number, military course title, training location, dates completed, or subject and level. The guide is updated daily.

official transcript to formally award credit, anything you receive at this point will only be an estimate.

3.　　*Check for inaccuracies (if applicable).* As with any document, a JST or CCAF transcript could contain errors. Information may be wrong or missing completely. Therefore, you should read through the entire transcript line by line. If you come across a mistake, note the issue and then take the necessary steps to correct it. Since every branch of the military has its own procedures regarding transcript errors, you'll need to follow the proper protocol for your specific branch of service. You might need to fill out a form and submit documentation.

## REQUEST YOUR OFFICIAL TRANSCRIPT

4.　　*Procure an official military transcript.* To award college credit for your military training and experience, your school will need an official JST or CCAF transcript. To request a JST, log in to the JST website, click on the "Transcript" tab, and then click on the "Official Transcript Request" tab. Find your current institution, verify the delivery method (online or U.S. Postal Service), and agree with the consent statement. There is no charge for a JST. To request a CCAF transcript, visit the Air Force Virtual Education Center through the Air Force Portal or mail a letter with your full name, last four digits of your Social Security number, date of birth, transcript recipient's address, and signature to CCAF/DESS, 100 South Turner Blvd, Maxwell AFB, Gunter Annex, AL 36114-3011. As with the JST, there is no charge for a CCAF transcript. But if you're in a rush and need overnight delivery, you'll have to order it through Credentials Solutions and pay for shipping and handling.

5. ***Ensure transcript delivery.*** Depending on the type of delivery method, your transcript might arrive at your school within a day or take several weeks. If your transcript is sent electronically or through FedEx, contact the registrar's office after one to two weeks. But if your transcript is sent through the U.S. Postal Service, contact the office after three to four weeks. They should have received your transcript and possibly even awarded you the appropriate credit.

6. ***Create a prior learning portfolio (if applicable).*** Some of your military courses and occupations may not receive a credit recommendation from the ACE. This unfortunate situation might occur due to any of the following reasons: the course has not been evaluated by the ACE, the course was not evaluated by ACE at your specific location, the course was not completed during the ACE evaluation period, or class attendance dates were not documented in your record. However, you might not be out of luck. If your school accepts prior learning portfolios, you could write about the college-level learning you acquired through this military training or experience and possibly earn credits. To explore this option further, go to FTO #22: Prior Learning Portfolio.

---

## ‖‖‖‖‖‖‖‖‖‖‖‖‖‖‖ DOUBLE-CHECK YOUR WORK ‖‖‖‖‖‖‖‖‖‖‖‖‖

### EXAMINE YOUR UNOFFICIAL TRANSCRIPT
- ❏ Register for an account (if applicable)
- ❏ View your unofficial transcript (if applicable)
- ❏ Check for inaccuracies (if applicable)

---

## REQUEST YOUR OFFICIAL TRANSCRIPT

- ❑ Procure an official military transcript
- ❑ Ensure transcript delivery
- ❑ Create a prior learning portfolio (if applicable)

---

||||||||||||||||||||||||||||||||||||||||||||||||||||||||||||||||||||||||||||||||||||||||||||||

# BONUS FTO #24:

## Professional Licenses and Certifications

||||||||||||||||||||||||||||||||||||||||||||||||||||||||||||||||||||||||||||||||||||||||||||||

CFP. MOS. RHCA. VT. Having these letters after your name won't just help your job, they might also benefit your education. Your institution might award credit for professional licenses and certifications issued by a state, national, or professional organization. They may need to be recommended for credit by the American Council on Education or the National College Credit Recommendation Service, or simply approved by your school. Ask for a list of all evaluated credentials. You might see items like real estate licenses and IT certifications. If your license or certification is on the list, submit a certified copy of the document to the appropriate office along with the fee, if one is required. But even if your license or certification isn't on the list, talk with your academic advisor. The school might review it and grant you credit.

# *FINAL THOUGHTS*

I played the first part of the game of LIFE differently. Instead of following all of the rules, I created some of my own. I still took the college path, but I attended school for only two years and thus successfully avoided student debt. And now my decision was about to be tested. I had just graduated. Just received my diploma. Just started the second and most important part of LIFE.

Like most other recent college grads, I felt apprehensive. Change is rarely ever a walk in the park. But even though I was about to embark into the unknown, I wasn't panicking. Because I had graduated early, I didn't have the same pressures as many of my classmates. With their student loan interest continuing to mount and payments due starting a mere six months after graduation, they scrambled to find work, sometimes settling for work they hated. Free from these concerns, I wasn't forced to settle on just any old job. I could discover my passions. Explore my interests. Chase my dreams.

And I had many dreams to chase. In high school, my dad proposed an idea to me: crafting a kind of bucket list, except instead of writing down things I wanted to do before I died, only including things I wanted to do while I was still young. On board with his suggestion, I grabbed a piece of paper and feverishly scribbled several items. After what seemed like just a matter of minutes, I had finished, folded the sheet into quarters, and stored it in a drawer for safekeeping. Over the next few years, I'd glance at it periodically and then return it to the drawer.

But on one particular occasion, I pulled out the list and stopped dead in my tracks. I had accomplished all but one item. (With a ring on my finger, I couldn't exactly be Miss America anymore.) Only in my early twenties, I had already visited Europe, worked in event coordination, attended graduate school, started drafting a book, and more. But I hadn't reached my goals because of pure luck or fate. I had reached them in large part because I had graduated from college early.

What's on your bucket list? Even if you've never put pen to paper, you probably have countless aspirations swirling in your head. Maybe you hope to travel the world. Or climb the corporate ladder. Or act on Broadway. Or volunteer in a women's shelter. Or something else entirely. If you'd gone with the crowd, you'd have to put these things off. But because you graduated early (or will in the near future) and seriously saved on college costs, you don't have to wait until after you've paid off a massive 10-year student loan. You can start going after your goals much sooner, maybe even right now. And with the same determination and dedication you've had throughout this entire process, I predict you'll achieve them all—and many, many more you have yet to even think up.

# APPENDIX A

|||||||||||||||||||||||||||||||||||||||||||||||||||||||||||||||||||||||||||||||||||||||||||||||||||||||||

# WHICH FAST-TRACK OPPORTUNITIES ARE RIGHT FOR YOU?

|||||||||||||||||||||||||||||||||||||||||||||||||||||||||||||||||||||||||||||||||||||||||||||||||||||||||

As you read the following list of contrasting statements, circle any you agree with. Consider adding one or more of the recommended fast-track opportunities under each statement you've circled to your graduation plan.

| I learn best through experience. | I learn best through classroom instruction. |
|---|---|
| • FTO #16: Gap Year Programs<br>• FTO #17: Intersession Abroad<br>• FTO #18: Alternative Breaks<br>• FTO #19: Internship<br>• FTO #20: Extracurricular Activities<br>• FTO #22: Prior Learning Portfolio | • FTO #2: IB Exams<br>• FTO #3: Pre-College Summer Programs<br>• FTO #4: Dual Enrollment<br>• FTO #12: Maximum Credits<br>• FTO #13: Summer Classes |
| I score well on tests. | I score poorly on tests. |
| • FTO #6: CLEP Exams<br>• FTO #7: DSST Exams<br>• FTO #8: UExcel Exams and ECEs<br>• FTO #9: TECEP Exams<br>• FTO #10: NYU SPS Foreign Language Proficiency Exams | • FTO #17: Intersession Abroad<br>• FTO #18: Alternative Breaks<br>• FTO #19: Internship<br>• FTO #22: Prior Learning Portfolio<br>• FTO #23: Military Transcript |

| I need a flexible schedule. | I need a 9 to 5 schedule. |
|---|---|
| • FTO #4: Dual Enrollment<br>• FTO #14: Distance Learning<br>• FTO #15: Independent Study<br>• FTO #21: Noncollegiate Learning<br>• FTO #22: Prior Learning Portfolio | • FTO #1: AP Exams<br>• FTO #2: IB Exams<br>• FTO #3: Pre-College Summer Programs<br>• FTO #13: Summer Classes |
| I only have availability during the school year. | I only have availability during the summer. |
| • FTO #1: AP Exams<br>• FTO #2: IB Exams<br>• FTO #4: Dual Enrollment<br>• FTO #5: Articulated Credit/Tech Prep<br>• FTO #12: Maximum Credits<br>• FTO #16: Gap Year Programs | • FTO #3: Pre-College Summer Programs<br>• FTO #13: Summer Classes<br>• FTO #14: Distance Learning<br>• FTO #17: Intersession Abroad<br>• FTO #19: Internship |
| I have a tight budget ($). | I have looser purse strings ($$$). |
| • FTO #1: AP Exams<br>• FTO #6: CLEP Exams<br>• FTO #7: DSST Exams<br>• FTO #9: TECEP Exams<br>• FTO #23: Military Transcript<br>• FTO #24: Professional Licenses and Certifications | • FTO #3: Pre-College Summer Programs<br>• FTO #16: Gap Year Programs<br>• FTO #17: Intersession Abroad<br>• FTO #18: Alternative Breaks<br>• FTO #22: Prior Learning Portfolio |

# APPENDIX B

||||||||||||||||||||||||||||||||||||||||||||||||||||||||||||||||||||||||||||||||||||||||||||||||||||||||

# SAMPLE SCHEDULES

||||||||||||||||||||||||||||||||||||||||||||||||||||||||||||||||||||||||||||||||||||||||||||||||||||||||

The following sample schedules contain two-year graduation plans for students in three common education stages: currently enrolled in high school, recently graduated from high school, and heading back to school. Each assumes a maximum of 18 credits allowed per semester and a minimum of 125 credits required to graduate. Since your plan must be specific to your college's transfer credit policy (as well as your personal needs, skills, and interests), these examples should only serve as guidance and inspiration to create your own plan using the Do-It-Yourself Schedule that follows the examples.

# SAMPLE SCHEDULE 1
## CURRENTLY ENROLLED
## IN HIGH SCHOOL

## HIGH SCHOOL: *JUNIOR YEAR*

| START DATE | FAST-TRACK OPPORTUNITY | END DATE | SEMESTER CREDITS EARNED |
|---|---|---|---|
| September | #1: AP Exams *(Human Geography, Statistics, World History, & Biology)* | May | 12 total (3 per exam) |

## HIGH SCHOOL: *SUMMER BETWEEN JUNIOR YEAR AND SENIOR YEAR*

| START DATE | FAST-TRACK OPPORTUNITY | END DATE | SEMESTER CREDITS EARNED |
|---|---|---|---|
| June | #3: Pre-College Summer Programs *(Fiction Writing & International Politics)* | July | 6 total (3 per class) |

## HIGH SCHOOL: *SENIOR YEAR*

| START DATE | FAST-TRACK OPPORTUNITY | END DATE | SEMESTER CREDITS EARNED |
|---|---|---|---|
| August | #4: Dual Enrollment *(College Composition I, Technical Writing, Precalculus, & Survey of Anthropology)* | December | 12 total (3 per class) |
| August | #11: One Major, No Minor | July | N/A |
| January | #4: Dual Enrollment *(College Composition II, Intermediate Spanish, Psychology of Aging, & Beginning Guitar)* | May | 12 total (3 per class) |
| | | **Earned in High School** | **42 Credits** |

## PRE-COLLEGE: *SUMMER BEFORE FIRST YEAR*

| START DATE | FAST-TRACK OPPORTUNITY | END DATE | SEMESTER CREDITS EARNED |
|---|---|---|---|
| May | #6: CLEP Exams *(Principles of Macroeconomics)* | August | 3 |
| May | #7: DSST Exams *(Principles of Public Speaking)* | August | 3 |
| | | **Earned Pre-College** | **6 Credits** |

## COLLEGE: *FIRST YEAR*

| START DATE | FAST-TRACK OPPORTUNITY | END DATE | SEMESTER CREDITS EARNED |
|---|---|---|---|
| August | #12: Maximum Credits | December | 18 |
| January | #12: Maximum Credits | May | 18 |
| Spring Break | #18: Alternative Breaks | Spring Break | 3 |

## COLLEGE: *SUMMER BETWEEN FIRST AND SECOND YEAR*

| START DATE | FAST-TRACK OPPORTUNITY | END DATE | SEMESTER CREDITS EARNED |
|---|---|---|---|
| May | #8: UExcel Exams and ECEs (*Earth Science*) | August | 3 |

## COLLEGE: *SECOND YEAR*

| START DATE | FAST-TRACK OPPORTUNITY | END DATE | SEMESTER CREDITS EARNED |
|---|---|---|---|
| August | #12: Maximum Credits | December | 18 |
| January | #12: Maximum Credits | May | 18 |
| | | **Earned in College** | **78 Credits** |
| | | **TOTAL EARNED** | **126 CREDITS** |

# SAMPLE SCHEDULE 2
# RECENTLY GRADUATED
# FROM HIGH SCHOOL

## PRE-COLLEGE

| FAST-TRACK OPPORTUNITY | SEMESTER CREDITS EARNED |
|---|---|
| #11: One Major, No Minor | N/A |
| #6: CLEP Exams (*American Literature, Natural Sciences, & Social Sciences and History*) | 18 total (6 per exam) |
| #10: NYU School of Professional Studies Foreign Language Proficiency Exams (*16-point in Italian*) | 16 |
| **Earned Pre-College** | **34 Credits** |

## COLLEGE: *FIRST YEAR*

| START DATE | FAST-TRACK OPPORTUNITY | END DATE | SEMESTER CREDITS EARNED |
|---|---|---|---|
| August | #12: Maximum Credits | December | 18 |
| January | #12: Maximum Credits | May | 18 |
| Spring Break | #7: DSST Exams (*Art of the Western World*) | Spring Break | 3 |

## COLLEGE: *SUMMER BETWEEN FIRST AND SECOND YEAR*

| START DATE | FAST-TRACK OPPORTUNITY | END DATE | SEMESTER CREDITS EARNED |
|---|---|---|---|
| May | #19: Internship | August | 6 |
| June | #13: Summer Classes (*Physics I*) | August | 4 |

## COLLEGE: *SECOND YEAR*

| START DATE | FAST-TRACK OPPORTUNITY | END DATE | SEMESTER CREDITS EARNED |
|---|---|---|---|
| August | #12: Maximum Credits | December | 18 |
| January | #17: Intersession Abroad | January | 6 |
| January | #12: Maximum Credits | May | 18 |
|  |  | **Earned in College** | **91 Credits** |
|  |  | **TOTAL EARNED** | **125 CREDITS** |

# SAMPLE SCHEDULE 3
# HEADING BACK TO SCHOOL

## PRE-COLLEGE

| FAST-TRACK OPPORTUNITY | SEMESTER CREDITS EARNED |
|---|---|
| #11: One Major, No Minor | N/A |
| #23: Military Transcript | 21 |
| **Earned Pre-College** | **21 Credits** |

## COLLEGE: *FIRST YEAR*

| START DATE | FAST-TRACK OPPORTUNITY | END DATE | SEMESTER CREDITS EARNED |
|---|---|---|---|
| August | #12: Maximum Credits | December | 18 |
| August | #22: Prior Learning Portfolio | December | 15 |
| January | #21: Noncollegiate Learning (*Corporate Communications* through the Saylor Foundation) | January | 3 |
| January | #12: Maximum Credits | May | 18 |

## COLLEGE: *SUMMER BETWEEN FIRST AND SECOND YEAR*

| START DATE | FAST-TRACK OPPORTUNITY | END DATE | SEMESTER CREDITS EARNED |
|---|---|---|---|
| May | #8: UExcel Exams and ECEs (*Science of Nutrition & World Population*) | August | 6 total (3 per exam) |
| May | #9: TECEP Exams (*Environmental Ethics & Introduction to Comparative Politics*) | August | 6 total (3 per exam) |
| May | #14: Distance Learning (*Art Appreciation*) | August | 3 |

## COLLEGE: *SECOND YEAR*

| START DATE | FAST-TRACK OPPORTUNITY | END DATE | SEMESTER CREDITS EARNED |
|---|---|---|---|
| August | #12: Maximum Credits | December | 18 |
| January | #12: Maximum Credits | May | 18 |
| | | **Earned in College** | **105 Credits** |
| | | **TOTAL EARNED** | **126 CREDITS** |

# DO-IT-YOURSELF SCHEDULE

## HIGH SCHOOL:

| START DATE | FAST-TRACK OPPORTUNITY | END DATE | SEMESTER CREDITS EARNED |
|------------|------------------------|----------|-------------------------|
|            |                        |          |                         |
|            |                        |          |                         |
|            |                        |          |                         |

## HIGH SCHOOL:

| START DATE | FAST-TRACK OPPORTUNITY | END DATE | SEMESTER CREDITS EARNED |
|------------|------------------------|----------|-------------------------|
|            |                        |          |                         |
|            |                        |          |                         |
|            |                        |          |                         |

## HIGH SCHOOL:

| START DATE | FAST-TRACK OPPORTUNITY | END DATE | SEMESTER CREDITS EARNED |
|---|---|---|---|
|  |  |  |  |
|  |  |  |  |
|  |  |  |  |
|  |  | Earned in High School | _____ Credits |

## PRE-COLLEGE:

| START DATE | FAST-TRACK OPPORTUNITY | END DATE | SEMESTER CREDITS EARNED |
|---|---|---|---|
|  |  |  |  |
|  |  |  |  |
|  |  |  |  |
|  |  | Earned Pre-College | _____ Credits |

## COLLEGE:

| START DATE | FAST-TRACK OPPORTUNITY | END DATE | SEMESTER CREDITS EARNED |
|---|---|---|---|
|  |  |  |  |
|  |  |  |  |
|  |  |  |  |

## COLLEGE:

| START DATE | FAST-TRACK OPPORTUNITY | END DATE | SEMESTER CREDITS EARNED |
|---|---|---|---|
|  |  |  |  |
|  |  |  |  |
|  |  |  |  |

## COLLEGE:

| START DATE | FAST-TRACK OPPORTUNITY | END DATE | SEMESTER CREDITS EARNED |
|---|---|---|---|
|  |  |  |  |
|  |  |  |  |
|  |  |  |  |

## COLLEGE:

| START DATE | FAST-TRACK OPPORTUNITY | END DATE | SEMESTER CREDITS EARNED |
|---|---|---|---|
|  |  |  |  |
|  |  |  |  |
|  |  |  |  |

## COLLEGE:

| START DATE | FAST-TRACK OPPORTUNITY | END DATE | SEMESTER CREDITS EARNED |
|---|---|---|---|
|  |  |  |  |
|  |  |  |  |
|  |  |  |  |
|  |  | Earned in College | _____ Credits |
|  |  | TOTAL EARNED | _____ CREDITS |

# APPENDIX C

||||||||||||||||||||||||||||||||||||||||||||||||||||||||||||||||||||||||||||||||||||||||||||||||||||||||||||||||||||||||||

# *SIDE-BY-SIDE EXAM COMPARISONS*

||||||||||||||||||||||||||||||||||||||||||||||||||||||||||||||||||||||||||||||||||||||||||||||||||||||||||||||||||||||||||

How do each of the college credit-by-exam opportunities compare in terms of cost, length, ACE recommended score, and more? Refer to the tables that follow to see basic info on each of the seven test options in this book.

# PART 1

||||||||||||||||||||||||||||||||||||||||||||||||||||||||||||||||||||||||||||||||||||||||||||||||||||||||

# COLLEGE CREDIT-BY-EXAM (FOR HIGH SCHOOL STUDENTS)

||||||||||||||||||||||||||||||||||||||||||||||||||||||||||||||||||||||||||||||||||||||||||||||||||||||||

| | AP | IB |
|---|---|---|
| GRADE LEVEL | 10th, 11th, or 12th | 11th and 12th |
| COST | $91 | $110<br>+ $160 candidate registration fee: $270 |
| OFFERED DURING | May | May<br>(most often Northern Hemisphere schools)<br>November<br>(most often Southern Hemisphere schools) |
| LENGTH | Most last 2 or 3 hours | 1, 2, or 3 papers<br>45 minutes to 3 hours each |
| POSSIBLE SCORE | 1–5 | 1–7 |
| ACE RECOM-MENDED SCORE | 3<br>(A score of 4 or 5 on some of the foreign language exams equates to more credit recommended.) | N/A |

# PART 2

||||||||||||||||||||||||||||||||||||||||||||||||||||||||||||||||||||||||||||||||||||||||||||

# COLLEGE CREDIT-BY-EXAM

||||||||||||||||||||||||||||||||||||||||||||||||||||||||||||||||||||||||||||||||||||||||||||

|  | CLEP | DSST | UEXCEL & ECE | TECEP | NYU SPS |
|---|---|---|---|---|---|
| **NUMBER OF EXAMS** | More than 30 | More than 30 | More than 70 | More than 30 | 3 types |
| **COST** | $80 + admin fee | $80 + admin fee | $95–$440 + admin fee of $50 (2-hour exams) or $60 (3-hour exams) | NJ residents: $35 per credit + admin fee<br><br>Out-of-state residents: $37 per credit + admin fee | 4-pt.: $120 12-pt.: $300 16-pt.: $400<br><br>+ registration fee of $20 (all exams) + shipping and handling fee of $20 (only for exams taken outside of NYC) |

|  | CLEP | DSST | UEXCEL & ECE | TECEP | NYU SPS |
|---|---|---|---|---|---|
| LENGTH (IN HOURS) | 1.5 or 2 (optional essays for comp and lit exams increase length) | 2 | 2 or 3 | 2 or 3 | 4-pt.: 1 12-pt.: 2 16-pt.: 3 |
| POSSIBLE SCORE/GRADE | 20–80 | 200–500 | A, B, C, D, or F | CR or NC | 4-pt.: 0–4 12-pt.: 0–12 16-pt.: 0–16 |
| ACE RECOMMENDED SCORE | 50 (higher for some foreign language exams) | 400 | C | N/A | N/A |
| NUMBER OF CREDITS | 3, 4, 6, or 12 | 3 or 6 | 1, 3, 4, 6, or 8 | 1 or 3 | Up to 16 |

# APPENDIX D

||||||||||||||||||||||||||||||||||||||||||||||||||||||||||||||||||||||||||||||||||||||||||||||||||||||||||

# COLLEGE CREDIT-BY-EXAM LEARNING MATERIALS

||||||||||||||||||||||||||||||||||||||||||||||||||||||||||||||||||||||||||||||||||||||||||||||||||||||||||

To prepare for a college credit-by-exam, you can utilize a variety of resources. While this list isn't comprehensive, you'll find several common study aids below.

## For CLEP, DSST, UExcel, ECE, and TECEP Exams

- **Textbook(s):** Borrow at least one from your public or school library or buy an older edition from a brick-and-mortar or online retailer. If possible, obtain a text recommended by the exam provider. Compare the book's table of contents to the exam's content outline, and read through only the chapters covered on the exam. Cost: varies, possibly free.
- **MOOC or OCW course:** Search for a MOOC through edX, Coursera, or Udacity, or an OCW course through MIT, Yale, Tufts, or some other university. Both Massive Open Online Courses (MOOCs) and OpenCourseWare (OCW) courses are free online courses available to anyone (optional certificate of completion from a MOOC can cost money). But whereas MOOCs typically have set start and end dates and allow interaction with instructors, OCW courses are self-paced and don't often give access to professors. Once you locate a class on your exam subject, work through the course. Depending on the course's contents, this may include watching lectures, reviewing notes, and answering questions. Cost: free.

- **InstantCert Academy flashcards:** Sign up for this subscription-based service. View online flashcards with a fill-in-the-blank format to quickly memorize the main points about your exam subject. You can also participate in InstantCert's discussion forum with other test takers. Cost: $20 for one month or $108 for six months of unlimited access to more than 60 courses.
- **iStudySmart class:** Purchase more than 50 courses directly from iStudySmart's online store. Each traditional course contains a study guide with a practice exam. Pick from three different formats: CD-ROM, printed version, or online access. Cost: $210-$240 for one traditional course, $750 for one year of online access to 14 courses, or $1,250 for two years of online access to all courses.

# For CLEP and DSST Exams Only

- **CLEP/DSST prep website:** Visit www.free-clep-prep.com. Peruse the contents. This site includes brief study guides for CLEP and DSST exams as well as more than 20 free, full-length practice tests. If you're willing to spend a little and one is available for your exam subject, you can also get a Quick Prep Sheet or Quick Prep Package (prep sheet plus an MP3 version and two additional practice tests). Cost: free (Quick Prep Sheet: $8.99 or Quick Prep Package: $15.99).

If you or a family member is in any branch of the military (regardless of activation status) or is a DoD civilian or contractor, you have free access to Peterson's DoD MWR Libraries Education Lifelong Learning Resource Center. Take advantage of its wide selection of CLEP and DSST practice tests and books. To register and confirm eligibility, go to www.nelnet solutions.com/dodlibrary.

# For CLEP Exams Only

- **REA study guide:** Purchase a guide directly from the online Research & Education Association, Inc. (REA) store (www.rea.com/clep). Unlike textbooks, MOOCs, and OCW courses, these books contain only the information you need to know to pass a CLEP exam. Go through the chapters and take one or more of the included practice tests. Cost $27.95 or $34.95.

# For NYU School of Professional Studies Foreign Language Proficiency Exams Only

- **Print media:** Gather books, magazines, and newspapers in your test language. Read through the text. If needed, consult a foreign language dictionary and remaster the forgotten word or phrase. Cost: varies, possibly free.
- **Electronic media:** Locate music, movies, television, and radio programming in your test language. Watch or listen to the content. Pay attention to the pacing and pronunciation. Cost: varies, possibly free.
- **Course:** Purchase from Rosetta Stone, Rocket Languages, Pimsleur, Fluenz, or Transparent Language. Depending on the program, the course may be available on CD, DVD, or CD-ROM or through an online service or mobile app. Increase your vocabulary and reinforce comprehension with one of these unique approaches to language learning. Cost: varies, either a flat fee or a monthly subscription (all of these programs also offer a free demo or trial).
- **Websites:** Visit BBC Languages, Livemocha, busuu, Internet Polyglot, and/or Word2Word. Discover lessons, audio, video, exercises, games, flashcards, and more. Cost: free.
- **Conversation group:** Meet up and discuss topics in your test language. Actively listen to each statement or question and respond accordingly. Avoid speaking in English as much as possible. Cost: free.
- **Online translator:** Use Google, Bing, Paralink, or Babylon. Translate a passage on the Internet into English and another into your test language. Check your work with the translator (but keep in mind that these aren't always perfect). Cost: free.

# APPENDIX E

||||||||||||||||||||||||||||||||||||||||||||||||||||||||||||||||||||||||||||||||||||||||||||||||||||||

# *TRIP PREPARATIONS*

||||||||||||||||||||||||||||||||||||||||||||||||||||||||||||||||||||||||||||||||||||||||||||||||||||||

If you're completing Fast-Track Opportunity #16: Gap Year Programs, #17: Intersession Abroad, #18: Alternative Breaks (AB), or another FTO that may involve travel, follow these steps (in no particular order) to ensure that you're well prepared for your journey. For international travel, work through any of the eight steps. But for domestic travel, skip over the first four steps.

1. ***Get a U.S. passport.*** For a new passport, gather the following documents: evidence of U.S. citizenship; photo ID (with copy); recent passport photo; and completed, but not signed, DS–11 form. Take these items and $135 ($60 more for expedited processing and $14.85 more for overnight delivery) to an acceptance facility for processing. For a passport renewal, simply mail your expired

I wish I had applied for my passport several months in advance of my trip. I waited until exactly six weeks prior to my intersession abroad trip to apply for a passport, which was a mistake. Just days before my scheduled departure, my passport still hadn't arrived. I had to drive to the city, pay for parking, and spend hours at the Seattle Passport Agency to follow up on it. Luckily, it came in time, but not without all this hassle and headache. Not to mention almost missing out on the trip of a lifetime!

passport, recent passport photo, completed and signed DS-82 form, and a $110 application fee to the National Passport Processing Center, P.O. Box 90155, Philadelphia, PA 19190-0155. To access the afore-mentioned forms or search for an acceptance facility, visit travel.state.gov/content/passports/english.html.

2. ***Get one or more travel visas.*** A visa is commonly a stamp in your passport, allowing entrance into a *specific* country for a *specific* purpose for a *specific* length of time. Depending on your nationality, intended destination, length of stay, and trip objective, you may or may not need a visa. If you're a U.S. citizen, visit the "Americans Traveling Abroad" page on the U.S. State Department website. Some countries can issue a visa upon your arrival, while others require you to obtain a visa prior to arrival. If you need one beforehand, go to the visiting nation's embassy or consulate website. Print out and complete the visa application forms. Gather these forms along with your passport, one or more passport photos, fee payment, and possibly proof of sufficient funds and an onward/return ticket (proof in the form of an airline or train ticket that you intend to leave the country after you arrive). Deliver by hand or mail the required materials with a self-addressed envelope. You should receive your visa and passport within a few weeks to a few months. You can often pay extra to rush this process, but it's best to apply as far in advance as possible.

3. ***Meet with a travel medicine physician.*** International travel can pose a risk to your health. In developing countries, exposure to hepatitis, typhoid, polio, and malaria are common. To minimize your chance of illness, your doctor may recommend a few vaccines or preventive medicines. While most are optional, some vaccines are actually required. For entrance into certain regions, you'll need to show an International Certificate of Vaccination for yellow fever or meningitis. To see a full list of recommended and required vaccines and medicines for a specific country, go to wwwnc.cdc.gov/travel.

4. ***Obtain an International Student Identity Card (ISIC).*** Recognized globally, this card proves your student status. But this isn't the only benefit. It also provides you access to more than 42,000 discounts world-wide, an ISIC prepaid MasterCard, and basic travel insurance. And all for just $25. If you want to upgrade your insurance coverage, you can pay extra for a premium or explorer plan. To apply for the card, go to myisic

.com or visit an STA Travel Store or ISIC Point of Sale. You'll need a valid ID (driver's license or passport) and proof of full-time student status. The card expires a year from the date of issue.

5. ***Purchase travel insurance.*** Before you request any quotes, review your current insurance and credit card policies. You may already have coverage. If not, research the different types. As a study abroad student, you'll probably need at least travel cancellation and interruption as well as health and medical evacuation insurance. Travel cancellation and interruption covers the cost of your trip in case of unforeseen illness, death, or inclement weather. Health and medical evacuation pays for medical care and transport overseas. Search for these and other kinds of travel insurance at travelguard.com, allianztravelinsurance.com, travelex insurance.com, or another site.

6. ***Book travel.*** Depending on your program, your trip might be completely prearranged for you. You simply show up, ready to learn. Others require more effort. You may need to secure your own transportation or accommodations. If you're stuck with part of the planning, head to www.expedia.com, www .travelocity.com, www.orbitz.com, www.kayak.com, or another typical

Don't forget to purchase bug spray. Mosquitos easily transmit diseases, some even deadly. And many aren't preventable with vaccines or medicine. To protect against bites, use insect repellent with DEET. Reapply according to the product's directions or when bites become noticeable.

Since the cost of an airline ticket can blow my budget, I start scouring the Internet for flights several months prior to my travels. If I come across a fairly unbeatable deal, I buy the ticket directly from the airline company (e.g., American Airlines, Virgin Atlantic) and aggressively search for a better price for the entire day. Thanks to a Department of Transportation regulation, passengers can get a full refund (no cancellation fees even for nonrefundable fares) as long as it's within 24 hours of the purchase and at least seven days from the departure date.

vacation site. If possible, purchase any tickets or rooms at least several months in advance.

7. *Pack your luggage.* Below is a packing list for international travel. Add or subtract items as needed.

---

|||||||||||||||||||||||||||||||||||||||| **PACKING LIST** ||||||||||||||||||||||||||||||||||||||||

### ATTIRE
- ❏ Clothing
- ❏ Shoes
- ❏ Jewelry
- ❏ Watch
- ❏ Sunglasses

### EQUIPMENT
- ❏ Camera (with charger or extra batteries)
- ❏ Electrical adapters and converters
- ❏ Prepaid cell phone (with charger)
- ❏ Tablet or laptop
- ❏ Blow-dryer
- ❏ Headphones

### HEALTH AND BEAUTY ITEMS
- ❏ Body lotion
- ❏ Contact lens solution
- ❏ Extra contact lenses and glasses
- ❏ Comb and brush
- ❏ Deodorant
- ❏ Face cleanser
- ❏ First-aid kit
- ❏ Floss
- ❏ Insect repellant
- ❏ Lip balm

- ❏ Personal hygiene items
- ❏ Medications
- ❏ Razors
- ❏ Shampoo and conditioner
- ❏ Shaving gel
- ❏ Soap
- ❏ Sunscreen (at least SPF 15)
- ❏ Toothbrush
- ❏ Toothpaste

## TRAVEL DOCUMENTS

- ❏ Driver's license or photo ID
- ❏ International Student Identity Card (ISIC)
- ❏ Contact information
- ❏ Travel guide and phrasebook
- ❏ Health insurance card
- ❏ Passport
- ❏ Photocopies of passport
- ❏ Travel visa(s)
- ❏ Vaccination certificate

## MISCELLANEOUS

- ❏ Debit and/or credit card (notify bank of travel beforehand)
- ❏ Light and healthy snacks
- ❏ Money belt
- ❏ International calling card or SIM card
- ❏ Travel journal
- ❏ Travel pillow and blanket
- ❏ FAA-regulation plastic bags
- ❏ Travel-sized detergent

I wish I hadn't packed two over-sized suitcases full of clothes for my intersession abroad trip. I had to lug those bags through several airports, train stations, bus terminals, and hotel lobbies and hallways. The other students had a much better idea. They brought only the essentials and then once or twice during the trip, washed them in the bathtub with detergent.

8. Reduce jet lag. When traveling across multiple time zones, you'll likely experience jet lag. You may feel deep fatigue, poor concentration, confusion, nausea, loss of appetite, or lightheadedness. To decrease these symptoms, adjust your sleep schedule at least a week prior to departure. If you're heading east, go to bed a half hour earlier each day. If you're heading west, go to bed a half hour later. During the flight, stay well-hydrated and eat light and healthy snacks. Upon arrival, immediately change your watch to the new time and follow the locals' routines. When they eat, you eat. And when they sleep, you sleep. If you're prone to severe jet lag, consult with your doctor. You may be prescribed melatonin or a stronger sleep aid.

# APPENDIX F

## *COMMONLY USED ACRONYMS*

| | |
|---|---|
| AB: | Alternative Break |
| ACE: | American Council on Education |
| AP: | Advanced Placement |
| CAC: | Common Access Card (for members of the military) |
| CCAF: | Community College of the Air Force |
| CLEP: | College-Level Examination Program |
| DoD: | Department of Defense |
| ECE: | Excelsior College Examination |
| FAFSA: | Free Application for Federal Student Aid |
| FTO: | Fast-Track Opportunity |
| IB: | International Baccalaureate |
| JST: | Joint Services Transcript |
| NCCRS: | National College Credit Recommendation Service |
| NYU SPS: | New York University School of Professional Studies |
| TECEP: | Thomas Edison State College Examination Program |
| TESC: | Thomas Edison State College |

# ACKNOWLEDGMENTS

College took me only two years; *College, Quicker* took me more than seven. While the book's time line was much longer than originally anticipated, the support for this project never fell short. I would love to mention each and every one of you here, but I don't have even close to enough room. With that being said, I still want to express my sincere gratitude to those people most influential and instrumental in this entire process. Special thanks to:

- My parents, Mark Reinhardt and Jane Neff, who encouraged me to obtain an *affordable education.*
- The Northwest University faculty and staff, who provided me with an *affordable education* and made my *early graduation* possible.
- My agent, Regina Brooks, who believed in my book idea about how to achieve an *early graduation* and sold my *proposal.*
- My first editor, Suzanna Bainbridge, who reviewed my *proposal* and, among many things, suggested adding *personal stories* to my chapters.
- My grandpa, Tom Blumhorst, and brother, Jackson Reinhardt, who allowed me to use their *personal stories* and include them in my *first draft.*
- My best friend, MJ Lunde, who typed in my *first draft* edits and gave my *unstable joints* a rest.
- My doctors, Dr. Richard Jimenez and Dr. Lew Estabrook, physical therapists, Scott Olson, Paige Raffo, and Leaza Armstrong, and occupational therapists, Jenny Mensching and Cary Eschenbach, who

minimized the pain in my *unstable joints* caused by my condition (Ehlers–Danlos syndrome) and enabled me to continue working on my *first and subsequent drafts*.

- My second editor, Michelle Lecuyer, who significantly improved my *first and subsequent drafts* and helped me produce a *polished manuscript*.
- The remainder of my publishing team at Sourcebooks, Inc., who turned my *polished manuscript* into a physical book and distributed and marketed the book around its *release date*.
- Last but certainly not least, my husband, Jeffrey R. Stephens, who offered his assistance on my book too many times to count way before and I can only assume long after its *release date*.

# INDEX

# ABOUT THE AUTHOR

At age 20, Kate Stephens graduated summa cum laude with a bachelor of arts in business administration from Northwest University, earning membership in Who's Who Among Students in American Universities & Colleges and receiving special recognition for the highest GPA in her entire class. By only attending college for two years, she saved nearly $60,000 and left school debt-free. With her undergraduate degree in hand, she spent the next few years serving as the event director at a local chamber of commerce, working as a behavioral therapist for children

© ALISA CLARK, 2015

with autism, and pursuing graduate level studies at University of Washington. Kate currently resides with her husband Jeff near Seattle, where she runs a home-based tutoring business and advocates for research and awareness for her connective tissue disorder, Ehlers–Danlos syndrome (EDS).